SEEDS OF CYNICISM

The Undermining of Journalistic Education

Sara-Ellen Amster

University Press of America,® Inc.
Lanham · Boulder · New York · Toronto · Oxford

Copyright © 2006 by
University Press of America,® Inc.
4501 Forbes Boulevard
Suite 200
Lanham, Maryland 20706
UPA Acquisitions Department (301) 459-3366

PO Box 317
Oxford
OX2 9RU, UK

All rights reserved
Printed in the United States of America
British Library Cataloging in Publication Information Available

Library of Congress Control Number: 2006924264
ISBN-13: 978-0-7618-3492-2 (paperback : alk. paper)
ISBN-10: 0-7618-3492-3 (paperback : alk. paper)

∞™ The paper used in this publication meets the minimum
requirements of American National Standard for Information
Sciences—Permanence of Paper for Printed Library Materials,
ANSI Z39.48—1984

Dedication

This book is dedicated to my sons, 5-year-old Noah and 1-year-old Gabriel, and my husband, Brian. It is a long time before either son will be a teenager, but Noah has already asserted his rights in advance, telling me, "Don't embarrass me, mom, and don't ground me."

The book also is for all the young people who try as best as they can to make the practice of journalism real and for those courageous adults who sacrifice their time regularly to guide them.

Table of Contents

Foreword: Toward a Lasting Democracy — vii

Introduction: Outsider in Journalism Class — ix

Chapter 1: History of the High School Press — 1

Chapter 2: The Advantages of Advantage — 37

Chapter 3: Why a News Class Resisted News — 81

Chapter 4: Make It a Great Day – Or Not — 135

Chapter 5: Constructing Professional Journalists — 189

Chapter 6: Afterword — 243

Works Cited — 250

Toward a Lasting Democracy

In January 2005, the John F. and James S. Knight Foundation released a report with significant implications for any investigation of high school journalism. The study found that one in three young people believe the First Amendment goes too far in its guarantee of free religion, speech, press and assembly. A surprising segment – 36 percent – said newspapers should not be permitted to publish without prior governmentapproval of stories.

The survey – billed as the largest of its kind – was conducted by researchers at the University of Connecticut. It questioned more than 100,000 students, 8,000 teachers, and 500 school administrators at public and private high schools nationally.

The study found students who take part in journalism activities are more likely to support a free press. This sounds correct, but it is unclear whether they are supporting the First Amendment because of their positive journalism experiences, or as a reaction to a school press that is not free. My own research demonstrates that all journalism experiences are not equally worthwhile. This book contends that inadequate journalism instruction, the kind that does not address students' legal rights, actually may be worse than no journalism at all. This study depended on extended observation of the way journalism was being taught and practiced at three Southern California secondary schools.

It was probably no accident that the Knight report hit the news wires just as Iraqis dipped their fingers in purple ink in hopes of starting a new society with their first free election. I agree that there is a danger of taking the right of free speech for granted. We will only remain a free and self-governing society if we have the support of the younger generation for democracy. Today, generations X and Y could weaken our freedom with their inattention to news.

Why safeguard newspapers if they are too much trouble to read, whether among teenagers or their parents? For teenagers, newspapers must often seem cumbersome reminders that learning, like reading, takes effort. Perhaps new technology will alter this reality, but technology alone cannot create a well-educated group of students wiling to use reporting and writing for high purposes.

This study is not bent on blasting youth for their apparent ignorance. When young people lack knowledge of something as important as the Constitution, then the schools must fill the learning gap. Journalism is taught primarily as an English course, and this might explain why history and government receive only passing attention. Adults in the schools are too often concerned about image and public relations and too infrequently about students' investigation of the world and their place in it. Maybe this is OK if those in power want a complacent citizenry. Allowing the society of the school to be a place for free and open debate is risky if the object of education is control.

This study, based on a small population of students in targeted journalism classrooms, has a different approach, but my experience reveals the results are rather ordinary. Few scholars have bothered to spend the time required for checking the quality of instruction in journalism. They either assume it is poor, or say they are promoting programs to improve the teaching of journalism, or suppose that any form of journalism is healthy. There are few methods of checking these programs.

Some might think this kind of qualitative study is onerous. But observation, if teachers and schools permit it, works. If students in journalism are alienated from the news, then there is less hope for other students. The schools are mistaken when they teach journalism that is not real.

Sara-Ellen Amster, Ph.D.
San Diego, CA
February 1, 2006

Outsider in Journalism Class

The terrorist attacks of September 11, 2001 changed America forever, but they were barely blips on the radar screen of many college-bound adolescents, as they enjoyed life and produced their high school newspaper in suburban Coastal City of southern California. "I know this is boring," declared co-editor Trevor, during a planning session for the October edition that year, "but we *have* to do it." When story ideas were dismally low, he said, "Guys we are way under ideas. So think of something. Can you think of anything?" The editors had turned out the first issue of the year on September 14, but news about September 11 was relegated to the bottom of Page One, inside a story about the delay of the pep rally and girls' volleyball game.

Steven, 17, was among the few students who felt the decisions of the editors were "irresponsible."

> The editors wrote an opinions article about how September 11 affected the football game. Come on! If that's all people go back and find, what does that say about this event? It says yeah, they knew about it, but they didn't want to address it.

The research of this book highlights many missed opportunities – not just the ones missed by young journalists but by the adults who were supposed to socialize them for the future. This work is not only about censorship but also subtler self-censorship and inadequate instruction in journalistic practices and norms. This book tells the story in depth of the way journalism has been practiced at three high schools in southern California, yet its details point to a much larger – and perhaps even universal – story of the way schools define and constrain young people. California should be among the most enlightened places for student journalists to function, given the fact that its state education code has restricted prior restraint by school officials of student publications for more than 25 years. To justify censorship in California schools, objectionable material must be libelous, obscene, or incite students to cause a "clear and present danger." Yet *de jure* law does not translate into *de facto* practice in the classroom.[1] Circumstances appear particularly troubling for working-class and minority youth involved in newspaper production. Two of the three schools in this study faced the regular threat of censorship, inconsistent (even absent) instruction, and contradictory messages about what the media are supposed to be about in a democracy. The third study school stood out as a higher quality, more stable location for learning.

While wealthier, suburban youth are not immune from staff changes or looming state budget cuts and all teenagers suffer from the growing national obsession with standardized testing that can pervert the real meaning of education, this study shows the stark disparity between upper-middle class schools serving mostly white students and a working-class school populated largely by Mexican-Americans. The schools serving middle- and upper-class youth supplied better facilities for journalism and more experienced teachers, but the school in the poorer community treated its newspaper as a poorly executed burden that could easily be eliminated if necessary. The most successful newspaper program in this study served the upper-middle class and enthusiastically supported the newspaper as another sign of academic prowess, treating journalism and teenagers with greater respect.

More than three decades after the book *Our Time is Now* (Birmingham 1970) was printed, I found few adults giving teens the sense that they could change their surroundings via journalism. Of high school press freedom, novelist Kurt Vonnegut wrote: "As to the people who tell these young adults that they must not speak as frankly as they do, because the officially adult community will be outraged: They are right in a way, but that way is cowardly. This is the home of the brave. Remember?" (x).

As I began this three-year project in the spring of 2001, I remembered Vonnegut's words. I expected to find lots of evidence that high school journalism instruction reverses the profound disinterest many young people have shown toward the news and government for the last 40 years. But instead, I found the opposite. Cynical instruction about the media is typical, largely disconnected from suggestions for reform or the inculcation of professional standards of writing and reporting. The schools are only partially at fault. The media themselves must take some of the blame as they are not always shining examples of journalistic excellence. Yet the small, local school press can empower youth and serve as an example of how things should be done in journalism. Quality journalism happens in some high schools, but they are a minority. The student press too often is stifled and dimmed.

Beyond the schools in my study, other Southern California high schools experience regular conflict between school authorities and student journalists, sometimes causing censorship battles. Ellen Kersey, recent president of the Southern California Journalism Education Association, was advisor to Adolfo Camarillo High School's *Stinger* in

Ventura County, Ca., when the principal of a neighboring high school illegally removed features mentioning contraceptives from a package of stories on pregnancy (*Stinger*, March 29, 2000, 1, 7). The district superintendent asked Kersey's principal to cut coverage of the incident from her students' paper. The student editor in chief stood his ground and ran a censored story from the neighboring school paper, called *The Spartan*, "When Children Have Children." This was not the only time Kersey and her students' newspaper challenged school authorities. After a shooting at a local high school the year before, Stinger launched an undercover investigation of school security measures, printing a first-person, front-page account of easy access to facilities and students on campuses ("Security found inadequate at district schools," *Stinger*, February 2, 2001, 1). Kersey, now retired, said her upper-middle class school was known as "the country club of our district," and its students were sharp, winning the most student newspaper competitions. "My kids were always seeking controversy and always wanting to deal with the big issues, then we got in trouble all the time. If you have an advisor and kids who don't, they are quite happy putting out a nice, little paper." The controversial stories won journalism awards. Had she not retired, Kersey believed, she would have been removed as newspaper advisor.

One advisor also willing to take heat at her school was a college and freelance journalist who taught working-class Latino students in a large county. Her high school (73 percent Latino) had no newspaper class, so newspaper production had to be conducted after school and on weekends. Often Spanish was the students' first language and constructing the newspaper presented a challenge, she said. Her willingness to give members of the newspaper staff significant freedom did not make her "a favorite person" with the administration, she said.

At the school, a student writing a story about protests surrounding the Iraq War interviewed an administrator who called students "opportunists" and a teacher who said protesters were "idiots." The young reporter then documented another case where a teacher was handing out pro-war leaflets to protesters and telling them "you're supporting murder," presumably because of Saddam Hussein's brutality.

For 25 years, the newspaper had required approval by the principal before each publication, a practice known as prior review, the advisor said. The principal had final authority over newspaper content, sometimes resorting to prior restraint by calling for the removal of certain stories. The school district made the principal the editor in chief of the newspaper and gave him the final authority for editing copy of the district's 11 high school newspapers. Such a practice violates the

California Education Code, which prohibits such censorship by school officials and gives student editors the responsibility for assigning and editing copy. But in this case, the school principal told the newspaper advisor she must not allow students to print the "inflammatory" Iraq War comments from teachers or administrators. She and students contacted the Student Press Law Center in Arlington, Va., and together they threatened a lawsuit, causing the district's policy to be rewritten in the summer of 2003. The First Amendment victory was "a huge thing" for the advisor's students. "It was like David and Goliath, and they thought, 'We can do something.' It was a life lesson you can't get from a textbook," she said.

The student editor said that the censorship "gave us the feeling that . . . because we are an under-performing school they don't feel that we have the capabilities of putting out a professional newspaper" (*Communicator*, Southern California Journalism Education Association, September 2003, 1). The district's policy was not employed at upper-middle class schools, where parents might object, just this advisor's school and two other schools comprised of working-class students, the advisor said. "Typically poorer schools have fewer teachers who are experienced," she said. "They pay their dues by initially being employed in needy schools and then they go to affluent schools closer to where they live." Teachers at suburban schools often do not have to confront a lack of computers, limited newspaper funding, and less skilled students, so that is easier for them," the advisor said. In addition, students arrive with extensive knowledge and preparation from home.

A. Methodology: Research Adds Insight to Teaching

This study uses a combination of qualitative methods including ethnography, participant-observation research, and journalistic techniques to collect data on student journalists and high-school newspaper programs. Few researchers have bothered to spend long hours watching the delivery of instruction in journalism classrooms. Most studies are quantitative in nature, requiring adults to answer a series of questions. Only the rare inquiry includes interviews with students in schools. Journalism teachers have written first-hand accounts of their own journalism teaching, but outsiders are not often invited in. Because I have been a professional newspaper reporter for nearly a decade and a three-time high-school newspaper advisor, my experiences deepen my interpretations.

I focused primarily on 15 students at each high school. The study population was selected to correspond to the nature of the newspaper project, where many students might contribute to the coverage of a single news event. Even so, main characters do emerge. I observed students in class and after school and I interviewed them for extended time periods, from 30 to 90 minutes each, usually more than once. At Homestead High School, there was instability and a higher turnover rate, so the study group changed composition throughout the year.

All answers during the classroom-based portion of my work were confidential. No students, teachers, or administrators at study schools are named in this report, and only pseudonyms are used to identify the three schools – Coastal, Homestead and Creekwood Canyon high schools. The particular locations in southern California are not specifically named. The schools in my study include two high-performing high schools and a low-performing school, based both on standardized test results and the perceptions of students and faculty. By recounting specific events that happened during observation sessions, classroom experiences retold during the extended interviews, and individual perceptions revealed verbally or in writing, I sought to examine the impact on teenagers involved in high school journalism.

The idea for this inquiry began during a conversation I had with Mark Goodman, executive director of the Student Press Law Center, early in my doctoral education. He was certain that the Supreme Court's *Hazelwood v. Kuhlmeier* decision, which granted school officials greater control over student publications for any legitimate pedagogical purpose, had bred greater self-censorship by high school students and advisors. Most studies finding little change after *Hazelwood* are inaccurate, he contends. They rely on different definitions of censorship, from simple editing, to prior restraint, to any adult interference. What was needed was direct observational research, which might outright uncover more subtle problems or incidents like the ones Kersey and others describe. Not only are many students unaware of their rights under California law, but many advisors are also uncertain, Goodman said. By observing, I could gain a sense of what was really going on in the classroom and how students understood their lessons, their own place in the school's power structure, and the value of the media. The idea was not only to uncover censorship, but also to discover what students were learning about the news.

I focused my research on the operations of the student newspaper, *The Coastal Chronicle,* at the end of the academic year 2000-2001 and during the school year 2001-2002. I stayed one to four hours at a time, sometimes visiting two or three times a week. The journalism elective had two advisors, April Hill and Laura Thompson. I watched the production of *The Homestead Herald* from August 2002 to June 2003 under the direction of one teacher, Stacey Webb, and a substitute, Dave Perez. And I also explored the operations of *The Creekwood Comet* from December 2002 to May 2003, while Advanced Journalism teacher Alexa Phillips ran the journalism program.

The students ranged in age from 14 to 18. They produced 10 editions per year at Creekwood Canyon, 8 at Homestead High, and 13 at Coastal High School. At students' request, I sometimes helped them on stories or accompanied them on assignments, to help improve their writing and reporting skills.

If the degree of independent judgment that students could exercise over editorial content following a news event was an important variable in this project, it was useful to assess those points at which students were allowed to set their own agendas. If the classroom teacher or school officials circumvented these agendas, it was critical to analyze those moments in detail as well as to collect student impressions of them. Even those times during which the teacher and school officials did not appear to influence the outcome of a story's coverage, the presence of these adults could have a chilling effect on student expression. Their intervention was their attempt to provide journalism instruction, yet their acts had both intentional and unintentional consequences. I paid special attention to the justifications given by educators for such intervention, including their ideas about how students might best avoid sensationalism. I found that an explanation of students' legal rights was often missing but critical to students' confident practice of journalism. As Michael Schudson asserts in *The Good Citizen* (1998, 309), the knowledge and assertion of one's rights is a hopeful sign that Americans are exercising their responsibilities as citizens:

> A rights-regarding citizenship does not 'answer' democracy's discontents, but it is a necessary part of any answer. Moreover, it automatically implies respect for the rights of others and the willingness to engage in public discourse according to public norms and a public language. We have to recognize that the claiming of rights, though it should not be the end of a citizen's political consciousness, is an invaluable beginning to it. It deserves to be nurtured, not condemned. We need to teach ourselves and our children more, not less, about rights.

Any education that is based on hiding major legal doctrine from student journalists is suspect at best.

Through an explication of specific classroom incidents or case studies, my intent was, as much as possible, to develop the "thick description" that Clifford Geertz invokes in *The Interpretation of Cultures* (1973). The idea of thick description can be traced to philosopher Gilbert Ryle. Geertz himself describes thick description as "our own construction of other people's constructions of what they and their compatriots are up to" (Emerson 2001, 59-60). I also modeled my research after such scholars as Angela Valenzuela (1999), who interviewed and observed working class Latino teens in Houston and Annette Lareau (1989, 2000), whose work with elementary school children and parents in northern California yielded insight into the way that family upbringing influences academic performance. Ethnographic researcher Valenzuela used techniques that looked closely at human relationships and how they affected students' motivation to succeed – factors I also examined.

Unlike my study, Valenzuela examined an entire school composed of Mexican-American youths, rather than one specialized classroom within the school. She visited a variety of classrooms and found that "rather than building on students' cultural and linguistic knowledge and heritage to create biculturally and bilingually competent youth, schools subtract these identifications from them to their social and academic detriment" (25).

Both of our studies look at the places where students conflict with official school authority figures and how these tensions affect the quality of their educations. Following Valenzuela's lead, I decided to supplement my observational results with quantifiable data. Student participants in my study answered a series of four question sheets on their home backgrounds, career goals, attitudes toward news and politics, and their media use. This information gave me more descriptive material, but it also allowed me to ask them relevant follow-up questions. I included questions on coverage of September 11 and the Iraq War.

I followed the examples of a host of other educational researchers who have conducted ethnographies both of teacher-student relationships and student friendship groups, from Paul Willis (1977) to Robert Everhart (1983) to Penelope Eckert (1989).

These studies shed light on the different ways that social class affects academic attainment. The background research of legal scholar Marjorie Heins (2001) and journalist Thomas Hine (1999) also proved invaluable. Journalism teachers were helpful in considering the process of how students produce news.

In general, I sought to follow the advice of George Spindler and Lorie Hammond who suggested taking notes and audiotapes, among other data. "The field ethnographer is also a collector of artifacts – drawings, documents, newspaper articles, editorials, memos, letters to the editor, essays, texts of speeches, and so forth."

My research principally came from what students had said on tape, usually in class, during conversations and in interviews. I employed no still photography with students or any video camera. I collected printed materials and examined data from essays students had written on why they wanted particular editorial posts. There were classroom assignment sheets, class story assignment and evaluation forms, raw notes on grade tabulation, stories in progress, newspaper issues and finished news articles and editorials, mock layouts, sections of the state education code, the students' class constitution (created during Mrs. Thompson's tenure at Coastal), awards lists and class enrollment forms. The more documents I reviewed, the more complete the picture of class operations became. The discussions with students and their in-class conversations, during formal and informal activities, form the bulk of this research, particularly those exchanges that related to case studies used.

David Buckingham's method in *The Making of Citizens* (2000) was critical to my observations and interviews, though Buckingham does not use ethnography. Buckingham included teens in Philadelphia and London discussing different styles of TV news programs aimed at audiences of young people. From focus group discussions about news and the news programs they had seen, he interpreted their attitudes toward news and politics. On the whole, he found young people continued to be alienated from the news but that they were also capable of insight about politics, at times as capable as adults. Buckingham analyzed the way young people talked about news and the way they used that talk to situate their own identities: "In expressing feelings and making judgments about what we watch, we are inevitably and simultaneously defining ourselves as particular kinds of people." (72).

Some students described news as upsetting and depressing. Some rejected politics as irrelevant to their lives. Others, no matter their material circumstances, believed they could not possibly influence society because of their position as minors. Issues upon which students were more likely to have an effect, such as school debates, held more interest for them, Buckingham found, but I found this interest was only slightly greater. Students were most interested in news expressed through humor or narrative, arts and entertainment. I chose case studies of conventional news, rather than entertainment, because students deemed these events more important, and they stood out as having sparked interest and debate. Like Buckingham's, my research has depended on talk, on students' verbal assessments of their own situations and beliefs. However, I gleaned more information about their perceptions of news by watching them attempt to produce news for others. Young people's attitudes toward news were revealed as they grappled with the presentation of their news stories. I viewed each story or newspaper page as a visual representation of teenagers' thinking.

Roy Peter Clark, in his book *Free to Write* (1987), demonstrates a journalism class that is student-centered and relatively unfettered. His book is based on his experiences teaching journalism to middle-school students in Pinellas County, Fla., and Clark believes "that journalism holds the key to improved writing instruction in America." Generating their own ideas largely motivated his journalism students. The investigation of these ideas allowed them to explore their immediate world. The journalistic process also makes students better citizens because they learn to question their assumptions and actively investigate issues of public concern. While neither Mrs. Thompson nor Mrs. Webb employed Clark's specific techniques, the class routine of brainstorming sessions, followed by story assignments and publication, appeared to follow the ritual of reporting the news. Despite this, I knew some students in my study found the process limiting as both teachers practiced it. A key factor was orchestration. Were the students allowed to investigate their own stories, or had brainstorming become an event circumscribed by the teacher and top editors, compromised by the assignment of grades? I wanted to explore the similarities and differences between the high schools and Clark's goals. Citing another well-respected writing teacher, Clark explained the student search for ideas this way:

> Teachers tell students what to write about. As a result, says Donald Graves, students go on 'teacher welfare' when it comes to ideas. They become passive and dependent and fail to recognize the value of their own experience. My students receive assignments as journalists do. But they must find many of their own writing ideas so we brainstorm, read and confer. Sometimes, I am reduced to taking dictation. (4)

The student editors' views about the news were reflected in decisions they made about story coverage, placement and play, which were sometimes contested by other students, the advisor or principal. The student writers constructed stories, but much like their adult counterparts, they were sometimes reluctant to highlight their own acts, which came from choices they made while reporting and writing.

My interviews included questions about student motivations for identifying journalism as a career goal or ruling it out, their ideas about the use of censorship, their conceptions of news and democratic ideals, their assessment of power dynamics, and their perceived level of autonomy in the classroom.

I started my contact with the students with the open-ended question of how they came to sign up for journalism, which often yielded longer conversations about their writing skills and college plans. We also discussed their relations with their families, their views of the news, both professional and at school, their views of the stories in the newspaper, their ideas about the high school audience or for the newspaper's improvement and their personal media habits. I found out who watched TV, what they watched, what newspapers and magazines they read, and whether they used any of these media for generating ideas for their newspaper. The journalist in me often would target particular points they had made for further discussion.

Along with students from working-class families, my sample included upper-middle class students because I sought to study up as George Marcus advocates (68, 85). My subsequent expansion to a high school with less privileged students and lower test scores was not for mere completeness or comparison, but was an effort to create a multiply situated project. In Marcus' words, I was "putting questions to an emergent object of study whose contours, sites and relationships are not known beforehand but are themselves a contribution of making an account that has different, complexly connected real-world sites of investigation" (Marcus 1998, 86). At all three high schools, I immediately knew I would need to consider my own reflexive understanding of my relationship to the dominant sphere of power. Was I more comfortable among the suburban middle class students because that is my own background and upbringing as the child of two professors? If so, how might that have impacted my research?

My subjects, too, often themselves were capable of considering their statements in light of their own positions on the newspaper, their motivations, family backgrounds, and loyalties. It was always important to recognize the teenagers at Coastal and Creekwood Canyon high schools for what they were – at once part of the powerful elite (by virtue of their class status) – and the powerless (because of their low position in decision-making chain of school governance). At Homestead, I needed to be careful not to underestimate students, repeating the same mistakes of their teachers. As Marcus points out, it is necessary not only to explore the relations of the powerful to the subjugated, but the ways in which there is contradiction, ambiguity and complicity in all of these positions (20-21).

B. Survey of Advisors

To find out the characteristics of other high school newspapers in Southern California and to situate the three study schools among their peers, I conducted an electronic survey of advisors with Kersey's aid. She sent 120 e-mails to advisors in the Southern California Journalism Education Association (SCJEA), receiving 20 responses. The survey is comprehensive in the questions presented, but limited by the pool of respondents and by the fact that not all high schools participate in professional journalism training. Advisors in the SCJEA represent the more involved schools that are already committed to journalistic aims. The response rate was close to 17 percent: responses came from schools situated in both upper-middle class and working-class communities.[2] Kersey said approximately one in seven high school newspaper programs in Southern California are part of the SCJEA, which runs competitions for student journalists and offers workshops and training for both journalism advisors and students. She confirmed that the answers to this survey were consistent with her experience based on a teaching career that spanned almost 50 years (Interview with Kersey, May 28, 2003).

The answers provide a glimpse of the practice of high school journalism in Southern California. Among the results:

• *Frequency of publication*: 70 percent of school newspapers in southern California are monthlies, coming out between 8 and 10 times during the academic year. A small number are weeklies, with the rare school attempting to publish a daily.

• *Time in the advisor role.* The bulk or 45 percent of newspaper advisors have held the job for two years or less, 25 percent stay three to five years and 5 percent stay six to nine years, with 25 percent staying more than 10 years, sometimes for entire careers. In other words, 70 percent have held the job for five years or less.

• *Journalism background.* The large majority of advisors were student journalists, either in high school or college. Forty percent listed no other experience besides on-the-job training and workshops, and 55 percent had taken college courses in journalism. About 30 percent were professional journalists at some point in their careers. This means about 70 percent of advisors do not have professional journalism experience.

• *Types of journalism class, teacher workload.* In almost every case, journalism is taught as a single production class. Between 15 and 20 percent of schools divide their classes into beginning and advanced. In one case, newspaper is strictly extracurricular but in two additional cases, it is both a class and an extracurricular activity. Forty percent of instructors teach a total of five classes including journalism, a typical experience that may be evidence of overwork. Fewer, 15 percent, teach four classes with journalism. It is rare to teach only three classes including journalism or to be saddled with six, but it happens. Most people affiliated with the Journalism Education Association were not running their programs as strictly extracurricular. Journalism usually was an English elective, but a history teacher taught the class at one site. Depending on the school, journalism could replace a regular English credit.

• *Extra pay for newspaper work.* Newspaper advisors most commonly were paid between $2,000 and $2,500 a year for their advising work, but there were some schools that paid $3,000 a year or more, even $6,000 a year. A smaller number of schools paid between $1,000 and $1,700. A handful paid a stipend of $1,000 or less, middle schools pay nothing extra, $600 at the junior high. The amount is sometimes dependent on a teacher's salary level and can vary. It is not much – usually about the same as a coach's stipend. A 25-year teacher with a master's degree and a top salary wrote: "I get a stipend that is less than the Academic Decathlon Advisor and less than that of athletic coaches."

• *Qualities of journalism students.* Journalism as an academic subject is fragmented and every class takes on somewhat different forms and populations. About 40 percent of advisors serve slightly more female students than males. Schools either try to limit their journalism programs to top students and writers, often excluding freshmen, or they take an inclusive approach, sometimes admitting non-traditional students who don't love school, as one advisor reported, and opening the program to all grade levels. Sometimes the school doesn't restrict the class, but the population ends up with primarily honors students anyway.

• *Funding of the newspaper.* Twenty percent of papers are entirely funded by advertising revenue. This is a hard benchmark to achieve and some schools find it difficult to maintain. Some papers are as much as two-thirds or more supported by advertising. Roughly 40 percent are supported by a combination of ads and student government money. A minority gains all their money from the school district, or 50 percent of their money from the school district and 50 percent from ad revenue. However, the more fiscally independent school newspapers are, the more editorial control they feel they enjoy. Larger papers cost more, as do papers using color. The average cost for a 12-page paper was about $400. The printing cost for a newspaper ranged from as low as $112 for eight pages to as high as $2,500 for 24 with full color. The cost also varies more depending on whether the paper is a broadsheet or a tabloid. The size of the school also is relevant: High schools ranged from 1,000 to 4,500 in size.

• *Purpose of a school newspaper.* I asked advisors: Do you feel that the newspaper is more of: a) an educational tool for students, b) a forum for student expression, or c) a public relations tool for the school? Five advisors, or 25 percent, saw all three factors as equal. Seven, or 35 percent saw its importance as an educational tool as being paramount. Five or 25 percent stated that its importance as a forum for student expression was most critical. Two, or 10 percent, said that it was equally a forum and an educational tool. One response listed the newspaper as a public relations organ and an educational tool. One advisor wrote,

> The students and I see the paper primarily as a forum for student expression. Secondly, but not very importantly, we also see the paper as an educational tool to improve writing and prepare students for college journalism. The administration insists that we also see the paper as a public relations tool and we rather grudgingly acquiesce.

Ultimately, what information about the media do most students take from their high school journalism experiences? I felt surveys were inadequate to determine this. The only way to know is to watch, to be the proverbial fly on the wall. Although some students reacted to my presence in class differently than others – and I am sure I interfered at times with the routine of the day – there were others who forgot I was there at all, that I was seeing and hearing what they saw and heard.

Notes

1 In addition to Cal. Educ. Code Section 48907 that protects students in public schools, the state has the Leonard Law, Cal. Educ. Code Section 48950, which prohibits school officials from censoring student speech that would have been protected had it occurred off campus.

2 Included in this February 2003 survey are SCJEA advisors from 17 high schools.

History of the High School Press

When students at the Public Latin School in Philadelphia distributed their hand-written *Students' Gazette,* the Revolutionary War was underway and British troops occupied the school building. Issued June 11, 1777, and published regularly for five years, *The Gazette* was the first known high school newspaper in America.[1] Philadelphia was the intellectual and financial center of the United States, soon to be the seat of government, and the Declaration of Independence had only been signed the year before. Philadelphia also was a birthplace of American journalism itself, second only to Boston, where the first newspapers were established. Benjamin Franklin's *Pennsylvania Gazette,* the most popular newspaper in the colonies, protested the British stamp act by printing the paper without the required date, number, masthead or imprint.[2]

It is unlikely that the young people in Philadelphia ever imagined each other merely as "adolescents" or "teenagers," but instead saw themselves as important members of a society in the throes of upheaval and reinvention. Psychologist and educator G.S. Hall would not popularize the term "adolescence" until 1904 to indicate a distinct time in child development and psychology. The term "teenager" was not even used until World War II (Hine 1999, 3-4, 225).

Journalist and social critic Thomas Hine, educational scholar David Buckingham, legal theorist Marjorie Heins and sociologist James Gilbert all have written about the teenager as a socially constructed phenomenon, a group variously afforded greater respect, status and power, depending on the era. Yet young people ultimately were forced to accept a definition of themselves as less than whole. The promise offered by adulthood helped them adjust to this weakened condition. Hine writes in *The Rise and Fall of the American Teenager* (1999) the notion of the teenager depends on "the idea of the adolescent as a not quite competent person, beset by stress and hormones." The definition of the teenager as immature and thus, deficient, remains so strong today that it can cripple the practice of journalism as young people first attempt it.

Before I explore three classrooms in depth, it is important to examine context, the history of journalism in the public school setting, and the way schools and society have come to cast a skeptical eye on the young. Public attitudes, made obvious in judicial decisions, as well as the attitudes of educators and school officials toward youth, are important because they influence the level of autonomy and trust teenagers can achieve in the classroom. The field of adolescent psychology also deserves consideration because it may identify the common strengths that young people can bring to journalism. There is a danger, however, in any over-reliance on psychological stages for describing teenagers' abilities, because of individual variation and the influence of social context in forming cognitive structures. These intellectual processes are more often constructed in discourse and adult-teenager exchange than they are predetermined, contributing to the distinct nature of every student journalist, journalism course and school newspaper. However, it is possible to chart the history of high school journalism, based on the commentary of journalism educators and textbook authors, scholarly research and legal rulings.

With the possible exception of the Revolutionary War period, when high schools were few and catered to the children of the elite, the history of high school journalism in America has not been very revolutionary. It has not typically been one in which wise and patient adults teach youth democratic ideals that will allow them to think critically about authority and challenge basic assumptions of the world. The ideal newspaper class might teach a critical pedagogy, allowing students to explore all aspects of the immediate environment – "critical thinking" is a catch phrase of educators – but such a concept is often missing from journalism courses.

The first edition of *Students' Gazette* was an experiment. It did not appear to be connected to a class, but rather was a kind of underground leaflet. Its young publisher promised on the front page that he would do "everything in his power to make this paper as entertaining as possible." The paper was produced more than a century before journalistic practices included the interview and other basic newsgathering techniques. It contained personal entries and letters to readers. The lead article thanked contributors and asked that subscribers "do everything to forward so useful an institution." There was an ad for a lost grammar book that offered a reward. A third entry was a wake-up call to classmates, saying that neither Newton nor ancient poets may offer much clarity about present-day times.

School journalism took a hiatus of more than a century while young people were not attending high schools but instead worked regular jobs, sometimes after apprenticeship periods. As a school discipline, journalism began in the early 1900s. Even then, it likely discouraged independent thinking and fostered self-censorship because of conflicting educational theories, legal constraints, and disciplinary methods of classroom teachers and school officials. History often showed the school to be a censor, squelching rebellion in favor of more superficial appearances, channeling youthful energy and impulses, and requiring young people to conform to strict regulation. Most high school newspapers did not become bastions of freedom.

Michael Moore's bestseller *Stupid White Men* (2001) describes the misery high schools unwittingly can inflict on students. He calls the contemporary high school "a two-thousand-plus inmate holding pen" and says that the result of constant intellectual abuse in high school often "means the kids learn to submerge any personal expression. They learn that it's better to go along so that you get along. They learn that to rock the boat could get them rocked right out of the school."

"Don't question authority, to do as you're told. Don't think, just do as I say. Oh, and have a good and productive life as an active, well-adjusted participant in our thriving democracy!" In fact, Moore calls the government of the high school "some sort of totalitarian dictatorship," a far cry from Revolutionary times, writing:

> The halls are packed with burned-out teenagers, shuffling from class to class, dazed and confused, wondering what the hell they're doing there. They learn how to regurgitate answers the state wants them to give, and any attempt to be an individual is now grounds for being suspected of being a member of the trench-coat mafia (115).

Of course, many educators would be appalled at Moore's cynicism, negativism and hyperbole. They have dedicated their lives to education. They would assert high schools provide worthwhile instruction.

A liability-conscious principal might say that teenagers are less experienced and mature than adults, that high schoolers are still mastering journalistic skills required to practice responsible reporting, writing and newspaper production, and that students are mere dabblers in journalism, so why give them freedoms accorded professional journalists? Their experience of the high school newspaper comes at a fixed time that is transitory, while the high school itself is more permanent and may need protection from reporters not fully accountable because they are preparing to leave the community for other opportunities.

Moore is convinced that students must take matters into their own hands and cannot place any faith in school authorities. He says that individual students can rescue themselves from the turgid educational system through journalism and calls upon them to "launch your own newspaper or webzine." His advice: "You have a constitutionally protected right to do this. If you take care not to be obscene, or libelous or give them any reason to shut you down, this can be a great way to get the truth out about what's happening at your school." Yet whether students nationally have a constitutional right to a free press remains an open question.

A. Liberation through Journalism?

Public high schools originated out of convenience – as places to send masses of young people in large numbers when workplaces no longer would accept them, to get them off the streets. As early as 1901, Stanford professor Edward Ross wrote that schools were "an economical system of police," assuring social restraint and social placement. The schools' chief goal, then, may not have been to secure individual intellectual and economic success, but more to seal societal conformity.[3]

High schools began serving large numbers of youths in part because the Great Depression left them jobless, and in part because child labor was losing its mainstream appeal, which led the young away from gainful employment. According to Hine, "It was during the Depression years that high school finally enrolled a majority of the school-age population and moved toward being the universal experience of America's young."

> While the Jazz Age had glamorized and eroticized youth, the Depression and the War that followed did something even more decisive to youth; they bureaucratized it. (204)

New Deal programs "actively discriminated against young people in the workplace." Many programs shaped the youth problems they sought to correct, he contends.

The major reason the schools gained acceptance, however, was parents. Parents opted to send their teens to high school not because they wanted them to learn about democracy or equality, but because they wanted to give their teenagers an advantage. Institutionalization in high school changed teenagers' lives irrevocably. High school enrollment grew from 4.3 million to 6.5 million students during the Depression, an increase of about 50 percent. By 1930, less than half of the nation's teens were students, but by 1940, two-thirds enrolled in school (Hine, 215).

Young people were anything but sheltered, Hine said. They were critical to the survival of their families. They were soldiers, sailors, cowboys, miners, schoolteachers and physicians. They also were poor and displaced, "left to scramble on their own as bootblacks or newsboys, or as pickpockets and prostitutes," Hine writes (300). Thus, students' current-day apathy toward political life and the media may be a fault of adults who dismiss their competence and ability to make a difference, writes Buckingham in *The Making of Citizens* (2000).

"It is clear that the declining interest in news journalism is seen by many commentators as an indication of a broader social crisis, and of the failure of older generations to adequately socialize the young – a situation that most suggest is likely to continue" (4).

In *After the Death of Childhood* (2000), Buckingham discusses how schools constrain youth by definition:

> The separation of children by biological age, rather than 'ability,' the highly regulated nature of teacher/student relationships, the organization of the curriculum, and the daily time-table, the practice of grading -- all in various ways serve to reinforce and to naturalize particular assumptions about what children are and should be. (7)

B. Vocationalism versus Progressive Education

Because parents must support the schools to ensure their viability and because parents can be career-oriented, one influential argument holds that journalism programs were inserted into secondary schooling for reasons of vocational preparation. This also may be because prior to the Depression, the American educational system had embraced business as the key to assuring social efficiency, but afterward, this unqualified endorsement began to fade, writes Herbert M. Kliebard in *Schooled to Work* (1999).

Youth were worst hit by Depression-era unemployment, an early cause of alienation. Fearful that disillusioned young people would turn to Adolf Hitler and communism, Charles W. Taussig attempted to add democratic education to New Deal vocational relief programs under Franklin Delano Roosevelt. The president was often skeptical of the ability of educators to boost participation in civic life, and he was more confident in his own rival programs directed at youth, which were part of the Civilian Conservation Corps and the Works Progress Administration. In 1935, Roosevelt created the National Youth Administration under the WPA to include "not simply job training but elements of the political education that Taussig and Eleanor Roosevelt had been supporting" (192).

Even when they only enrolled a substantial minority of youth, secondary schools helped socialize both middle- and working-class young people. According to historians John Modell and Madeline Goodman

(1990), the evolution of capitalism and the modern welfare state extended youth and expanded its significance.

"The period from 1870 to 1930 (later in European countries) marks the transformation in America from the nineteenth century's 'useful child' to the twentieth century's sentimentalized 'priceless child,'" they write.

This shift worked against student journalists just as they were starting out. Youths were urged to remain in school because education would later equal opportunity. At the same time that schools emphasized social mobility, self-government and choice, rejecting inherited status, they also sharply constrained young people for their own good with the justification of protecting them. While having their decisions made for them enabled young people to avoid exploitation in the workforce, it also made it easier for them to avoid thought and individual self-will that the educational system was supposed to encourage.

The emphasis on vocational education at the time school journalism was launched led DeWitt C. Reddick, author of the textbook *The Mass Media and the School Newspaper* (1976), to conclude that the original purpose of high school journalism classes was "to stimulate and guide young people in the development of communication skills that prepare them for careers with newspapers, magazines and other information publications and agencies." However, this was a narrow view. While most American young people did not yet attend high school, many indeed may have taken these courses with the goal of gaining a trade. Yet the original purpose of journalism was more sophisticated and directed at a broader audience – at least in the minds of the few who launched early high school programs.

Evidence suggests that journalism courses sprang out of the English curriculum. Today English teachers run the classes. The introduction of journalism to secondary schooling was not a direct invention of John Dewey's progressivism, although it shared much in common with the goals of his experience-based and "learning by doing" education. It also was not an outgrowth of the vocational movement, though journalism programs launched lifelong careers for many cub reporters.

Researcher David Knott of the University of Toledo (1981) contends that it is no accident that "the growth and proliferation of high school newspapers and national and state journalism education associations occurred in roughly a 10-year period – 1920-1930. It was the same decade in which Dewey and his disciples gained momentum. This was the period in which education for democracy enjoyed its first promising bud. Journalism education and high school newspapers have extremely close ties to this theory" (14). Dewey's theories were tested

CHAPTER 1: HISTORY OF THE HIGH SCHOOL PRESS 7

at his Laboratory School at the University of Chicago. If Dewey was not directly responsible for high school journalism, his theories helped provide a philosophical justification for its spread.

Journalism was politically partisan until the 1830s when the penny press began directing its news to the masses. The Civil War brought a demand for more dependable and standardized news-gathering. Yet major changes in the way people received their news did not happen overnight. The partisan press died slowly.

"By 1890, the modern conception of the newspaper with a capable staff and huge circulation had emerged, and the need for trained personnel led to interest in journalism education," wrote Paul Dressel of Columbia University's Teacher's College (21).

Dewey opposed the idea of job training in the public schools, but his "vague and loosely defined identification as an educational reformer seeking to infuse active occupations into what had become a passive, almost archaic, curriculum probably served to associate him in the popular mind with the very position he tried to oppose," argues Kliebard in *The Struggle for the American Curriculum* (1995).

Dewey argued, "When education is tied above all to one's predicted occupational or social role as distinct from one's present reality, the remoteness of school from life is accentuated rather than diminished." He felt an emphasis on the "here and now" might be the best preparation for the future. He was critical of the way vocationalists seemed to accept the structure and conditions of the workplace in order to prepare young people for specific jobs, not for analytical thinking. "Vocationalists directed their criticisms not at the way workers were being made appendages to their machines and at the inequality of opportunity in the job market but at schools for being inadequately attuned to the workplace," writes Kliebard. "This was just what Dewey was afraid of" (228).

Before journalism education was a recognized discipline, some high schools produced extra-curricular newspapers, most of them four-page, mimeographed editions printed monthly. Depending on location, what was in these newspapers may have been quite tepid. Among the exceptions: New York City's *The Horace Mann Record*, which became a biweekly because "the news got cold before it reached the public" (Abbott 1910, 659). This difficulty in providing timely news still makes news in most high school publications bland and less relevant as students struggle to adopt professional news standards. One school, Shortridge High School in Indianapolis, actually published a daily in 1898, writes Knott of the University of Toledo (1981).

For his doctoral dissertation, Knott found that formal journalism classes were rare in high schools before the 1930s, but he listed courses in 1900 at North High School in Des Moines, Iowa; in 1910 at Kearney High School in Kearney, Neb.; in 1912 at Washington High School in Milwaukee, Wis.; and 1914 at Decatur County High School in Oberlin, Kan. (Knott 1981, Campbell 1939). But these programs were isolated and unaware of each other, and it was not until 1940 that journalism was considered part of high school life. Cora Dolbee was credited with launching the first high school journalism class in the nation (Boyd 1960), but this is mainly because she took the time to document her effort, not because she was first.

She wrote that journalism was in its infancy as an academic subject – "so new in all high schools that there are as yet no records anywhere" (520). Her article showed excitement about journalism's potential. "A boy who was naturally one of the most careless writers in the fall developed before the end of the first term into the best news writer, and at the end of the second term, surprised not only the class but the instructor by writing the best short-story in the division – the most unified in plot, the freest in style."[4]

C. Shaping High School Journalism

Few subjects privilege the "here and now" more adeptly than journalism, and the subject historically has been seriously misunderstood and underestimated, treated very skeptically by its critics, including many English teachers themselves, perhaps because they questioned its academic status. Charles R. Foster in "Extracurricular Activities in the High School" (1925, 144-151)[5] advises schools not to "overemphasize the news value of high school publications" but focus on community relations and students' English skills.

In a May 1919 piece for *The English Journal*, Frances Perry similarly argues a main purpose of school publications is to promote the school.

"Boost," he writes. "Boost everything and everybody. Boost!" Perry explains by saying, "The school paper exists primarily for the good of the school. . . " (299-301).

In American history, the concept of high school journalism was controversial at first, unthinkable for some, because it necessarily invoked professional journalism in the greater society. Many educators were skeptical about giving young people the power of the press, and they were unsympathetic with journalism's connection to democracy and civics. Although they have achieved notable successes, journalism programs have never been standardized or turned into much more than a sidelight to the traditional core courses offered by secondary schools. As a result, one journalism program, the philosophies and expertise of its educators, and the quality of its student newspapers can vary widely from the next, even in a single county.

Different educational theorists have had different uses for journalism, saying it offers a range of benefits. Many journalism educators have stuck to their ideals about journalism's potential to provide both better literacy skills and a democratic education. Wrote Grant Milnor Hyde in an early high school journalism textbook (1922):

> Much has happened in high-school journalism since the first edition of this book was written in 1920-21 under the title, *A Course in Journalistic Writing*. The introduction of anything journalistic into high school was a very debatable subject at that time; many English teachers looked upon it as a new form of heresy; most of the university schools of journalism were vigorously opposed to it. The author was earnestly warned against 'advocating journalism in high school' (v).

Like Dolbee, who recognized high school journalism's value for addressing media education and for evaluating publications outside school, Hyde saw journalism's myriad uses.

Willard Bleyer of the University of Wisconsin-Madison spoke out in 1919 against the idea that students could get high school training then leave directly for the professional journalism world where their stories would inform millions of Americans about political life (593-601). That many did this anyway was beside the point. "We cannot afford to let high-school boys and girls harbor the mistaken notion that, because they have developed a certain facility in writing for the school paper, they are ready, on leaving school, to enter the profession of journalism."

Instead, Bleyer argued that the basic purpose of journalism training was to prepare students for democracy, but he suggested high school students also would need a liberal college education before they could function as journalists. This view would slowly gain mainstream acceptance. Bleyer felt media education could remedy "loose thinking":

> Boys and girls need to be taught how to read a newspaper to the best advantage. Unless they learn to discriminate between the mere episodes, such as accidents, fires and athletic contests, and significant events that are making history, they may go through life, as many

people do, enjoying the chewing-gum of the news while the flavor lasts, and scarcely realizing that they have been neglecting the food of thought (597).

It did not take very long for other educators to recognize the value journalism held for teaching critical reading along with written expression. Hyde's *Journalistic Writing* (Hyde, 1922, 1929) suggests that the purpose of high school journalism be three-fold:

> 1. To use journalistic subject matter and methods to arouse interest in advanced composition courses that will be quite as valuable to future businessmen, plumbers, teachers, lawyers and stenographers as to future journalists. 2. To teach young people to read the newspaper intelligently, to discriminate in selecting newspapers, to support the better type of journalism, and to get the greatest personal benefit out of their newspaper reading. 3. To provide a try-out and perhaps the first steps for those who are thinking of the profession of journalism as a career (vii).

While he was unusually progressive for his era, Hyde still displayed an elitist bias toward what media are acceptable and useful for young people to read. In addition, he clearly anticipates that there will be controversy and conflict in the process of producing school newspapers, writing that the individual circumstances of journalism classes will vary, depending on such factors as "the relation of the journalistic class to the enterprise, the problems of financial and editorial responsibility, possible faculty censorship, and the relation of the newspaper to the student body and faculty."

He suggests school newspapers have boards of control, including newspaper staff heads, teachers and alumni, with monthly meetings to provide advice on matters of editorial policy and resolve disputes. "If the staff and Board are properly conducted, the only censorship needed is to insure good taste in humor columns and such small matters" (328).

A decade earlier, Allan Abbott had argued in an article he wrote for *The School Review* that censorship is "rarely if ever necessary. The teacher should tell his editors how, and not what to write" (666).

In his doctoral dissertation for Indiana University, John Allen Boyd wrote that "although the thought then seemed to be that the faculty should have complete control of the editing and censoring," Abbott's article offered a different viewpoint and "may have been the spark that started the fire for journalism education in the secondary schools" (11).

In a 28-page booklet he wrote for the University of Missouri called *Journalism for Teachers* (1912), Frank Martin said journalism advisors "should stir up opinion in favor of school improvements." The first textbook used by journalism classes was *Newspaper Writing in High Schools* by L.N. Flint, head of the Department of Journalism at the University of Kansas (1917), and more textbooks followed, offering a variety of opinions on how to operate a school journalism program and defending the aims of teaching journalism in high school.

Journalism teachers today still recognize the importance of instruction in media and democracy. Yet many get caught up in the imperative of production and focus on creating the school newspaper to the detriment of instruction in other goals, including the teaching of professional ethics and standards.

In his textbook, *Journalism for High Schools* (1919) Charles Dillon wrote that the school newspaper should give students writing practice but he also expressed optimism that "the school paper should be a real paper, not a toy, no matter how small it may be" (1).

D. Steady Growth?

E.H. Redford of Stanford University noted that "journalism was being taught in 40 states and that there were more than 12 city and state high school journalism advisor's associations of high school publications"[6] In his *Secondary School Journalism: Current Practices and Trends*, Alan Scott writes:

> By 1940 the work of the high school journalism instructor and the outlines of what he should teach had developed with due reference to recognized aims and generally accepted principles of education. The confusion of the early years had not been completely swept aside, but secondary school journalism was widely accepted and had not only survived the depression years but had expanded (21).

During the war years, high school journalism's popularity either remained stable or decreased because of competing demands on students, but the 1950s increased participation in high school journalism. By 1957, there were 4,686 people attending the Columbia Scholastic Press Association meeting in New York City, a jump of 1,220 from 1947. In 1927, there were 1,100 at the annual conference, 2,100 by 1937, Boyd wrote (15).

A paragraph in a post-war journalism guide for West Virginia secondary schools made clear that journalism's aim was not to impart extensive technical skills, "but rather long-range goals which will contribute to a student's fuller life and more interesting education. It must make its contribution to society as a course which will bring to maturity persons who will speak and write their language in a clear, correct and forceful manner" (6).

In James Agnew's 1951 text, *Today's Journalism for Today's Schools*, Agnew writes about the numerous ways journalism can be transformative not only for young people's lives but also for the school curriculum. He lauds journalism for its ability to change with changing times. Agnew argues in favor of the benefits of journalism's practicality when students have trouble relating other academic subjects to their day-to-day existences:

> As the aims of education have shifted from subject matter to the individual, journalism has assumed a role of increasing importance in the modern school curriculum. With the new emphasis directed toward the problem of helping the student learn to make satisfactory adjustments in a rapidly changing world, came the need for radical revisions in the curriculum. Many traditional subjects, when weighed in the light of the new emphasis, were found wanting. Journalism was not one of these. . . .

Each story is judged by peers and is "not just another composition" for the teacher, Agnew writes.

If Agnew wanted journalism to spark major curricular revisions, it was not to be. The idea that students in high school might have a constitutional right to freedom of expression was not even considered plausible in most places in the 1940s and 1950s. Students did not question the authority of school officials – punishment was swift if they did. Researchers often follow the evolution of high school journalism by tracing the steps students made through the legal system. They mark the changes in high school journalism by referring to three eras, all surrounding the U.S. Supreme Court decision in *Tinker v. Des Moines Independent Community School District* 393 U.S. 503 (1969), which made high school students "persons" and granted them Constitutional privileges. The three periods are pre-Tinker (1948-1968), Tinker (1969-1987) and the Hazelwood era (since 1988). Tinker was a watershed decision for the student press because since Tinker, "almost every court facing a question of student press rights has started its analysis with the Tinker . . . decision and found student journalism entitled to extensive First Amendment protection," write Goodman of the Student Press Law Center and J. Marc Abrams in the *Duke Law Journal* (September 1988).

CHAPTER 1: HISTORY OF THE HIGH SCHOOL PRESS

In contrast, the Hazelwood era refers to the period after the Supreme Court's *Hazelwood v. Kuhlmeier* decision 484 U.S. 260 (1988), which stripped high school students of press freedoms that many had known to exist over the previous two decades. Students live under the Hazelwood law today, although a number of states, including California, supply student journalists with greater legal protection.

E. Evolution of Student Press Law

Robert Knight wrote in *Journalism Educator* (Summer 1988) about the attitudinal atmosphere in high schools before students were granted more legal rights:

> The pre-Tinker era, 1948-1968, was an 'in loco parentis' environment in which things were placid, rules were rules, and daily dangers for teenagers were the exception. Teachers considered themselves publication sponsors, and some had proprietary feelings about their newspaper or yearbook. . . Principals did not see themselves as publishers for they rarely had students trying to sneak things past the sponsor (42-43).

A survey of advisors, high school principals and editors conducted by Don Horine (1965, 1966) confirmed these observations of an oppressive environment for high school journalists. In addition, students may abandon the idea of becoming journalists because they are "allowed virtually no editorial freedom," he wrote (339). Some schools he studied even had written policies stating that the school newspaper should be a public relations instrument of the school. Ironically, he found that at [Benjamin] Franklin High School in Los Angeles, the policy stated, "It shall be the policy of the Franklin Press to promote loyalty to the school and to individual members of the Franklin student body." At South Bay Union High School District, the newspaper policy permitted criticism but said "any statement or article about members of the local school or district staff shall be cleared with the person involved before being printed." Horine wrote that advisors had "a tight rein" over the student press whether they claimed to offer freedom or not.

Some student editors appeared to have an attitude of deference to adult authority. One wrote:

> The high school paper shouldn't take sides on such a touchy issue as Viet Nam; personally, I feel we would do more harm than good with such an editorial, for we would certainly offend someone. A metropolitan paper can afford to do this. The high school paper should carry (articles) about outstanding students, notices of coming sports events and dances, and the like.

L. Erwin Atwood and Malcolm S. MacLean Jr. (Spring 1967) found that "anti-journalism" attitudes toward high school journalism instruction, school newspapers and journalism careers were destructive to the development and viability of high school journalism programs, even if the views were held by "a substantial minority." Their survey of principals, advisers and students in Iowa found major rifts in attitudes about journalism, its value and purposes.

"Opponents feel that school newspapers are inaccurate, and since few people expect anything worthwhile from high school papers, it doesn't matter what is printed," the researchers wrote in *Journalism Quarterly*.

Parents opposed to journalism instruction "the most negative of opponent groups, feel that no one in his right mind would seriously consider journalism as a career."

Opponent and proponent principals alike "express a preference for the yearbook over the newspaper, presumably because they see a greater public relations value for the yearbook." However, principals do not advocate strict control of publications content with the exception of P.R.-types who feel there should be no criticism of school policy, no publication of anything that might reflect unfavorably on the school, Horine wrote. Such principals feel "that they themselves are best qualified to determine publication content" (70-78). The negative attitudes about journalism instruction have never totally died out.

The '50s brought the most regressive school attitudes toward high school journalism because these years reflected a time in which youth were not trusted and the media was considered to have a negative impact on youth. In *Cycle of Outrage* (1986), James Gilbert argues that adults blamed the changing social climate after World War II, including juvenile delinquency, on the media's profound influence on modern society. The problem was that the emerging American society seemed to crave Hollywood, radio and comic books more than literary classics and other works considered evidence of taste. By the early 1960s, Baby Boomers were the largest group in America and the attitudes toward the media shifted, Gilbert contends. "Already set apart in high schools, [young people] constructed a subculture that drew energy from the peer group culture of school, retail stores, drive-in theaters, and early versions of fast-food restaurants where the many of them worked" (215). The changing nature of public attitudes toward the media coincided with the negative way journalists were viewed. Journalism programs today continue to function in an atmosphere of significant disapproval toward the media.

In contrast to the 1950s and early 1960s, the late 1960s might be seen as the heyday of high school journalism, if such a period ever existed. Those who viewed high school journalism programs more positively experienced a victory with the U.S. Supreme Court ruling in *Tinker v. Des Moines* (1969). The case involved three Des Moines teens, siblings John and Mary Beth Tinker and Christopher Eckhardt, who were suspended after wearing black armbands to school in protest of the Vietnam War. School officials had known about the protest in advance and issued a policy prohibiting the armbands.

In the majority opinion, Justice Abraham Fortas said the "fear of disturbance" did not justify prohibiting the students' symbolic speech. Because the school allowed other political statements such as campaign buttons, the court found the regulations restricting speech were not content-neutral and targeted one subject.

"First Amendment rights, applied in light of the special characteristics of the school environment, are available to teachers and students," wrote Fortas. "It can hardly be argued that either students or teachers shed their constitutional rights to freedom of speech or expression at the schoolhouse gate." In addition, the court viewed public schools as limited public forums, not "enclaves of totalitarianism."

"School officials do not possess absolute authority over their students," Fortas wrote. "Students in school as well as out of school are 'persons' under our Constitution. They are possessed of fundamental rights which the State must respect, just as they themselves must respect their obligations to the State."

While Tinker focused on a protest, the ruling's pronouncements about young students' Constitutional rights were so sweeping, that many educators and lawyers believed they were directly relevant to the school newspaper. They were to be proven correct by subsequent legal decisions. The Tinker judgment had relied to some degree on a precedent set by W*est Virginia State Board of Education v. Barnette* 319 U.S. 624 (1943), In that case, several children of Jehovah's witnesses would not salute the flag because they believed they were being forced to bow down to an image. The ruling overturned a previous decision and sided with the students. The majority opinion said the school was dictating speech to students or, in other words, it was compelling their speech. Compulsory unification of opinion achieves only the unanimity of the graveyard," Justice Robert Jackson warned.

F. Captive Voices Again?

The *Tinker* decision, many believed, should have settled the question of whether student journalists had the right to free speech. However, more regressive policies and attitudes about the school press, present for a half-century, were difficult to erase. The best evidence for this point is in Jack Nelson's book *Captive Voices* (1974), which found Tinker did not cause school districts to alter their practices on freedom of expression significantly, and high school journalism remained bland, subject to routine censorship.[7] Nelson found that school newspapers suffered widely from "taboos that spring from the house organ concept of the school newspaper." He also found students were ignorant of their Constitutional rights because teachers emphasized restrictions and downplayed legal protections of free speech. At that time, the only material that could be censored had to be deemed obscene, libelous or disruptive to the school.

Yet the Commission compiled plenty of evidence that showed school censorship was rampant. It focused on three areas:

1. Controversial political issues such as racism, students' rights, and, at one time, the Vietnam War.
2. Criticism of school administrators or faculty policies or unfavorable images of the school, such as criticism of athletic teams or of school censorship policies.
3. Lifestyles and social problems, such as birth control and drug abuse (41).

Parents did not seem eager to help students fight school censorship and many supported strict school rules. This finding was supported by a 1969 Lou Harris poll that found nearly two-thirds of parents and 27 percent of teachers surveyed believed that "maintaining discipline is more important than student self-inquiry." In fact, the Commission reported about the teachers that "no matter how blatant the act of censorship or how harsh the treatment of students who rebel at the act, administrators generally find wide faculty support for their policies, for many teachers as well as administrators find a free high school press a threat to their own concept of institutionalized control of students."

In the late 1960s and 1970s, educators and students rethought ideas about how much input students should have into their own educations, in both high school and college. The high school press found itself in conflict with school authorities over issues of control. Some high school newspapers were ordered not to cover student protests, according to the Commission. The Commission's content analysis showed that 52 percent of news coverage was devoted to sports and social events, and 75 percent of newspapers contained no news of student suspensions or expulsions. A poll of students indicated that 53 percent believed the school newspaper was used to create a good impression on visitors of the school.

Nelson wrote, "Censorship more than any other factor has a greater adverse effect on the quality and relevance of high school journalism. Good writing, editing, layout and production are important but the essential purpose of a newspaper is to communicate a message" (44).

The debate over what the schools should become – and what kind of education they should foster – was discussed in *Crisis in the Classroom*, Charles Silberman's report as director of the Carnegie Study of the Education of Educators. Cited in the Commission report was Silberman's declaration that "the most important characteristic schools share in common is a preoccupation with order and control." He presented a drastically dim picture of American schools:

> It is not possible to spend any prolonged period visiting public school classrooms without being appalled by the mutilation visible everywhere – mutilation of spontaneity, of joy in learning, of pleasure in creating, of sense of self. The public schools – those 'killers of dreams' to appropriate a phrase of Lillian Smith's – are the kind of institutions one cannot really dislike until one gets to know them well. Because adults take the schools so much for granted, they fail to appreciate what grim, lifeless places most American schools are, how oppressive and petty are the rules by which they are governed, how intellectually sterile and anesthetically barren the atmosphere, what an appalling lack of civility obtains on the part of teachers and principals, what contempt they unconsciously display for children as children.

Other studies confirmed that censorship was hardly extinguished by Tinker (Kristoff 1983, Broussard and Blackmon 1978). In 1980, Robert Trager and Donna L. Dickerson surveyed schools in Indiana, Illinois and Wisconsin and found that 73 percent of respondents – students, advisers and principals – agreed that administrators have the power to review material prior to publication. This was true despite the fact that in *Fujishima v. the Board of Education*, the Seventh Circuit Court of Appeals, relying on *Tinker*, said that schools could regulate the time, place and manner of distribution, but could not insist that permission be granted before printed materials were distributed. This decision actually endowed high school journalists with the same rights as professional journalists, but as a legal matter nationally the issue never quite got settled. The Seventh Circuit ruling only affected public high schools in Indiana, Illinois and Wisconsin. However, Trager and Dickerson found that the ruling did not cause an increase in underground newspapers, nor did it spur greater disruption by student publications. Yet the researchers said confusion reigned after various legal rulings in the post-Tinker period:

> By not ruling on the question of prior restraint in high school, the Supreme Court has allowed Courts of Appeals to announce decisions at variance with one another. The finding of a lack of consistency in freedoms believed in and granted within one circuit shows that the state of First Amendment protection granted high school students remains based on the whim of those in charge, not the law (138).

If Trager and Dickerson truly were seeking clarification, the Supreme Court gave them their wish in *Hazelwood* (1988). But if they wanted students to enjoy greater freedom, they may have preferred that such a ruling had never been rendered. *Hazelwood* limited student rights if their newspapers were part of the high school curriculum. The ruling "eviscerates the Supreme Court's decision in *Tinker*, overrules many lower court decisions protective of the student press, and curtails student press rights . . ." Goodman and Abrams wrote (Summer 1988).

G. Hazelwood Replaces Tinker?

Under previous case law, once a state designates a place or form of communication for public use for assembly and speech (for use by certain speakers, or for discussion of certain issues), it must show a compelling state interest in restricting the speech that occurs there. In addition, the speech must be content neutral and narrowly tailored to achieve the government's interest. Goodman and Abrams wrote:

> Courts also recognize school auditoriums, airports and city parks as public forums and have protected the right of such groups as the Hare Krishnas or the Nazi party to engage in expressive activities in those forums free of government censorship. Further, the Supreme Court has consistently and unambiguously stated that prior restraints on expression are among the acts most disfavored under the Constitution. This disfavor has been, presumptively, no less true in the context of our nation's public schools (2).

Abrams and Goodman list examples of student speech that courts have protected -- a four-letter slur about a university president; a photograph of a burning American flag; an editorial calling for continued racial segregation; advertisements about race relations, unionization and the Vietnam War; criticism of a governor and a state legislature; articles by non-students containing alleged obscenity; and "derogatory, profane and blasphemous" criticisms of the Catholic church. Courts have protected stories on teenage sex, birth control and abortion as well as articles about drug abuse and criticism of school policy and staff; articles without bylines; and materials offensive to good taste or that presented a negative image of the school; and articles on such non-school related topics as the draft and the Vietnam War, Goodman and Abrams wrote.

In the spring of 1983 at Hazelwood East High School in St. Louis County, Mo., Kathy Kuhlmeier, Lee Ann Tippett and Leslie Smart were students in the Journalism II class that produced the high school newspaper, *Spectrum*. The newspaper considered itself a forum for the student body and printed a disclaimer saying "all non-bylined editorials appearing in this newspaper reflect the opinions of the Spectrum staff, which are not necessarily shared by the administrators or faculty of Hazelwood East." In addition, school board policy stated: "School-sponsored student publications will not restrict free expression or diverse viewpoints within the rules of responsible journalism."

Students planned a two-page section in May 1983 that would deal with teenage pregnancy, including a discussion of birth control and abortion and a feature about three Hazelwood East students who became pregnant. Other articles dealt with divorce, teenage runaways and juvenile delinquents. After reviewing the special section, the school principal Robert Reynolds directed the faculty adviser to remove the two-page spread, saying the articles were "too sensitive" for the newspaper's immature readers and there was insufficient time to fix two objectionable stories before publication. He was concerned pregnant students would be identifiable, and their boyfriends and parents would have their privacy rights compromised because there were so few pregnant students at school.

In siding with school officials, the court referred to a 1981 decision of the Third Circuit in *Seyfried v. Walton*, involving a superintendent's decision to cancel a production of the musical "Pippin." It found that "*Spectrum* was an integral part of Hazelwood East's curriculum, as opposed to a public forum for free expression by students." The court based its reasoning on established public forum doctrine, arguing that public schools do not have the qualities of traditional public forums such as streets and parks for purposes of assembly and debate, unless they designate certain facilities, such as the student newspaper, for public use. The court judged *Spectrum* to be part of the school curriculum with "the imprimatur of the school," an activity partly funded by the school and run by the journalism teacher, for which students received credit and grades. The majority opinion viewed the teacher, not the students, as having the final authority over Spectrum's content. Thus, the school did not deviate from its written policy that "(s)chool sponsored student publications will not restrict free expression or diverse viewpoints within the rules of responsible journalism" because the school decided what it was that constituted responsible journalism.

The court's decision rejected the arguments of the Eighth Circuit Court of Appeals, which had adopted the *Tinker* standard that student speech could not be restricted unless a ban would prevent "material and substantial interference" with schoolwork or discipline or the rights of others.

"It was not unreasonable for the principal to have concluded that such frank talk was inappropriate in a school-sponsored publication distributed to 14-year-old freshmen and presumably taken home to be read by students' even younger brothers and sisters," the Hazelwood court determined.

Falling short of overturning *Tinker*, the court weakened it considerably, saying its decision applied to all activities that might "fairly be characterized as part of the school curriculum, whether or not they occur in a traditional classroom setting, as long as they are supervised by faculty members and designed to impart particular knowledge or skills to student participants and audiences."

The decision named the public school the "publisher" of a school newspaper and the "producer" of a play. As such, the school could censor speech that was "ungrammatical, poorly written, inadequately researched, biased or prejudiced, vulgar or profane or unsuitable for immature audiences."

The high court ruled that schools "do not offend the First Amendment by exercising editorial control over the style and content of student speech in school-sponsored expressive activities so long as their actions are reasonably related to legitimate pedagogical concerns." However, there can be many definitions of what constitutes a legitimate pedagogical concern, and the case left the student press vulnerable to improper censorship.

Justice William Brennan dissented, dismissing the fears of school authorities and saying that the "mere desire to avoid the discomfort and unpleasantness that always accompany an unpopular viewpoint" did not justify censoring student expression. He said the court's decision could never be reconciled with *Tinker* as it seemed to flout much of it. "The young men and women of Hazelwood East expected a civics lesson, but not the one the Court teaches them today."

Goodman and Abrams said students now face "a Hobson's choice" between launching an underground newspaper to have editorial freedom and remaining with the school-sponsored publication, which may restrict them:

> The likely effect of such a message is student cynicism. Students who might have eagerly awaited a chance to participate in our system as adults may instead pursue more parochial concerns. Students who might have considered careers in journalism will turn instead to other interests. These cannot be the messages that the Supreme Court intended to send the youth of America.

They called the Hazelwood decision "a serious step backward," saying that the majority of newspapers in America are student newspapers and the majority of journalists are students. "Students participate in journalism for the education, the experience, the opportunity to improve their skills and the lessons they can learn from the individual stories that they cover and the overall process of newspaper production. . . those lessons are best learned in an environment as free as possible from censorship."

H. Controversial Speech

The Supreme Court actually began weakening *Tinker* in a decision two years earlier, *Bethel School District No. 403 v. Fraser* 478 U.S. 675 (1986). Senior Matthew Fraser had spoken at a voluntary assembly of 600 students on behalf of a candidate for student election by using an extended sexual metaphor. Teachers had warned him beforehand that he would face "severe consequences" if he delivered his "inappropriate" address. School rules prohibited the use of obscene language or gestures, as well as "conduct which materially and substantially interferes with the educational process." Fraser spoke anyway to an audience that reacted with hoots, yells and sexual gestures. He was suspended for two days, then sued school officials alleging a violation of his First Amendment rights. He prevailed in state court. The school district was denied an appeal in the Ninth Circuit, then the Supreme Court reversed the state court's decision, 7 to 2. In the majority decision, Chief Justice Warren Burger focused on the schools' mission to promote civic values. "Surely, it is a highly appropriate function of public school education to prohibit the use of vulgar and offensive terms in public discourse." Burger wrote. Fraser's speech was "acutely insulting to teenage girl students," Burger wrote, adding that it "could well be damaging to its less mature audience, many of whom were only 14 years old and on the threshold of awareness of human sexuality."

But Marjorie Heins, author of *Not In Front of the Children* (2001), blasts Burger's paternalism. Heins was an American Civil Liberties Union attorney in *Reno v. the ACLU 521 U.S. 844* (1997), the Supreme Court case that called the Internet a traditional public forum. Heins faults the chief justice because he "cited no empirical basis for his twin assumptions that 14-year-olds are seriously damaged by sexual jokes or that teenage girls are offended by (and would themselves never engage in) sexual innuendo" (132). Heins supported the dissenting opinion of Justice John Paul Stevens that Fraser "was probably in a better position to determine whether an audience composed of 600 of his contemporaries would be offended by the use of a four-letter-word – or a sexual metaphor – than is a group of judges who are at least two generations and 3,000 miles away from the scene of the crime."

In fact, Heins saw both the *Fraser* and *Hazelwood* rulings as examples of contemporary attempts to protect young people from the assumed harms of controversial speech, based on shaky assumptions about youth that date back to the time of Plato. Heins cites a string instances of censorship in which school board punishments of teachers were upheld by state courts: a high school drama teacher who was transferred to a middle school for picking the play "Independence" (with themes of divorce, homosexuality and unwed pregnancy) for her advanced acting class in North Carolina; a Missouri creative writing teacher who did not remove obscenities from her students' fiction; and a Colorado history teacher who showed Bernardo Bertolucci's film "1900," despite its nudity, violence and implicit sex. Indeed, censorship of public school curricular materials and library books "had become so common in the United States by the 1990s that hardly any work was immune from challenge," Heins writes (4). "Among the targets were Maya Angelou's *I Know Why the Caged Bird Sings*, Toni Morrison's *Beloved*, John Steinbeck's *Of Mice and Men* and Mark Twain's *Huckleberry Finn*."

Heins points to a widely held assumption that exposure to certain "art, literature, advertising and other forms of communication" might be acceptable for adults, but young people are "either too fragile to handle vulgarity, sex, and controversy or lack the intellectual freedom rights that the First Amendment grants adults – or both" (5):

CHAPTER 1: HISTORY OF THE HIGH SCHOOL PRESS 23

Even if adults could agree, moreover, on what is truly inadvisable for young people, the rarely asked question remains, In what sense is it harmful? And does it justify censorship?

The results of broadly accepted and vague theories about youth and media effects have been Internet rating and filtering systems in the public libraries, stores that will not carry music with warning labels affixed, and laws curtailing indecency on cable TV. All are examples of government censorship based on the emotional appeal of sheltering children, not on scientific study.

The *ACLU v. Reno* case resulted in the Supreme Court declaring the federal 1996 Communications Decency Act unconstitutional because it had criminalized offensive or indecent online speech. But ironically, the ruling only served to bolster the popularity of censorship measures designed to shield youth from sexual or other "low-value" speech related to violence, racial hatred or drugs and alcohol, and other controversial topics. Like those of the CDA, the measures designed to replace it relied on the assumption that young people need to be guarded from what they see or hear before they are ready to see or hear it.

The Supreme Court has "zigzagged dizzily – on the one hand recognizing minors' free speech rights and on the other moralizing on government's interest in protecting them from too vigorous an exercise of those rights, particularly when the subject was sex," Heins contends. She reveals cultural differences of attitudes and approaches toward youth and sexual information that "suggest that we really know very little about how sexual, violent, or other media content will affect any individual young person." Still, censorship initiatives that supposedly protect minors serve symbolic purposes and rarely encounter much political resistance.

Heins builds a case against censorship because it is often justified on perceived harm to children, as opposed to actual harm. "Given the overwhelming difficulty in even defining what it is we want to censor, and the significant costs of censorship to society and to youngsters themselves, we ought to be sure that real, not just symbolic, harm results from youthful pursuit of disapproved pleasures and messages before mandating indecency laws, Internet filters, and other restrictive regimes,"(11) she says. Young people "need access to information and ideas precisely because they are in the process of becoming functioning members of society and cannot really do so if they are kept in ideological blinders until they are 18" (12). She calls on adults to involve youth in policymaking and journalism.

I. Media Effects

The difficulties that journalism programs have experienced in the high schools leading to the *Hazelwood* decision are the result of the faulty logic that high schools need to engage in aggressive child protection, even of older teenagers. School officials must not inflict censorship on young people unless there's an established link between perceived and actual harm to them, or else the censorship could inflict the greater harm. The potential harm is so great because of psychological factors that have been identified as unique to teenagers. The fears of school authorities about what young people can and cannot handle must be backed up by research, not emotion. Blaming the media is much easier than resolving intractable social problems, agrees media scholar Henry Jenkins. In testimony at a Congressional hearing on media violence after the Columbine tragedy in 1999, he said:

> the key issue isn't what the media are doing to our children, but rather what our children are doing with the media. The vocabulary of media effects, which has long dominated such hearings, has been challenged by numerous American and international scholars as an inadequate and simplistic representation of media consumption and popular culture. Media effects research most often empties media images of their meanings, strips them of their contexts, and denies their consumers any agency over their use.

Censorship of high school newspapers is part of broader censorship of materials reaching young people.

Material in high school newspapers may be all the more threatening because high school students devise it. What is considered inappropriate for a high school journalist to write often is based on ideas about how the school should meet its obligation to protect minors from knowledge for which they are thought to be ill prepared. Students express themselves in what they produce for the high school newspaper but also in what media they use as well as the clothing, hairstyles and peer groups with which they associate.

There has been no scholarly agreement about the extent of the damage to student expression brought on by *Hazelwood*. First Amendment scholar Louis Ingelhart, however, found that in curbing students' free speech rights, the Hazelwood court ignored various facts: that children can be treated like adults in court, 16-year-olds may marry, girls can become pregnant by age 11, 18-year-olds can vote and serve on juries and 17- and 18-year-olds can see R-rated movies.[8]

Thomas Eveslage, another First Amendment scholar, called the Hazelwood ruling "frighteningly broad and repressive" and said "the Court has stirred smoldering cinders that threaten to erupt in damaging ways." He said administrators, advisors and students were not surprised by Hazelwood because in most places, they thought censorship was allowed or at least they functioned as if it were.[9]

There has been no scholarly agreement about the extent of the damage to student expression brought on by *Hazelwood*. Thomas Dickson's 1989 study of high school principals in Missouri just after Hazelwood found that just 20 percent planned to "look more closely at student publications" because of it. In 1990, Click and Kopenhaver similarly found that 89 percent of high school principals knew about Hazelwood, but a slim 12 percent of advisors said their publications had faced censorship since the decision. In that study, three-quarters of advisors said that prior restraint had not increased since the ruling. In Tennessee, Bowles reported similar results, based on a questionnaire sent to advisors in 1989. One study that interviewed students (Crow, 1992) concluded that there was large-scale agreement between students and principals in Texas over the extent of prior restraint. Students reported that no stories had been withheld from publication because they were too controversial, invaded a student's privacy, or criticized a teacher.

Yet it is clear that these studies do not tell the whole story of what is happening to the high school press. Goodman's views are based on anecdotal evidence, including phone calls and e-mails to his Student Press Law Center. He argues that Hazelwood has increased censorship in high schools and bred more self-censorship by students out of "a systemic presumption" that censorship will be inevitable. He said those studies that have questioned students are likely inaccurate because students do not know when they are being censored. He represented that at conferences, students claim they are uncensored, yet most raise their hands that no, they could not write an editorial critical of a decision by the principal. Just as students are uncertain of their rights, so are many advisors, Goodman said.[10]

The more restrictive acts of high school principals must be at least partially attributed to the legacy of *Hazelwood*. The Supreme Court sided with those in authority, so that even in a state that claims to provide maximal freedom for young people, there can exist a climate of self-censorship, fear and conformity for students. California is one of the few states with additional legal protections for high school journalists, but these legal protections are not consistently employed. In 2001, 13 percent of calls to the Student Press Law Center relating to censorship complaints came from California public high schools, the highest percentage of any state, in part because of its large population. This trend continued in 2002. Such evidence indicates that *Hazelwood* is part of the push by adults who want to protect young people from worrisome ideas, rather than prepare them.

At the 1988 summer meeting of the Association for Education in Journalism and Mass Communication in Portland, Ore., Professors Louis Day and John Butler formulated a defense of Hazelwood, arguing that the decision was sound educational policy and restored "the proper balance between the pedagogical mission of the public schools and the role of the student press."[11] They contended that Hazelwood represented the reemergence of a cultural transmission perspective popularized in United States schools with need to absorb diverse immigrants from around the world. In this view, schools were supposed to mold American youth, not act as sites where they could develop themselves. The roots of this ideology are in the classical Western academic tradition. The ideology states that "schools had to help synthesize people around a demand for a new, functional and positive conceptions of the school's role in society." The Hazelwood ruling marked the demise of the progressive educational theories of John Dewey, Day and Butler contended.

> High school newspapers are not public forums established to facilitate an unfettered marketplace of ideas. These school-sponsored publications are educational tools, designed to teach journalistic knowledge, skills and ethical behavior. Administrative restraints on articles which the principal feels are in poor taste, contain objectionable material or are likely to violate the interests of third parties do not abridge the general free speech rights of student reporters. . . (A)dministrators and journalism teachers must have flexibility in formulating and implementing policies regarding the ethical and legal 'standards' to be incorporated into scholastic journalism instruction.

Hazelwood marked a conservative shift in the way the courts viewed young people. Day and Butler identify five standards underlying *Hazelwood*: 1) free speech values are not as important in schools as in the larger society; 2) regulation of the high school press is necessary to maintain academic standards; 3) local – not national – standards should govern the high school press; 4) students are immature, justifying a "limited capacity" right to free speech; 5) student journalists can find other outlets for expression so that they are not totally denied free speech.

CHAPTER 1: HISTORY OF THE HIGH SCHOOL PRESS   27

These rationalizations for *Hazelwood* gloss over what the schools have accomplished to fight racism in the name of education. Where it takes place, the emphasis today on multicultural education and diversity is healthy and leaves room for the clash of perspectives in the classroom. The operators of the modern schoolhouse must know that those they call teenagers are more capable than they might imagine and deserve input into their education. They can handle the demands and ethical conundra of the newspaper, perhaps with enlightened guidance from experienced journalism teachers. Proof of this can be found in those moments when students surpass the expertise of those who have been hired to instruct them, but the analysis of Day and Butler does not seem to recognize this. While young people can be impressionable, schools only will be more valuable for them if they avoid censorship and give students the license to experiment. Journalism programs must teach codes of professional ethics and responsibility, encourage creativity, then stand back.

J. Adolescent Psychology and Journalism

Depending on how one interprets the psychological research, one could find a way to argue either for or against teen involvement in journalism. With his two-volume treatise in 1904, G.S. Hall is credited with giving rise to a movement to safeguard the teenage years as critical. His concepts created a springboard for adolescent psychology and contributed to its connection with the greater school bureaucracy and legions of professionals for preserving child welfare. According to Hall, write historians John Modell and Madeline Goodman (1990, 102), "Adolescence was a phase of upheaval and trauma, storm and stress, corresponding to mankind's evolutionary progress from savagery to civilization." Hall romanticized youth, portraying adolescence as a state in which the mind is most elastic and fraught with potential. He felt that the stage signified the "rebirth of the individual, embodying both the possibilities and the uncertainties associated with radical change and thus was congruent with an era of unprecedented social and economic change." If Hall was to be believed, youth were not a vexation on an ordered society. Rather, their vulnerable condition during the transition to adulthood required understanding.

Hall could be compared to an overprotective parent. He feared adolescents' apparent adult-like capacities and independence as manifestations of disease that required treatment. If self-directed discovery and the capacity to question authority are essential aspects of journalism, Hall might have condemned them as premature and unhealthy. It then would be easy to see why a free press in high school would conflict with his vision. He thought that teenagers must not be exposed to ideas best restricted to adults. Relying on Hall's theories, it is possible to view teenagers not merely as innocents, but also as fragile souls with disturbed minds or even partial people coping with hormonal imbalances.

Perhaps most influential in contributing to notions of child protection was Jean Piaget, who divided childhood development into universal stages, a steady march from concrete to abstract thinking. Piaget made it easy for adults to discount the ideas of adolescents about the world as "a stage" they were going through. However, the theories of child psychology also can be used to support the argument that adolescents' psychological makeup makes them perfect candidates for school newspaper production. There are a variety of reasons that neither censorship nor the shielding of young people from painful world events is in their best interests. In fact, it is developmentally appropriate to instruct teenage journalists in matters of journalistic responsibility and to allow them to explore sensitive subjects. Psychoanalyst Erik Erikson (1968) suggested that adults focus on teenagers' strengths, their "vital virtues," rather than their inadequacies.

For instance, professional lore posits that journalists are supposed to be in search of the truth, but this is also true of teenagers, whose psychological proclivity often involves the dogged search for ideals to believe in. "The evidence in young lives of the search for something and somebody to be true to can be seen in a variety of pursuits more or less sanctioned by society," writes Erikson in *Identity, Youth and Crisis* (235). "It is often hidden in a bewildering combination of shifting devotion and sudden perversity." Erikson contended that what appears to be shifting behavior actually demonstrates that young people are looking for consistency or "durability in change," whether it be greater accuracy, sincerity, fairness, authenticity or genuineness. "The adolescent fears a foolish, all too trusting commitment and will, paradoxically, express his need for faith in loud and cynical mistrust," Erikson writes (129). This is why cynicism in the young is complicated and perhaps a necessary ingredient of both growing up and practicing journalism.

Thus, it may be a happy coincidence for any journalism teacher that real-world journalists are supposed to find the discrepancies in what people purport to believe and what they actually believe, revealed in how they act. Teenagers are not merely cynical but they may have a built-in expertise for distinguishing pretense. The journalistic maxim, "If your mother says she loves you, check it out," also could be emblematic of some teenagers' rocky familial relations. Journalists, as part of the Fourth Estate, often take an adversarial stance toward public officials. So, too, may teenage rebelliousness toward authority figures, be turned into an asset. If not used for constructive purposes, of course, their extreme behavior can lead to deviant, self-destructive or delinquent acts (Erikson 236). Taken as an asset, though, teenage estrangement from others, which Erikson sees as part of "identity confusion," may work to boost students' empathy for the underdog in society and ally them with victims on the margins of school life. Interestingly, the concept of David Elkind (1967) that teenagers often imagine themselves as the heroes in their daily dramas also may be seen as an attempt by young people to view themselves from the outside and to understand how others view them. This could be viewed as a critical disposition that also helps their journalism.

Psychologist Piaget argued that children achieve "formal operations" in the middle of their teen years, indicating that they can grasp hypothetical concepts and the relation of one abstract concept to another. This is especially helpful as teens shape and reshape their political, occupational and social identities, requiring them to think in a sophisticated way about future events. This "new set of identification processes" constitutes both the strength and weakness of teenagers, Erikson writes. Young people consider their own self-concept during a period Erikson names "moratorium," in which they struggle with questions of who they are and who they will become, trying on different roles and perspectives. Without a solid sense of the self, young people may grapple with what Erikson termed "identity crisis." Susan Harter (1990, 376) argues "the process of identity formation also involves the selective repudiation of possible roles or selves. One must not only make a commitment to certain choices but also give up others."

A fundamental lesson of journalism is the ability to place yourself in other people's shoes. An undecided but skeptical student journalist, provided with instruction, potentially could seek more and more convincing evidence to achieve a comprehensive and balanced report.

In the end, just being young is an asset. It means greater energy, unburdened by burnout or a jaundiced attitude. Erikson writes that young people also express their personal search in their persistent desire for locomotion – such as in work, sports, dancing "and the employment and misuse of speedy animals and machines." But youths also find an outlet for expression in "the movements of the day," – "whether the riots of a local commotion or the parades and campaigns of major ideological forces, if they only appeal to the need for feeling 'moved' and for feeling essential in moving something along toward an open future." If this is true, the ideology of journalism itself may provide inspiration because it allows young people to feel a part of an operation larger than themselves and to become engaged in the task of shaping their peers' minds by providing information to the wider school community.

Philip Cowan, author of *Piaget: With Feeling* (1978), writes that teenagers function differently from children because second- and third-order formal operations allow teens "to be introspective in an analytic mode, to think critically about themselves and about the way they think and behave" (289). It is this thinking that can make the discussion of journalistic ethics feasible and even a beneficial part of the learning process as they discuss different actors' roles and intentions. If young people appear self-absorbed, it is not because they cannot see the world through others' eyes, writes Cowan, but because of the need for identity and to understand larger social systems and networks (292).

Young people are often engaged in thinking about the world as it should be, and this idealistic nature, combined with healthy skepticism and "a strong proof orientation" may add to their strength as journalists. "Along with a preoccupation with themselves and their identity goes an equally strong concern with transforming society in the direction of some utopian ideal," writes Cowan (291).

Because of the nature of young people, democracy "must present adolescents with ideals which can be shared by young people of many backgrounds, and which emphasize autonomy in the form of independence and initiative in the form of constructive work," contends Erikson (133). The same could be said for the journalism classroom. Teenagers may bristle easily at the slightest perceived unfairness and at infringements upon their personal autonomy. Journalists, also, value their independence from official authority. This is not a matter of immaturity but of values and ethics for both the journalist and the teenager.

As persuasive as Erikson is about the stage of being a teenager, his theories also are generalizations. They become less applicable to older teenagers, who have left Piaget's concrete reasoning stage behind and become closer to adults. Cowan is mindful that cognitive structures provide only one set of information about an individual and social context is a very important factor in shaping personality. Perhaps social context is the most important factor. This view was championed by the Russian social theorist Lev Vygotsky, who contended that social interaction and discourse help shape cognitive structures. Personality develops through interaction with the culture and adult-child exchanges.

Not only are there differences in the speed at which some people develop but there are adults who never achieve the point of formal operations, never seriously finding their identities, Cowan points out. Thus, there is a strong justification for rejecting blanket assertions about teenage behavior, for placing too much reliance on Piagetian stages. This is because the stages mark achievements, but also set limitations. The influence of Piagetian theories is so strong that there are those social scientists that suggest postponing certain instruction for later, when young people are developmentally ready for it. However, such theories are part of a deficiency model attacking the capacities of young people. Daniel Keating (1990) writes:

> At a practical level, it is clear that using theories of brain maturation to guide educational or other interventions is at best, premature. In particular, the practice of revising curriculum to lessen the cognitive challenges for preadolescents and early adolescents while educators await some specific physiological maturation, is not supported by the best available data.

Keating favors more studies of adolescent decision-making that examine the ways teenagers use skills in practical situations, arguing that societal "attachment to an imagined social order in which teenagers are immune from the necessity of making important decisions is itself a barrier to enhancing adolescents' decision-making abilities" (73). This problem results in adults who automatically assume teenagers will act irrationally. My own investigation of journalism programs follows Keating's call for future research engaged with "more meaningful content in more natural contexts."

Cowan, too, echoes the point also made by Erikson that adults must build on the strengths of teenagers, not search out their deficiencies. Cowan points to the relevance of Lawrence Kohlberg's studies of prison populations in the mid-1970s, which proposed that "the way to influence moral reasoning . . .

> is to enhance role-taking; the major way to enhance role-taking in prisons is to restructure the society so that prisoners participate in creating and enforcing the moral-conventional rules which they are attempting to understand (295).

Cowan extends these conclusions to the schools where teachers must involve students in acting upon moral and ethical principles. Journalism is ideal for teaching these skills because students, given sufficient autonomy, realize that the process of producing the newspaper may affect people's lives and reputations, requiring them to tread carefully.

Cowan elaborates:

> I have described how many of the new cognitive achievements of adolescence contribute to clashes with parents and other adult members of society. Mostly, however, these characteristics (skepticism, idealism, individually determined principles, independence, hypothesis testing, experimenting with roles and identity, values and aesthetic orientations) are traits which many parents and teachers value and hope that their children or students will ultimately possess. It seems to me that we need to find ways of incorporating adolescent strengths into adolescent education (297).

Journalism educators, then, would do well to use basic principles of adolescent psychology as a justification for increasing the credibility and importance of journalism as an academic discipline, and not as an adjunct to the high school curriculum. If educators seek better citizens and critical thinkers and writers, as they claim they do, then many more resources must be allocated to journalism. Teachers trained as journalists must teach journalism. It should be made a subject on par with any other to give students, as Keating says, "meaningful opportunities to construct ideas, to discover facts, to create theories, to test hypotheses, and to exchange viewpoints." Such an expansion of journalism would create greater challenges for adults, who are often more concerned about their own community image, job security or controlling young people in schools, but it would also pay greater dividends, if schools are truly determined to educate the young.

Giving young people more of a say into their education is hardly a new idea, but it is one that is slow to catch on, because of a stubborn insistence by state officials on the importance of traditional means of assessing students' abilities. In particular, Frederiksen (1984) has argued that schools influence what is taught by over reliance on standardized testing. "Tests of critical skills and higher-order thinking, for example, are difficult to create for mass administration," writes Keating. Neither do standardized tests add much insight to teen intelligence. "We need to entertain the possibility that engaging in advanced thinking may be more hindered than helped by current educational methods," he writes.

K. Conclusion: Importance of Autonomy

From the subject's very early entry into schools, journalism has confronted non-committal adults who are conflicted about the purposes of school newspapers. To be sure, there are well-regarded school journalism programs, but they are not the norm. Teenagers still suffer from community mistrust and so do the media products they embrace –

from movies, to video games, to music lyrics. Those media produced by youth, namely school newspapers, are not even considered worthy of criticism because they are given scant credibility in the wider society. This has not been helped by the confluence of historical and psychological forces. Neither American law, nor psychology, has helped clarify the confusion about student capacities or Constitutional rights, and even if they did, schools often exist within isolated enclaves under the direction of principals with their own educational agendas. To many of them, the school newspaper is considered no more important than a sports team. A major problem lies in recruiting teachers qualified to provide journalism instruction.

Interestingly, the bulk of high school journalism advisers nationally are "volunteered" or forced into their positions, according to *Death by Cheeseburger* (1994), which describes a wide-ranging Freedom Forum inquiry into high school journalism. It refers to a 1991 survey by Jack Dvorak of the Indiana University High School Journalism Institute, which found 43.1 percent of journalism instructors first thought of being newspaper advisers "after assignment by administrator" (22). Because of a lack of qualified, well-trained journalism instructors, schools "frequently 'volunteer' individuals with no background, experience or even inclination for the job. This reinforces the idea that high school journalism is not a serious subject" (*Death by Cheeseburger*, 13).

On the whole, journalism has developed in the United States in a very disjointed fashion, as if different educators all around the nation were discovering its merits and motivational value independently. The rise of journalism organizations, camps and workshops, has helped improve this situation, although journalism may never be completely coordinated as a school subject. Journalism instruction in high schools sprang from the English curriculum, but it owes much of its success to progressive educational ideals and the ideals of democratic education. The qualifications of journalism teachers remain a vexing issue that can create the opposite effect than is intended. Conflicts in the way different educators have viewed journalism's mission reduce the effectiveness of journalism programs. The legal system, too, has given schools mixed messages over the years, and its effect on high school newspapers has varied.

Journalism continues to fight both its history in the schools and historical perspectives about teenagers. Yet this could change with political will, leading to a better democracy. However, change is notoriously slow in schools and the actual encouragement of critical thinking rather than only the rhetoric endorsing it takes a great deal of courage.

It would involve serious revisions to the American curriculum. In addition, the psychological theories that have helped to limit and control youth must be reinterpreted to focus on teenagers' beneficial traits as well as their deficiencies. A focus on individual distinctions and social context may erase notions of universality applied to teenagers. In effect, what is considered least valued needs to become most valued in both teenagers and the public school. In particular, criticism of the outside media should not be extended to the school media because the schools are not governed by the same forces and might have the chance to do journalism better. A major step involves giving teenagers more autonomy.

This concept also was identified in a landmark 1984 study that gave pagers to teenagers and had them document their daily activities and feelings. Like many adults, the study found that teens often preferred anything to work, but they could become engrossed in those constructive activities that they enjoyed. In part, their preference for leisure time was because they chose what they wanted to do, and choice was a pivotal issue. "Teenagers have to learn how to enjoy what they are doing, and they must learn how to give meaning to the events unfolding in their lives by relating them to freely accepted goals," wrote the researchers Mihaly Csikszentmihalyi and Reed Larson (5). The researchers attempted to identify what they called "flow experiences," which created cognitive order out of chaos and were intrinsically motivating. Schools, they said, are not especially good at making education motivational for teens.

They found at least half the time students were not paying attention to teachers:

> The curriculum is an assembly line that pushes ideas and activities in front of the student at a fixed rate, ready or not. What is manufactured, however, is a great deal of internal discomfort. To save time, schools concentrate on academic subjects to the exclusion of the issues teenagers really care about.

Not surprisingly, the study found when classes are enjoyable, when they give students some sense of autonomy, students learn more and earn better grades. This is true of journalism because it allows students to excel in front of their peers, the most important audience for teenagers. They can learn to love journalism because it puts them on a more equal plane with adults. Moreover, newspapers provide an outlet for youth to explore identity, learn the value of hard work, and affect their communities for the better. Newspapers can be a seed for democracy, making young people more aware of the world. Like real journalists, high school students must learn to make each story assignment their own.

Notes

1 *Students Gazette*, Vol. 1, No. 1, Norris of Fairhill Papers, Vol. 44. Historical Society of Pennsylvania Archives. Cited as first school newspaper by Knott 1981,
2 See Library of Congress, Washington, D.C. web site: <http://memory.loc.gov/ammem/today/jan17.html>
3 Cited in Hine, 155.
4 After addressing Dolbee's class one day, the editor of *The Salina Evening Journal* wanted to try out another boy as a reporter, but it would have compromised his school attendance too much.
5 Quoted in Boyd 1960, 11.
6 His 1910 master's thesis is not available. It is detailed in Boyd 1960.
7 Nelson's book is based on a report by the Commission of Inquiry into High School Journalism convened by the Robert F. Kennedy Memorial.
8 Dvorak, Lain and Dickson 246.
9 Ibid 260.
10 According to Goodman, the studies' definitions of censorship are inconsistent. They range from an advisor's simple editing for spelling and grammatical mistakes to the advisor or principal's cutting out potentially disagreeable features to any type of interference by school authorities.
11 Dvorak, Lain and Dickson 252.

The Advantages of Advantage

According to Anthony Giddens, whose work builds on the theories of Max Weber (1946, 1947, 1958, 1968), societies are considered "closed" to the extent that they limit young people's social mobility or in fact, rule it out altogether. Youth are sentenced to lives of limitation and poverty when they are channeled into a permanent underclass, sometimes by the very educational systems that purport to offer a chance at advancement:

> In general, the greater the degree of 'closure' of mobility chances -- both intergenerationally and within the career of the individual -- the more this facilitates the formation of identifiable classes (1973, 158).

However, Giddens notes that no law exists to limit individual mobility and "hence, it must be emphasized that there is certainly never anything approaching complete closure."

More and more scholars repudiate the schemes of old-school class theorists who rely strictly on Karl Marx' conception of history as a series of struggles between large blocks of identifiable social groups, such as workers and capitalists. They find that class systems are more fluid, dynamic, and difficult to define today, but they cannot be ignored because of their real and lasting impact on society. These theorists are not ready to declare class privilege in America dead. It is easy to observe that some communities wrestle with problems of poverty for generations while others prosper and thrive. The debate is ongoing over the extent to which the United States is a society where people's social standing can be predetermined by the places and families into which they are born. Class distinctions are made socially in the way people dress and live, in their educations and occupations, the materials they read, what they watch on TV (if they claim to watch TV at all), how they talk, and in their very expectations for their lives and their children's achievement.

People may belong to categories heavily influenced by their occupations, social affiliations, or leadership groups. As early as the mid-1980s, Michael Useem (1984) defined an American elite as an "inner circle" of corporate leaders who shared common concerns that transcended the immediate welfare of their own firms to make up the values of a wider business class. This new power elite represented an upper class that more well-off students in this study aspired to join.

The greater complexity of social classes does not mean that such classes have been eradicated or that social inequality no longer afflicts the nation's schools. A great social divide concerns social scientist Charles Tilly in *Durable Inequality* (1998). Tilly contends that such inequality exists in the classification systems employed by disparate groups to accept and exclude people. In the identification of class differences, he adopts a relational view that goes beyond wages to consider issues of "wealth, health, nutrition, power, deference, privilege, security and other critical zones of inequality that in the long run, matter more to well-being than wages do" (24).

Social classes are created through interpersonal relations. Among the causes of inequality, Tilly argues, are unequal schools or "authoritatively organized differences in the acquisition of capacities for performance." He posits that family backgrounds "affect children's school performance and teachers' evaluations of that performance, which in turn channel children into categorically differentiated, career-shaping educational streams."

If the channeling of social classes is aggravated by public school practices, sociologist Annette Lareau, author of *Home Advantage* (1989), traces the roots of this inequality to the different ways the working and affluent classes socialize their young and interact with the educational system. Most affluent parents see the education of children as a shared responsibility, she finds. They treat their children's teachers as employees who work for them, form social networks with other parents, and more closely monitor their children's performance and assignments. Working-class parents, on the other hand, see the home and school as separate spheres and prefer not to interfere with the job of teachers. Not having attained a high level of education themselves, they are often intimidated by the official school world, Lareau contends:

> Relations between working-class families and the school are characterized by separation. Because these parents believe that teachers are responsible for education, they seek little information about either the curriculum or the educational process, and their criticisms of the school center almost entirely on non-academic matters. Most working-class parents never intervene in their children's school program; their children receive a generic education (8).

CHAPTER 2: DEMOGRAPICS AND BACKGROUND

Upper-middle class families see themselves as partners in their children's education, taking steps at home to reinforce the children's learning.[1]

The context of the schools in this study gave each newspaper its unmistakable texture and the promise of journalism as an instructional element in the school curricula was fulfilled or frustrated. Two groups of students were mostly upper-middle class and white at Coastal and Creekwood Canyon high schools, although Coastal High School had slightly greater diversity that it had achieved through busing. These two institutions were once rated among the top 100 public high schools nationally by *Newsweek* (June 2, 2003). The third site, Homestead High School, drew neighborhood students who came from working-class, Latino homes. It was counted among the state's 500 lowest performing high schools, put on probation, and given two years to improve.

Creekwood Canyon's school newspaper *The Comet* was often used as a model at Coastal. *The Comet* won awards that gave it a standing – judged by a national press association – as among the top high school newspapers in the nation. The school's high parental income and parent educational levels helped to keep student expectations high. Also contributing were the actual structure of the class and its reputation, built over 27 years, as well as its power to motivate and bring young people together, teach them leadership skills, and allow them broad autonomy. The newspaper at Creekwood Canyon had become a self-perpetuating institution and students sought to keep it strong. I theorized elite teenagers would more likely enjoy a freer rein and greater self-determination on the school newspaper than youth struggling academically and financially.

There was a significant divide between parent involvement at the two upper-middle class schools and at the working-class school. Parents at Creekwood Canyon High School prepared a feast – large tins of barbecued chicken and lasagna with fancy desserts – for the student journalists working late at night to finish *The Comet* on May 6, 2003 while parents at Homestead encouraged their children not to stay for after-school layout but to get home as quickly as possible to help with family responsibilities, such as child care and cooking. Students at Homestead were poorly served by the school's emphasis on discrete testing and point-by-point accountability while testing was viewed as a necessary poison among upper-middle class students. A wide variety of factors affect the quality of any high school journalism program, not the least of which are the teacher's knowledge and school officials' stance toward press freedom. Most important, my study suggests that issues of social class also dramatically affected the quality of education at the three study schools. Journalism was particularly influenced because of its dependence on students engaged in the news and politics, interests more often of households with higher income and educational attainment. Students working for *The Homestead Herald* were damaged by a halfhearted effort to practice journalism. No one had high expectations for them. This is not to say that there are no places where similarly situated Latino students can find journalism practiced at a high-functioning level. There are, but they are rare. More time would have provided an opportunity to expand this study, and even more would afford the chance to follow the journalism students beyond high school to learn how they are received in the working world.

As I conducted my study, the California schools were bracing for state budget cuts, and many teachers were worried about higher class sizes. Per-pupil spending in California already was considered grossly inadequate by critics -- the state ranked as low as 41st in the nation by 2003 (Gumbel, April 2003). The state faced criticism for being unable to meet the needs of all its students equally. In 1971, the California Supreme Court had sided with the plaintiffs in *Serrano v. Priest*, finding that children of "equal age, aptitude, motivation and ability" lacked equal access to educational funding. This violated the 14th Amendment or the equal protection clause of the U.S. Constitution.

The state attempted to solve this educational inequity among its 1,000-plus districts in 1978 with Proposition 13, which allotted property tax money, residential and commercial, directly to the state, instead of to individual school districts. The state then reassigned the dollars using a complicated formula. The problem was that this ultimately led to the shrinking per pupil expenditures because while districts were being funded equally, schools were not. Some districts had both schools with upper-middle-class parents and with working-class populations. California's 2000-01 budget provided \$6,837 per student, but the national average was \$7,640, meaning that the state was then ranked 33 in per-pupil spending nationally.[2]

A report by the Public Policy Institute of California (2000) suggested that the failure to support the schools adequately had increased class sizes, which in turn, may have led to California's sub-par performance on standardized tests. By the late 1990s, the state's pupil-teacher ratio was almost 40 percent higher than the average for other states. As doubtful as they often can be, standardized tests may demonstrate that school finance reform has not worked – at least that it has not done what policymakers wanted. These circumstances made the

CHAPTER 2: DEMOGRAPICS AND BACKGROUND   41

budget crisis of 2003 yet more calamitous for education, which comprises half the state budget. The disastrous effects of education spending actually had been building for more than 20 years. "In 1978, California's per-pupil outlay on public education exceeded the national average" but spending fell seriously by the 1990s, according to a 1995 Rand study. Budget reductions could affect school newspapers that rely on district money, especially where decision-makers consider them a luxury.

It is important to view the schools in this study in the context of their unequal treatment: Upper-middle class parents subsidized their children's schooling through private donations and foundation fund-raising while schools serving the working class had fewer benefactors. Thus for public schools with a higher-income population, the parents try to make the vagaries of state finance irrelevant:

> Families have responded in various ways to the perceived decline in public school quality. Some have enrolled their children in private schools; others have donated time and money to public schools . . .both reactions have been modest and mostly confined to high-income families. While private school enrollment rose from 14 to 21 percent among families in the top 10 percent of the income distribution, there were no increases at all among families in the bottom 60 percent of that distribution.[3]

In three school districts in my study, private school enrollment had gone up since 1990, from hundreds of students among low-income families to thousands of students in the higher-income locales.[4]

While specific data regarding these schools may change from year to year, this study offers a snapshot of these journalism programs as they functioned within their settings at the particular times under consideration. Many of the observations concerning the economics of student life may prove rather similar to other secondary school journalism experiences around the state and nation.

A. Homestead High School

With more than 2,600 students, Homestead High School is the only high school serving its California city of more than 15,000 households in one of the poorest areas of the state. Nearly 70 percent of students are poor, measured by their participation in the federally subsidized free or reduced lunch program. More than 75 percent are Latino, so that the Spanish language is often the currency of social life. As students delivered their school newspaper *The Homestead Herald* on March 20, 2003, they spoke Spanglish. "Quieres un newspaper?" Delia (15) asked a classmate along the concrete pathways that are the school halls. With her was Ana (also 15), a Mexican immigrant who relocated at age 5. For many young people, Spanish was their first language, and more than one-fourth of the school's students were considered "English Language Learners," with 69 percent of them scoring below the 25th percentile in reading on the Stanford 9 achievement test.

The school's makeup offered a clue to its educational dilemmas, not because students were minorities or less capable, but because of poverty-related ills and the link between family income and school success (Mehan et. al 1996, Lareau 1989).

One of the biggest obstacles faced by the high school, which operates on a year-round block schedule, is transience, principal Harold Frank said. In any given year, fully one-quarter of the Homestead population was transient -- either coming in (not as new freshmen) or leaving prior to their graduation date.

A number of students are Mexican immigrants, legal residents or undocumented, because of the school's proximity to the Mexican border. The year-round schedule was among the tactics designed to offset the effects of poverty and immigration on the students' schooling. Year-round schedules, which sought to replace the traditional, 180-day school year, took root in California in the late-1960s, mostly to ease school overcrowding (Zykowski et. al 1991). In the United States, year-round schools can be traced as far back as 1645. Immigrant families supported the year-round calendar in the 1880s in hopes that their children would adjust to English and American culture more quickly without the extended summer vacation. During breaks that occurred throughout the year, students who had failed courses at Homestead could take make-up instruction. However, the issue of transience hurt the outlook for children in poor and working--class families because they might start months behind whenever they relocated from schools with regular timetables. When they left Homestead, they could not easily switch to other schedules.

Mr. Frank contended that he could improve students' academic performance, if they stayed at Homestead long enough to absorb their lessons:

> If you give me students who are here for four years, we can have them do more than four years of work in that time frame because they will be here, they are staying, they come to school every day, and they are prepared to learn. But if I have someone who is transient, they're normally behind credits or not doing well – especially if they come from a traditional setting. They are seven weeks behind because they come in September and we have been at school since July. So the facts are that our population is the way that it is. We can't control it. We can't dwell on economics or anything else. We can only work with the student that comes every day and hope that we can give them the best quality education (Interview with Harold Frank, September 17, 2002).

The transience factor was related to poverty and not necessarily immigration, Mr. Frank contended, although he was not sure of the actual reasons. It meant that English teacher Stacey Webb, who ran the high school's journalism class, had difficulty building a sense of community or the newsroom culture that might exist in other student newspaper settings. Because students were transient, targeting instruction to their needs also was hard because the student who was present today might be gone tomorrow. Thus, there was little notion of a student-run press with student editorial control or autonomous news judgment. Nor was there the intrinsic motivation necessary for producing a high-quality student publication. The structure of the class and to some degree, the content of *The Herald*, was largely teacher-directed. In Mrs. Webb's estimation, nothing could be achieved any other way.

Mrs. Webb faced tremendous odds. If not immigrants, many students were the children of immigrants. A number had single mothers supported by public assistance or Social Security benefits. Some of the students in this study told stories of upheaval and turbulence, making it difficult for them to keep permanent addresses or achieve real stability. Their academic record – and the endeavor of producing the school newspaper – could rightly be secondary to those more pressing concerns. These were challenges of extreme disadvantage, even lack of nutrition, of families losing their homes or facing internal strife and sporadic trouble with the police. Mrs. Webb was frustrated by what she saw as a lack of motivation in as many as half her class. She admitted f probably knew more about where her students were coming from, the particular challenges they faced outside the classroom, than she did. Given her own level of journalism knowledge and training, mostly gleaned from a past teacher and the textbook, she tried to do what she could. She also was responsible for recruiting her own students into journalism class, but the other classes she taught were for those with low reading ability. Although some were recommended by their English teachers, many students came to the journalism class because they were Mrs. Webb's former students from the reading lab. They were the students she had encountered. Mrs. Webb had trouble turning struggling readers into journalists.

So many students required extra help at Homestead it was unclear whether the school could reach more than a small number. Bureaucracy often contributed to an official school culture that did not really know its students. For example, one journalism student, Carlos, 15, a first-generation American, was placed in the wrong world history class for more than six months because he was confused with another boy who shared the same Hispanic name.

"They [the school authorities] don't care," said his classmate Tony, also 15, during a student discussion of the Iraq War and the way political leaders may send young people off to die without considering the impact of their policies.

"They don't even know our names," said Carlos of school officials (Field notes, February 25, 2003).

The two boys were among three journalism students placed in a new intervention program, launched in January 2003, the school's attempt to improve student performance. The program worked with 600 freshmen and sophomores who had earned three or more Fs. Just three months prior, it had started with 969 students. Substitute teacher Dave Perez, a Latino man in his late 20s,[5] was brought in to teach journalism and reading during Mrs. Webb's maternity leave in spring 2003. As a former intervention teacher, he had said he found student grades would go up as soon as they knew someone would be checking up on them. Some of the journalism students could make inroads out of resilience and resourcefulness, but mostly they were passive and silent. I did not see evidence that they were connecting with adults who sought to help them, including Mrs. Webb. They had only a short-lived relationship with Mr. Perez. Like many teens, many considered adults hypocritical or hopelessly out of touch. That both Carlos and Tony felt the school did not care about them was important to grasping their academic grief.

In *Subtractive Schooling* (1999), education theorist Angela Valenzuela contends that "the mainstream curriculum is demonstrably accessible through a route responsive to students' definition of caring" (267). Mexican-American young people are particularly resistant to education that does not demonstrate this sense of caring, she argues, writing:

> The feeling that 'no one cares' is pervasive -- and corrosive. Real learning is difficult to sustain in an atmosphere rife with mistrust. Over even comparatively short periods of time, the divisions and misunderstandings that characterize daily life at the school exact high costs in academic, social and motivational currency. The subtractive nature of schooling virtually assures that students who begin the year with only small reserves of skills, as do most regular-track U.S.-born youth, will not succeed; and conversely, those who come with more positive orientations or greater skills, as do Mexican-born students, are better equipped to offset the more debilitating aspects of schooling (5).

Although evident around the school, students' Mexican heritage was not particularly valued in the journalism classroom. The school had an "English immersion" approach that did not stress competence in students' native language. While the Creekwood Canyon newspaper always included a Spanish-language story, [6] the Homestead newspaper did not print any.

Kate Browning, coordinator of the school's effort to improve student performance under the state's Immediate Intervention of Under-Performing Schools program, said she believed Valenzuela's assertions about a lack of caring. The school's students were victims of "low expectations," including ingrained teacher views that they would not be attending college. Changing this involves a major shift in thinking that "most kids will go to college," she said. Too many Homestead teachers had "given up."

An unwavering sense of duty to their families was a positive trait, but it also could reshape and constrict students' plans for themselves. Delia, who wanted to attend an art college in San Francisco for fashion design, could not convince her father of her hopes. He told her such independence would put her in harm's way. Her mother had dropped out of school at age 13. The family, legal U.S. residents, was forced to leave their home and find a new one, but high rents meant they had to return to Mexico, keeping Delia and her two younger sisters in school by making a brutal four-hour daily commute from Tijuana. In order for this to be possible, the parents had to supply an aunt's local address to school authorities. This was a common ruse because many other students came from Mexico illegally, Delia said, but no one could write about such an issue for the school newspaper without facing expulsion for obvious reasons, she said. It also was not the kind of story *The Homestead Herald* usually would choose to tackle. Purely by happenstance, I met another student who told me she was making the same commute from Tijuana, using a relative's address to stay at Homestead. We talked as she waited for her ride in front of school. The commute often left Delia and her sisters hungry and gave them migraines, but it showed the parents' resolve to educate them in U.S. schools.

Alejandro Portes and Ruben Rumbaut in their landmark study *Immigrant America* (1996) contended that the stereotype of immigrants coming to America to escape the destitution of foreign lands is inaccurate. The poorest of the poor often cannot come here. Even unauthorized immigrants had above-average education levels and job skills compared to the population of their homeland.

"Although the socioeconomic origins of most immigrants are modest by U.S. standards, they consistently meet or surpass the average for the Mexican population," the authors wrote (10-11).

Immigrant literacy rates are higher than commonly thought, they contended. The authors argued that Mexicans leave Mexico because they seek the expanded opportunity America can offer. I could see one example in Ana, the sole freshman in the Homestead classroom, whose mother had been an elementary school teacher in Mexico. Her mother and an older sister were attending community college together. Delia, who had come to California at age 2, also showed a persistent desire to succeed no matter the obstacles.

When Mr. Frank instituted a system of checking parental records that was supposedly more rigorous at the start of the 2002-2003 school year, he said, he dropped more than 100 students from the rolls on the third day of school. Mr. Frank was then accused of being part of the Immigration and Naturalization Service.

"Now I am not in the immigration business," he said. "I am not a border patrolman . . . In fact, I was not allowing people to come to this

CHAPTER 2: DEMOGRAPICS AND BACKGROUND 47

school who lived in [a local big city] or other places. It had nothing to do with living in another country." Mr. Frank downplayed the impact of immigration on the school. At the same time, his very language reflected a sensitivity to the controversy over California's Proposition 187 (1994), which sought to deny public benefits to illegal immigrants and to turn school staff into enforcers of immigration policy. The measure was approved by voters, but most of it was declared unconstitutional four years later.

The rights of schoolchildren whose parents have brought them here illegally were established by the U.S. Supreme Court in *Plyler v. Doe* (1982). In that case, the court ruled that Texas could not withhold schooling from children not legally admitted to the United States. It held, "The Texas statute imposes a lifetime hardship on a discrete class of children not accountable for their disabling status. These children can neither affect their parents' conduct nor their own undocumented status."

The school's emphasis on English may have been because most immigrant parents opted for English-only classes for their children. However, the state's Proposition 227, approved by voters in 1998, also required that students remain in bilingual education for no more than one year. This untenable demand was controversial. The U.S. Department of Education's Office for Civil Rights issued a statement after the ballot initiative was approved that it "does not relieve school districts of any of their obligation to comply with federal civil rights requirements. These requirements afford recipients of federal funds considerable latitude in selecting an instructional approach so long as it effectively addresses the educational needs of limited English proficient children." The U.S. Supreme Court sought to protect the rights of these children with its 1974 ruling in *Lau v. Nichols*.

Under the district's methods, it usually took three years for immigrants to leave bilingual education entirely, according to Superintendent James Regan. It required more like four to seven years to learn academic English, Regan wrote. Students whose parents request a bilingual program are tested at least once a semester, he said:

> Ongoing testing gauges growth in language mastery and helps determine students' ability to add more mainstream classes to their schedules. Even from the start, students receive high levels of immersion: three to four hours of English classes each day. And as they quickly increase the load, their progress is supported through talented teachers who have been specially

trained by the district in using 'sheltered English' techniques such as visual aids, group-work and hands-on activities that make it easier for all students to understand the material. Lastly, before graduation, students must demonstrate their English skills on a writing test. It's been this way in our district for 20 years!" (Superintendent's message, June 1998).

In a May 1998 message, the superintendent bemoaned the state's requirement that students just learning English take standardized exams. "While this approach may provide politicians with great TV sound bites, it seriously shortchanges students by failing to provide a true picture of their genuine abilities."

Mrs. Webb was not bilingual, and that made it more challenging for her to be among the caring teachers that Valenzuela discusses. She was a friendly woman liked by many of her students, but she also was conservative and fearful of taking risks. She believed in individual responsibility, having pulled herself through difficult times as a teenage mother herself. Her life story was something she did not share with students, afraid of what message it might send. She also showed she was not particularly interested in students' lives and experiences, which could have been the starting point for their newspaper stories. The students in her class often were silent and passive during her attempts to spark class discussion. Brainstorming sessions usually became an exercise in reading aloud from the school calendar. This was not necessarily evidence that students did not care about school or even the news, but that they did not care about what she wanted them to care about. Carlos, a new student in the class, found it especially challenging when he was assigned a story about President's Day. As I walked with him to interview other students, he complained about the assignment but said he took it without comment so as not to create a bad impression. His assignment was one most professional newspapers would not cover.

The Homestead teenagers I met were concerned about important issues in their lives. Like others their age, they had dreams, only some of which were unrealistic. Besides their perceptions of a lack of caring, which differed from student to student, they also were unaware of the stages and incremental steps involved in planning for college admission or careers, information normally imparted to more affluent adolescents. This is the cultural capital discussed by Pierre Bourdieu in *The State Nobility* (315-320, 1989) and other works. Parents pass on values to their children but they also give them resources -- a familiarity with the language, art and music-- that they can use to gain power in the world.

Upper-middle class students enter school accustomed to the speech patterns, authority structure and instruction used in educational institutions. Students' background knowledge, accumulated during their upbringing, adds to their overall cultural capital. In addition, the school bureaucracy perpetuates class distinctions by which some subjects are esteemed and others devalued (Bourdieu 1977, 130, 152-153). I argue that journalism is one of these devalued subjects.

The students' imaginations were limited because although they wanted successful lives, most could not grasp the world's immense possibilities. Many did not wish to go far away for college or a career, but this was directly related to their financial state and discouragement from parents who had not been to college themselves. Ironically, parents who had struck out for improved opportunity in America sometimes sabotaged their children by limiting them unnecessarily. For such students, financial aid and scholarship programs existed. The Compact for Success in the district where Homestead was located, matched students with the local campus of the state university, encouraging them to succeed academically. The university guaranteed admission to the seventh-grade class of 2000, 2001, and 2002 if they passed all their classes and maintained a 3.0 GPA in required courses. This offer had been expanded to eight of the district's 10 high schools, including Homestead, which was trying to boost the number of students who attended four-year institutions. But fewer than 25 percent of graduates completed the course requirements for admission to California State University or the University of California in 2001, a low rate in the school district.

Homestead High School is in a city that is only eight-square miles. The Pacific Ocean is on the west side of the city, a larger school district to the north and east, and a river to the south. The school is across the street from a gas station, a tire store and a stereo supply business.

The district also includes schools on the west side that have students who come from higher socioeconomic backgrounds. Dave Perez, the substitute teacher, had grown up in one of those areas.

Mrs. Webb teaches in the oldest building, which was constructed in the 1940s. Today, renovation is sorely needed. The school was built for 2,400 students but is overcrowded by 200. In four years, it is expected to admit 1,000 more students. The school district built a $9.5 million gym (with five new classrooms) through a $187 million voter-approved bond measure, but teachers and students questioned the choice to construct a gym before fixing up aging classrooms.

Mr. Frank said the decision to construct the gym project first was made by a committee but that he supported it because it was less disruptive to student learning. The age of the school was a source of pride (a few students told me they and their mothers shared the same teachers), but peeling paint and cracked pavement was not: Unlike other schools, Homestead could not turn to its parents for money. Less than 7 percent of the population had completed college, and the median household income was under $30,000 a year. Just over 40 percent of the population over age 25 had not graduated from high school, and an additional 25 percent had never gotten beyond high school. Some 30 percent of residents earned less than $20,000 annually. Like the high school, the city population was mostly Latino – just more than 59 percent, according to the 2000 U.S. Census. Whites made up just more than 14 percent. Almost 65 percent of the population over age 5 spoke a language other than English at home. Some 35 percent of students lived with grandparents who did not have high school educations.

Homestead was typical in that it was experiencing many of the same problems with its Hispanic student population as many other similarly situated schools, whether near the Mexican border or not. Hispanics were expected to become the largest minority group in the nation by 2005. Hispanics had made gains in academic achievement in the previous 20 years, but key gaps remained for Hispanic students when compared to white students. These gaps probably would continue to exist once students entered the job market where Hispanic men were expected to earn lower incomes than whites at most educational levels, according to a Census report.[8] Poverty for Hispanics in America exceeds 21 percent, compared to the poverty level for non-Hispanic whites of less than 8 percent.

Homestead High School had a school newspaper since 1924, even publishing during World War II, though there have been periods with no newspaper and the publication schedule has varied, judging from the records of the local library and the school. *The Homestead Herald*, almost entirely funded by the school district, was produced eight times from July to June in the 2002-2003 school year.

Mrs. Webb's small building offered journalism and reading in two classrooms. The journalism students alternated between the rooms, which were also not far from the school's central offices and other classroom wings. The walls of the reading classroom were decorated with color posters of the parts of speech – noun, adjective, verb and so on – and the parts of the essay. One often could see books for much younger children around, such as "The Little Engine That Could," part

CHAPTER 2: DEMOGRAPICS AND BACKGROUND   51

of the English language immersion approach. The other classroom, known as the newsroom, contained a poster of the parts of the news story and tips on writing the lead or first paragraph along with a list of current newspaper editors. Two dry erase boards announced the story assignments slated for the upcoming edition. The journalism program had no shortage of computers with about 20 laptops and the same number of desktops, all of which had the PageMaker layout program. This was proof technology alone does not make a successful newspaper program.

Mrs. Webb, in her mid-30s and starting a second family, taught middle school for 10 years, then moved to Homestead, where she at first taught English to five classes of freshmen and sophomores in four different rooms. She initially rejected the idea of taking over the newspaper class, but she ultimately became convinced, tired of juggling classrooms. "[The principal] said the newspaper class was a must," Mrs. Webb recalled. "I compared my current schedule to this schedule. I thought, OK, I can handle the newspaper class. Whatever it is, I can learn it."

When she first took over the class, students ran the paper and she facilitated. They were confrontational and more liberal than she was, Mrs. Webb said. The last advisor also was more flexible with them about what topics they could choose, perhaps too flexible, according to Mrs. Webb, because she allowed obscenities and foolishness, such as an entire page of one girl's computer Instant Messages to her boyfriend. The previous editor in chief, a senior who graduated in 2001, considered Mrs. Webb "oppressive." Mrs. Webb said she did not care what students chose to write about, as long as there were no profanities, the subject was appropriate for school, and the work was well-researched.

In 1997, the principal prior to Mr. Frank's tenure, had removed the 26-year newspaper advisor, but Mr. Frank was unclear as to the reasons why. The ousted teacher Carol Schultz had run the newspaper program prior to the advisor before Mrs. Webb. Mr. Frank said she allowed students to print "gang-related material," but 19-year-old Jerry, who had the ousted advisor as a journalism teacher when he was a freshman, said nothing could be further from the truth (Interview with Jerry, April 10, 2003). He said she was removed for the content of her students' newspapers, particularly an editorial denouncing the JROTC program. The former advisor Mrs. Schultz confirmed this (Interview with Carol Schultz, May 22, 2003). In a private meeting, students begged Mr. Frank to allow the ousted advisor to return, but he refused, said Jerry, who became editor in chief during his senior year. "I don't think he knew the whole situation, and I don't think he really cared."

The advisor was ousted because the administration wanted a different, less controversial kind of student press, and that has been the result, Jerry said.

The decision sacrificed the longtime advisor's 26 years of experience. After her removal, she retired early. His experiences on the newspaper soured Jerry on journalism, he said. Once this "liberal" group of students graduated, new students joined the class. They did not take to journalism easily, Mrs. Webb said. Although Mrs. Webb gave instruction in journalism at the beginning of the year, they either did not remember her teachings or chose not to. Students would write stories without gathering information or interviewing sources, except perhaps each other.

Typically, the editor in chief is supposed to have significant input into the operation of the newspaper, but in this setting, the teacher did the bulk of the work involved in managing the newspaper and editing stories and layouts. Mrs. Webb encouraged the editor in chief she had appointed, Lali, to lead some brainstorming sessions, but the Samoan girl, polite and quiet, was uncomfortable with being in charge, particularly with assigning work to other students when they had not volunteered for it. This irked some students, as they saw assigning stories as part of her job. Mr. Frank was happy with Mrs. Webb's imposition of structure on the class. Although he disavowed any responsibility for the advisor who had been removed, that experience and others made him more cautious and strict. He said he would feel free to censor the newspaper – he considered himself the publisher. He denied ever censoring the newspaper by using prior restraint, but Jerry said he had done so.

I asked Mr. Frank, "You said you have to live with what's in the local press. But you don't take that attitude with the school newspaper?"

"I will control what's in that paper," he said, "That's different. I'm responsible for it."

Still, I never directly witnessed Mr. Frank take a heavy-handed approach with the newspaper. This probably was because it presented virtually no threat by the time I came on the scene, or because my presence would have made him uncomfortable. Jerry said he used to have to defend his columns before they were published because Mrs. Webb had given Mr. Frank copies. Mr. Frank would take issue with certain words.

CHAPTER 2: DEMOGRAPICS AND BACKGROUND 53

Mrs. Webb had regularly ceded Mr. Frank a fourth of one editorial page for a letter from Mr. Frank to students, a decision that left less space for student expression and was journalistically questionable because of Mr. Frank's powerful role in the school. In theory, Mr. Frank said, he believed he would be justified in pulling a story prior to publication because of *Hazelwood*. He had no idea a 1977 state law prohibited the censoring of the public school press in California, banning acts of prior restraint, except in very limited circumstances. The law rendered *Hazelwood* potentially moot in California.[9] Our conversation about this proceeded this way:

> SEA: In California, there's a state law that says you can't censor kids --
> HF: Oh, yes you can!
> SEA: To a certain extent, or how do you view it?
> HF: I look at it that there's censorship. It's my newspaper. I'm paying for it. It's mine. Absolutely. And I have the right to censor you because this is an elective class. You can run your own newspaper underground, or if you're paying for it. But I have had that discussion and some people will say 'You can't deprive me of my freedom of speech.' Well, this is not a safe haven. Schools are not safe havens. You have a freedom of speech as long as you're not ripping on anybody, as long as you're not wearing condoms around or making statements that are inappropriate. As long as you're not belittling anybody, you are entitled to your beliefs. And there is a fine line there, and I will have the final say. I'm very strong on that.
> SEA: There was that Supreme Court decision in '88, *Hazelwood*, which basically said the same thing you are saying to me right now.
> HF: That's where I got it from. I didn't know it was called *Hazelwood*, but the fact is I may censor the school newspaper. End of story. (Interview with Harold Frank, September 17, 2002)

Mr. Frank's seeming unwillingness to consider the possibility that students had press rights clearly could not be reconciled with existing caselaw. Other California principals have taken his stance, based on information from other advisors and accounts of the Student Press Law Center. The principals at the two other schools in this study were aware of student press rights, though they sometimes acted to constrain student free speech in particular cases, more at one school than the other. *The*

Herald was usually so tame that there was little need for heated discussion or debate.

    Mrs. Webb, too, was not about to encourage the kind of critical journalism that would facilitate students writing about their own life circumstances and social position as less powerful. The idea that journalism could correct wrongs that the students identified was not stressed and neither were their First Amendment rights. When two white students, Jessica and Kimberly, both 16, entered in the middle of the school year, their political nature stood in sharp contrast to the attitudes of most of the other students. Jessica recounted for me her attempts to sit down during the daily Pledge of Allegiance and the way other students and the teacher reacted in past classes. Kimberly told me about the leadership role she had taken in protests against the Iraq war. Yet when I suggested the teacher encourage the first student to write a column about her refusal to stand for the pledge, the teacher told me that kind of behavior was not something the school newspaper should be encouraging.

    I felt this was a lost teaching opportunity and gave the teacher a copy of the Supreme Court's ruling in *West Virginia State Board of Education v. Barnette* (1943), which gave students the right not to stand. Justice Robert Jackson wrote the "compulsion of students to declare a belief" and "compulsory unification of opinion achieves only the unanimity of the graveyard." Mrs. Webb promised to read the opinion, but I had the impression it would go in the circular file.

    Mrs. Webb's claim that her students were "not very political" was true of many, at least where conventional politics were concerned, She was not doing much to trigger political thinking either. She tried at times, pressing students to write about terrorism when they wanted to write about body image. But the students did not cover a possible teacher strike or state budget cuts or changes in the high school graduation requirements. These difficult news stories would have required her help during both the reporting and writing process. Journalism is a subject that could be employed to aid students' intellectual transformation into critical thinkers. However, the students needed a stronger understanding of professional journalistic practices and standards in order to overcome apathy and use journalism for their own self-actualization. Journalism at Homestead did not have to be apolitical. Mrs. Webb believed many of the students in the journalism class were unmotivated because the greater school climate did not motivate them, but as they got to cover stories they regarded as important to their immediate lives, they grew more excited and involved.

One example was Tony, who sought my help to write a column about an inadequate library system for checking in book returns that resulted in some students being improperly charged, including Tony himself. He and other students felt that they should do more of this type of story in the school newspaper. It resulted in the school erasing the charge from Tony's bill and relocating a book bin that was open to theft.

Yet Mrs. Webb pointed to other examples of the lack of motivation prevalent in the school environment that she argued made running a journalism program much more difficult. Most times, her students seemed to be actively trying to avoid work, she said. Students lacked motivation, but while Mr. Perez, the substitute for Mrs. Webb, might conclude from this that they were "lazy," their environment and life circumstances were so difficult that any achievement in this setting could seem remarkable. Some school reform efforts focus on the psychological needs of underachieving students for exactly this reason, writes Hugh Mehan in *Constructing School Success* (1996). His psychiatric expertise led reformer James P. Comer to conclude "students' academic and behavior problems result from unmet psychological needs rather than willful badness."[10]

It could not have helped students' psychological health that Homestead was engaged in what some teachers and students saw as a frenzy of testing. One veteran English teacher said she had little time to do anything but prepare students for tests. Mrs. Webb said that this mentality frustrated some teachers, but there were others who would give instruction directed at a particular test for half a period, then give students the rest of the time off. Some teachers had trouble adapting to the school's two-hour block schedule. This meant some journalism students would ask Mrs. Webb if the rest of the class time could be free, instead of spent working on the newspaper. Students who refused to take seriously the English section of the graduation exam took a subversive stand when they stared at blank pages, then stayed longer to avoid returning to class. A six-year accreditation study in March 2003 heralded the new intervention program, but recommended the school "increase rigor and relevance in the classroom."

Yet student resistance to specific teaching styles in the school seemed to be connected to larger patterns of docility that often result from authoritarian teaching methods. Even in cases where the journalism instruction was not authoritarian, the students were in classes all day where there was no room for their input, so they often assumed there was no room here either. It seemed that school officials tried to boost performance through an aggressive focus on preparing students for standardized tests, among Superintendent Regan's top priorities. "Through extensive data analysis and research, we developed a comprehensive system of support to ensure students are prepared to answer questions about everything from measurement and geometry to vocabulary and literary reading. There's extra help for those most in need. Depending how far a student falls below the passing grade of 350 [on the high school exit exam] a range of test support options are in place" (Superintendent's Message, February 2003).

Passing tests is an important step to college. The problem with this approach was that it made high school education itself unbearable for many students. In the second to the last paragraph of the Superintendent's column (the rest is focused on improving performance on the graduation exam), he mentions other tactics of improving student learning, "cutting-edge teacher training, broader parent involvement at our campuses, and greater use of educational technology in the classroom." These things sound like add-ons to the greater importance of the tests. Yet Regan was recognized nationally as a top superintendent. He had a reputation for sound fiscal management.[11] At the same time, the focus on testing obviously was a reality of the American educational system he was forced to accept.

The focus on test scores must have had some effect because the school's Academic Performance Index or API, an indicator that combines the Stanford 9 national achievement test scores with the California Standards Test, had risen every year from 461 in 1998 to 555 in 2002, though it was still 245 points below the state's goal for all high schools, said Mrs. Browning. Unless the school could raise this score by 5 percent, Mr. Frank could lose his job by state law, she said. Improvements in test scores probably came at the expense of other more important but less quantifiable educational achievement, journalistic excellence being one of the sacrifices. Under the current U.S. education system, high test scores would give students more of a chance for a college education. Unfortunately for those students who would not attend college, high school might be their last connection to formal education.

The pressure of constant testing irritated Jessica, who said the tests made her feel like a machine. She ridiculed the California High School Exit Exam and the Stanford 9 achievement tests in reading and math. In a March 18, 2003 column, she wrote:

CHAPTER 2: DEMOGRAPICS AND BACKGROUND 57

Obviously, this test is a burden to everyone who has to take it. We have to leave our classes, which on any other day would be fine, and go to either the new or old gym and sit, in very uncomfortable chairs, for up to four hours taking a test we did not want to take to begin with. (*Homestead Herald*, March 18, 2003, 9)

In 2002, only 21 percent of the class of 2004 had passed the math section and 38 percent had passed English. In *Punished by Rewards* (1993), Alfie Kohn argues against tests for evaluating students. Kohn writes that better teaching places less emphasis on testing:

> Assuming that classes are kept at a reasonable size, a competent teacher has a pretty good sense of how each student is doing. Anyone who requires a formal test to know what is going on may need to reconsider the approach to instruction being used and whether he or she is talking too much and listening too little. Indeed a series of interviews with fifty teachers identified as being superlative at their craft turned up a strikingly consistent lack of emphasis on testing, if not a deliberate decision to minimize the practice. In particular, a classroom that feels safe to students is one in which they are free to admit when they don't understand something and are able to ask for help. Ironically, grades and tests, punishments and rewards, are the enemies of safety; they therefore reduce the probability that students will speak up and that truly productive evaluation can take place (203).

There is little tolerance by top officials for any kind of "deliberate decision to minimize" testing. In fact, journalism itself may be devalued as an academic subject because it does not lend itself to standardized tests and quantitative evaluation. These student productions are obvious ways to assess performance and any journalism advisor knows that the process of producing a newspaper -- of reporting stories, meeting deadlines and working cooperatively with others -- also must be judged along with the final product.

The subjective reality of important subjects was not something valued in this environment. Perhaps it couldn't be because so many requirements were imposed by the state. Such testing is part of a "banking' notion of teaching described by Brazilian educator Paulo Freire, as though students were blank slates that could be lectured at, with the information inscribed and then spit back during examinations. Freire, a champion of the urban poor, explains in *Pedagogy of the Oppressed* (1970) that the problem-posing education he advocates will enable people to develop their power to understand critically the way they exist in the world, which is not static but always in transformation. He describes the differences between banking education and the more enlightened variety:

> Banking education resists dialogue; problem-posing education regards dialogue as indispensable to the act of cognition, which unveils reality. Banking education treats students as objects of assistance; problem-posing education makes them critical thinkers. Banking education inhibits creativity and domesticates (although it cannot completely destroy) the intentionality of consciousness by isolating consciousness from the world, thereby denying people their ontological and historical vocation of becoming more fully human (Freire 1970, 83-84).

Education theorist Anne Haas Dyson's book *Writing Superheroes* (1997), credits Freire and education reformer John Dewey for advancing the argument that "freedom must be continually renewed, or else shelters become cages." Transformation occurs through interaction with students' immediate surroundings, which is a central ingredient of journalism. Mrs. Webb needed to intervene in the newspaper more subtly by challenging students' story ideas and getting them more deeply involved in additional subjects that interested them.

"Adults . . . cannot give children freedom by turning them loose with a paper and pencil, any more than they can by turning them loose in the wild. But they can challenge children, helping them sense social and textual possibilities beyond their current borders," Dyson writes (166).

B. Coastal High School

The young people of Coastal City predominantly were raised in upper-middle class households. The median household income is at least $70,000 a year, the median home value, more than $650,000, according to data from the 2000 Census, which counted almost 18,000 households. Citizens have higher than average education levels, and the city is home to research and development firms and a prominent university. Those who show up at town council or for school board meetings are often leading experts in their fields. Coastal High School is set in a residential neighborhood, where locals sometimes complain about teens' noise and cars. The school is walking distance from shops and restaurants. The area has near perfect weather and a cool breeze from the ocean.

Most students at Coastal High School are protected in their suburban enclave. They often have access to computers, sometimes one for every member of the family (in contrast, most Homestead students must use them at school or the public library), allowances as high as $400 a month, and the use of a family or personal car. If a student needs something for school, a ticket or a uniform, even an advertisement for the school newspaper, parents can usually supply the money.

Academically, Coastal is the most successful secondary school in its district. This is a factor of more than standardized testing. More than 90 percent of the graduating class of 2002 went on to four-year colleges, including highly prestigious institutions. The students have much less difficulty coping with the pressure of standardized exams: 98 percent of the class of 2004 had passed the English section of the California High School Exit Exam, and 86 percent had passed the math section as of 2002. Both are needed to graduate. The high number of students who were planning to attend four-year institutions could be seen in the more than 86 percent of seniors who took the Scholastic Aptitude Test or SAT, almost 320 out of a grade 12 enrollment of 370, according to a county K-12 achievement report for 2002. The average total score was more than 1150. In addition, more than 500 Coastal students took more than 1,050 Advanced Placement exams in 2002, with 860 exams scoring a 3 or better, the cutoff for college credit. The school offered Advanced Placement courses in 22 subjects. By comparison at Homestead, fewer than 30 percent of juniors and seniors took the SAT, with an average total score of 818. More than 370 students took more than 600 AP exams, with close to 30 percent scoring 3 or better. Homestead offered 15 different AP subjects to students, a mark of pride in its struggling environment. In fact, the same *Newsweek* report that ranked Coastal and Creekwood Canyon top performers placed Homestead 277th in the nation for its AP program. The only misleading part of this was that the school's effort to have as many students as possible take the AP Spanish language and literature tests might have skewed the magazine's results. The ranking was based on the number of AP tests taken at the schools.

One reason for these results could be found in the high-performing students' family backgrounds: More than 30 percent of Coastal parents had graduated college, and an additional 47 percent had completed graduate school, according to the California Basic Educational Data

System, based on a 2002 standardized test form that students had filled out. On a scale of 1 to 5, students rated their parents' educational levels more than 4 on the same form. The 2000 Census found the percentage of those who held a bachelor's degree or better in the school's zip code to be almost 70 percent. Almost 70 percent met the requirements for admission to the University of California or California State University systems while at Homestead, a mere 25 percent had met the same standard. A story in the local daily (January 7, 2001) said the student who was ranked 50th in the Class of 2000 attended Yale University and 55th, Cornell.

With more than 1,600 students, the population of Coastal High School is mostly white at 66 percent, 21 percent Latino, and 9 percent Asian, along with a small fraction of other ethnicities. Many of the students traditionally had come from the immediate community, yet as recently as 1996, the majority were non-residents. This fact led the local daily newspaper to run a feature story in 2001 that bemoaned the dismantling of the Voluntary Ethnic Enrollment Program or VEEP, which accounted for the bulk of Coastal's diversity. VEEP had supplied free busing to mostly Latino students from inner-city neighborhoods. Referring to Coastal's academic success, the article's author said: "Amid this consistent excellence, a change is occurring. [Coastal High School] as social laboratory is in retreat. Racial diversity engineered by decades of busing is giving way to a whiter, richer, more local student body. . . . The gates of [Coastal High] are shutting against students from poorer neighborhoods, so the locals are missing opportunities to interact with students of different races, economic classes and zip codes." Principal Evan McCormick said this might be unavoidable because the school's academic success now was blocking many low-income and minority students. This was because more local residents, who get first priority, were opting to send their teenagers to public school. Overall, the school's Latino population dropped from more than 27 percent in 1994 to 21 percent in 2002. There were once 300 VEEP students, but that number was cut in half. No students were being taken from VEEP waiting lists because Coastal was admitting only those who were part of the program in middle school.

Previously, busing for integration, those students who attend the school from other neighborhoods as part of the gifted program, and intra-district transfers combined to give Coastal a more diverse ethnic mix:

CHAPTER 2: DEMOGRAPICS AND BACKGROUND 61

> What we are finding now is as the residential community comes back, the non-residential community doesn't have as many chairs to occupy. I don't know what is going to happen as soon as we finish off this new science building, this new aquatics center and we're done with the new athletics field. This campus visually and physically is going to be very attractive, so I don't know what that's going to mean for the community. They may say, 'Why should I pay $70,000 a year to go someplace else?' (Interview with Evan McCormick, August 3, 2001)

The school's High School Expansion Facilities Committee raised more than $5 million in private donations for an advanced Science and Technology Center, new classrooms, and an Aquatics Complex. The construction may have caused more parents to keep their children in public school. The resulting more limited use of VEEP, plus the placement of most Latino students in three-hour remedial English classes that left little room for electives, meant fewer and fewer underrepresented minorities could take journalism.

With only one Latina student in journalism class, most student journalists were what David Brooks described as "bobos" or bourgeois-bohemians in his book, *Bobos in Paradise* (2000). They were largely children who struggled to meet the high expectations of their parents, working hard in school and weighing themselves down with extra-curriculars in order to gain entrance to top universities. They sought to enter fields that would earn them good money while they also sympathized vaguely with those who were less well off or "lucky" than they. They strongly identified with their parents. Most held liberal values that would allow them to make a difference in the world. They were an eclectic bunch whose values mirrored the contradictions of those now in the nation's most powerful roles, an elite class not always comfortable with its wealth or bourgeois status. The journalism class of between 31 and 35 students also was a reminder that Jews are gaining acceptance from non-Jews. Jewish students comprised 25 percent of the class, and they became its leaders.

Rejecting the district superintendent's master plan for the schools, Coastal High fought to turn its academic gains into official autonomy from the district, achieving that designation as the school year closed in 2002. The faculty had at first threatened a vote to make Coastal an independent charter school, spending almost two years developing the plan. School officials and staff disagreed with the superintendent's plan, taking special exception to mandatory freshman physics classes (physics is usually taught after biology and chemistry) and the three-hour English periods for students who required remedial help, an approach called "Genre Studies."

"Teachers have complained that the long English courses required by the master plan have driven up class sizes in other classrooms," according to a story in the local daily (Magee, April 3, 2002). "The blueprint also imposes rules on how money can be spent at each campus." The district may have been focusing on its schools with higher percentages of homes where students had non-English speaking parents and were at greater risk of poor performance.

The teachers felt they were being disrespected by district staff, and 59 percent reported that they enjoyed teaching less this year, the report found. The problem with such top-down reform efforts is that real reform must have the support of those expected to implement it.

If Coastal had opted to become a charter school, the district would have lost a secondary school with a high performance record. By granting Coastal autonomy, as long as it kept up its academic standing, the district allowed the school to determine its own academic affairs while retaining it within the district. Mr. McCormick made it clear that he would keep the charter proposal "for a rainy day," the newspaper story said.

Coastal's faculty and staff supported autonomy because the centralized district plan for the schools applied uniformly to every school, even though each one had its own unique educational challenges and needs, Mr. McCormick said. Latino students were languishing in the three-hour literacy classes, he said. The English Department wanted to change that to two-hour literacy blocks. Mr. McCormick, mocking the superintendent's one-size-fits-all school plan, said it was too standardized:

> Where is the human response to the individual needs of the child? That's what underlay the concerns of this campus, and it's not that we want autonomy for us. We want autonomy for every school, and then I want every school to be held publicly accountable for what's going on. But at the same time, I want every school to have the capacity to make the changes in operations it needs to try and get things to where they need to be. . . . It's a matter of wanting to have the chance to tailor what's going on to the needs of the kids. (Interview with Evan McCormick, May 29, 2002).

Of course, there were skeptics and some opponents of Coastal's plan for autonomy. Despite the fact that the School Board's vote was unanimous in favor of the move, "at least one member warned that such special treatment for a school fortunate enough to serve a high-income, well-educated community could threaten to balkanize the district," wrote a journalist for a major education publication. In the story, the school board member called Coastal "the Cadillac school of the district in terms of socioeconomics."

"If the school district's academic [policy] is flawed enough that the jewel of the district wants to withdraw, maybe we should offer the same instructional autonomy to all schools," the School Board member said. In an issue of the local daily, he went so far as to call the special arrangement with Coastal an elitist policy directed at the powerful and wealthy. "Every kid in this district deserves what [Coastal] High gets," the School Board member said (April 10, 2002, B1). The superintendent responded to the School Board member's criticisms in the education magazine story story by saying, "This is a conflict that existed long before I arrived. [Coastal] has always been a flagship school without much of a fleet in its wake. From my point of view, this is a suitable resolution to a generation-long controversy."

After the story about the minority population shrinking at Coastal, students at other schools scoffed at Coastal's publicity as the district's top high school. One young man wrote to the local daily that he had chosen a competing urban high school for its educational quality and diversity. "It gave me a much broader social perspective than I feel I would have obtained at a school in a more affluent neighborhood," he wrote (January 13, 2001). A girl wrote that students at her school were dealing with real-life struggles. "The reason why we do not do as well as [Coastal] in test scores is because we have a lot more on our minds than school," she wrote. "Parents should realize that diversity shapes character and helps children integrate when they're out and on their own. Caucasians are not the only race around." A third writer in the issue suggests expanding Coastal, instead of shutting minorities out, "School integration has resulted in educational achievement and greater community satisfaction, contrary to the dreary outcomes its critics predicted. But the paradox at [Coastal High and possibly other schools as well, is that its very success may lead to its demise simply because of space limitations."

Coastal's student newspaper, *The Coastal Chronicle*, was a product of its high-performing environment, complete with all the debates and controversies. The journalism classroom was made up of advanced students, the majority of them female, but it often suffered from its reputation as "a gut." Coastal students won awards in local and state writing competitions and attended summer journalism camps while Homestead's teacher and students chose not to enter these contests or apply for the camps out of a sense of inadequacy, because they felt the school newspaper at Homestead was not at the level of other school papers. Students produced *The Coastal Chronicle* on a three-week schedule, 13 issues each academic year under the direction of an advisor who graded all the students with input from the editors, based on two different point systems. My research focused on the end of academic year 2000-2001 and the school year, 2001-2002. The journalism elective saw two advisors in that time, April Hill and Laura Thompson. Mrs. Hill held the advisor role eight years and was retiring at 66. Mrs. Thompson took over.

Students could stay in journalism class as long as three years, working their way up to 14 editorial posts, including copy editor, section editor, and editor in chief responsible for overall management and editorial-writing. During this study, students at Coastal were between age 15 and 18; 14-year-old freshmen could be part of the journalism program at the other schools, but not Coastal. The Coastal press run called for 1,800 copies, distributed free to more than 1,600 students and 100 faculty. The journalism class generated and divided story ideas, gathered information around the campus, wrote news, features and opinion pieces then designed, distributed and critiqued the newspaper. They planned for new editions even when they had just completed the previous ones. In a way similar to professional newspapers, student roles combined to make the newspaper's production seem cyclical. This was not to last by 2003.

Mrs. Hill ran the class in 2000-2001 with an iron fist. Mr. McCormick, who had been the advisor before her, said he "tricked" Mrs. Hill into taking the job. She took it reluctantly but grew to love the informal contact with students. She even allowed students to produce stories on a few controversial topics, such as gun violence, possible cancerous substances in the portable classrooms and the nighttime theft of AP tests. However, her students saw her as a routine censor of their work, too controlling and arbitrary. The next teacher I observed was Mrs. Thompson, who was in her mid-20s as she entered her third year at Coastal, having "volunteered" to teach journalism. Her decision could be traced to the fact that she was inspired by her own high school journalism advisor as a teenager. An African-American,[13] she was ambitious and intelligent. She also was less likely to forbid stories, particularly as she began the year (when she saw herself as "a renegade" who sought to help underdog students). She had taken journalism classes in college and taught journalism for a year as a beginning high school teacher in New Orleans where boys 20 and 21 would address her with "yes, ma'am" and " no, ma'am." The students there had great respect for adults and the newspaper did not print anything "that might make a teacher or the administration look bad," she recalled. Before coming to Coastal, Mrs. Thompson taught three years of middle school locally.

Her attitude about allowing her students "to stretch out" and "push the envelope" changed as the year progressed at Coastal High. This was mainly because she had underestimated the basic journalism instruction students would require, such as in recognizing news stories, finding angles, writing leads, and grasping the inverted pyramid. She also underestimated the amount of time being journalism advisor would take her and probably the abilities of the pre-selected editors-in-chief. The class had the popular *Journalism Today* textbook, but did not use it much, and a large portion of the transmission of knowledge was accomplished from student to student. As with Mrs. Hill, Mrs. Thompson's students attempted to write about some controversial topics, including a section on sex and substance abuse and an editorial that criticized the school superintendent. This demonstrated latitude. The students saw themselves as unnecessarily constrained by Mrs. Thompson, too. Yet many students would attest the class (maybe not them but other students) needed to be strictly controlled to avoid sensationalism.

Because Principal McCormick had served as journalism advisor, he said he sympathized with the demands of the job and the aims of *The Coastal Chronicle*. He remembered his own contributions to the Coastal newspaper, which at first only published four or five times a year. He expanded this to monthly and sometimes more frequently. He also boasted that he was able to add color to the pages. Despite the soft spot he had in his heart for student journalism, Mr. McCormick could act in ways that belied those intentions, probably because of the pressures of being principal that came from all quarters, especially parents. He saw California student press law as "indistinct," with gray areas, a view that helped him take a number of controversial steps as "publisher" of the paper. He would apply district guidelines that may or may not have been Constitutional. In one example, he said the student newspaper had to remain "scrupulously neutral" by supporting George W. Bush as well if they decided to endorse Al Gore. He also required that all student polls be submitted to him prior to their use. However, this reading of the law seemed overly narrow and relied on district guidelines that, according to the Student Press Law Center, might have referred not to the student newspaper but to in-house school publications. He was in a difficult position:

> I try to be careful not to pound the creativity out of them, but there are lines that can't be crossed, legal lines, libel lines, slander lines, those kinds of things, and issues that have to be dealt with in a different way because we are a public institution using public funds (Interview with Evan McCormick, August 3, 2001).

Before she left for an English teaching job at another school at the end of the 2001-2002 school year, Mrs. Thompson said she saw Mr. McCormick as inconsistent:

> In many ways, when he talks to the journalism class as individuals, he is very much for them being a journalist and doing the hard stories. He says, 'Yeah, you're a journalist. This is what you do.' Then he turns around and he'll censor things. But I think part of that comes from being an administrator. It's not an easy thing to be a principal because every day, you are making difficult decisions. And I think probably he was a journalism advisor. So I am sure at least part of him wants to say, 'yes, go, do, do, do.' But then you are also an administrator with pressures from parents, teachers and students too. So you make the best decision that you think at the time (Interview with Mrs. Thompson, May 31, 2002).

Students at Coastal were sophisticated and willing to fight for their rights, but they were often on the losing end of such battles because of their relatively powerless position.

In the September 14, 2001 issue – less than a week after the September 11 tragedy on the East Coast, – students chose to keep a centerfold planned earlier that was devoted to the fact that this was the 75th anniversary of the school newspaper. This was evidence that September 11 seemed distant from their lives of sun and surf. The sheltered environment that the school offered its students may have been a false front, but students were more inclined to protect than abandon it.

CHAPTER 2: DEMOGRAPICS AND BACKGROUND 67

The centerfold revealed that the first edition was published on Feb. 12, 1926. Its slogan dubbed it "the official organ" of Coastal High School. The centerfold reprinted a feature that discussed the disbursement of $20 to the swim team in 1933 and students' "pet peeves" in 1946, which included girls who peroxide their hair for boys and "boys who don't know how to dance" for girls. A 1957 column offered etiquette hints on what to do if you fall on the dance floor accidentally, take a good napkin from your best friend's party, or get caught chewing gum in class. There was an excerpt from an interview with Jim Morrison printed in 1967 and a reprint of a short story on a visit by President Richard Nixon.

Amid papers that betrayed nothing more than a genteel innocence was a 1987 issue that contained news of a major drug sting at the high school by a female undercover cop. This was proof that the students had spending money and were not spending it in the most judicious way. The police officer reported making 28 drug purchases from the students, with the purchases including marijuana, PCP, cocaine and methamphetamine. A timeline in the retrospective showed that the newspaper returned to cover less shocking news after that. Its list of milestones included a 1991 interview with supermodel Cindy Crawford. The year 2000 heralded the school's major construction project funded by parents to build the new swimming pool and science center. Steven, the boy who designed the centerfold, was disturbed at the scant attention the newspaper issue had paid to September 11, but it did not seem surprising in light of its past coverage. Steven also saw a darker underbelly developing at the high school, revealed in his attempt to conduct a controversial student poll on sex and drug use.

By the 2002-2003 school year, any semblance of class organization had disappeared, mostly because the class had seen a high turnover of advisors, some students said. There were problems with all aspects of journalistic performance and students felt that the papers were more difficult to produce because of the lack of useable material. At the same time, the journalism students managed to produce 13 issues, the same number as the previous year. Jamie, the features editor, was proud of the coverage in an issue that attacked the superintendent's reforms and budget cuts because it was within the students' press rights, he said. The issue named the man personally in headlines and asked why he wasn't listening to the school, as in "Can you hear us?"

"The law is on our side," Jamie said. "I am fed up with people not wanting to make a fuss." At the same time, even Jamie was concerned about the March 28, 2003 edition. "I was thinking it was out of line because it was so single-minded. I understand [the superintendent] has constraints due to the state budget and I don't think we can blame the whole issue on him... He was made a scapegoat in this issue."

C. Creekwood Canyon High School

Creekwood Canyon's district is about 15 miles from Coastal City, but it is close enough that the two schools sometimes view each other as rivals. Students and their families often know one another and share similar community activities and goals. Creekwood's record is the only one in the area that matches and exceeds the milestones achieved by Coastal. For example, Creekwood earned an API of 858 in 2002 (down from 872 in 2001), placing it among the upper echelon schools in California. If a higher-performing or less diverse school than Coastal was conceivable, then Creekwood was it. It was almost double Coastal's size, with an enrollment of almost 3,000 students. Of that number, nearly 80 percent of students were white and 13 percent Asian, with the remainder Latino, according to the county K-12 2002 achievement report.

Although state budget cuts threatened to change this in 2002-2003, the school had kept its English classes small, with an average size of 23. Special programs sought to personalize the learning environment, including the Peer Assistant Listeners (PALS) program, which provided academic and social support to freshmen, and a peer tutoring center that gave help in all subjects after school and two nights a week. "Although our culture is one of high expectations and student achievement, we work hard to ensure that no student is left behind," Principal Marla Hooper wrote in the School Accountability Report Card for 2000-2001. "Personalized instruction is enhanced by the two-hour block schedule, which provides plenty of time for students and teachers to interact in class."

The school sits on a major suburban thoroughfare, but it is nestled amid expensive homes and quiet, well-kept streets. The Creekwood Canyon area, from which students are drawn, has a median household income of more than $90,000 a year, and a median home value of almost $475,000.[14] The 2000 Census also reported that the Creekwood Canyon zip code contained more than 10,500 households. While a slight 15 percent of students at Coastal received free lunch, only 2 percent of Creekwood students qualified for such federal assistance. By Creekwood's estimate, 93 percent of its parents either attended or graduated from college. The 2000 Census listed the percentage that graduated from college or graduate school as almost 75 percent. On the Stanford 9 national achievement test, almost 80 percent of students scored above average (50th percentile or higher), almost 90 percent in language and math. The scores were well above county and state averages. More than three-fourths of juniors and seniors took the SAT, compared to just 42 percent countywide and 37 percent statewide. The average scores were 561 on the verbal portion and 601 on the math section. Nearly three-fourths met the requirements for University of California or California State University admission, and almost 80 percent of seniors took and passed AP classes. The school offered its students the use of nine computer labs and a library that was open two evenings a week. More than 100 classrooms were connected to the Internet, compared to an average of 40 countywide and 33 statewide. The school had seen rapid growth in the last five years, adding about 800 students, and in 2000, it completed a building to house English classes, including the journalism class, and two computer labs that served the newspaper and yearbook. The school offered a relatively safe location. In 2000-2001, fewer than 4 percent of students were involved in incidents that required suspension (not counting in-school suspensions), and expulsions were less than one half of one percent.

The school has managed to keep its educational standards high despite California's Proposition 13 that capped the state's property tax rates and made it more difficult for communities to issue bonds for schools. A public school foundation, launched in 1993, was successful raising private donations for Creekwood. Relying on the foundation, Creekwood's district is among the lowest in funding per student in the county and one of the last in the state, which already spends almost $1,000 less per pupil than the national average. District leaders have decided to target what state funds Creekwood receives for use in the classrooms, so that all money for extracurricular activities must come from private sources. However, this is not a problem for *The Creekwood Comet* because the newspaper generates 100 percent of its funding through advertising. The district supplies the classrooms, computers and salaries for the full-time newspaper advisor Alexa Phillips as well as the Beginning Journalism teacher Betsy Baker. No student at Creekwood, according to the foundation, is ever turned away from activities for lack of money because of the availability of scholarships. The foundation works for a 100 percent parent participation rate in donations to support the high school.

The *Creekwood Comet* is the brainchild of an advisor who taught at the high school for 27 years. Franny Eastwoood started small in 1974, overseeing a black-and-white newspaper that was only eight pages, produced on a Compugraphic typesetting machine. Today, The Comet publishes 24 to 28 pages and uses color. Students sell more than $2,000 in ads each issue. According to a local newspaper story published on her retirement at age 60 (December 21, 2001), Mrs. Eastwood had guided her students to win enough plaques and trophies to fill eight shelves in "the pub" or publication room, where students hold staff meetings. Mrs. Eastwood was a literature major at her Iowa college (she enjoys Mark Twain and Leo Tolstoy), but she learned journalism during weekend workshops sponsored by the Journalism Education Association. She picked up news story writing techniques and the latest journalistic tools and resources. She passed this knowledge on to her students. She also learned from her own students and from taking them to state and national conventions. Her most important insight, as stated to the local paper: Do not specialize and instead, allow students to take part in all aspects of newspaper production. "They could all write, sell ads and lay out the paper. It makes for a very cohesive team," Eastwood told the local daily. She also took care to keep the newspaper fun, often holding parties and providing opportunities for students to bond.

Her system was still going in 2003. The current advisor, Alexa Phillips, shadowed Mrs. Eastwood during the 2000-2001 school year, her last, in order to grow accustomed to it. In her late 20s, Mrs. Phillips had attended Columbia University and wrote for *The Columbia Spectator* before transferring to a warmer, University of California school. The California native also had experience interning at a local newspaper. She had initially applied for a job as a speech and debate teacher at Creekwood but then switched her interest when she found out the newspaper advisor position would be available. The school also was considering a math teacher because of his design background, but journalism is an English elective, so Mrs. Phillips and her newspaper experience won out. "The person who was retiring after 27 years, she built this," said Mrs. Phillips. "I'm just lucky to take it over."

The first issue Mrs. Phillips produced with students alone occurred after the September 11 tragedies in New York, Washington and Pennsylvania. Coverage was a challenge for the press everywhere, but Mrs. Phillips said she "had it easy" by having trained with a veteran, compared to the experience of others who may be just thrown into the advisor role.

The Creekwood program worked this way: Students could sign up for the Beginning Journalism elective as early as first semester freshman year. In order to write for *The Comet*, they had to earn an "A" in the introductory class and gain the teacher's recommendation for the advanced journalism class, which produced the newspaper. In Beginning

CHAPTER 2: DEMOGRAPICS AND BACKGROUND   71

Journalism, students first absorb lessons of journalistic ethics, professional behavior, and story formation and style. They then produce what is known as "the baby paper," each taking leadership roles similar to the ones on the actual student newspaper. In total, between the two classes, there could be as many as 70 students participating in journalism at any given time. In addition, there are always other students waiting to join the newspaper because spots only open up as seniors graduate. The structure of the journalism program at Creekwood means that those students who get on the newspaper are there Coastal had no such requirements. The open method of allowing students into the journalism classes at Coastal and Homestead was more democratic because it allowed students of different academic abilities to participate, but it also resulted in journalism students with only a passing interest in producing the newspaper. Mrs. Phillips used to teach beginning and advanced classes, then a second teacher was hired "because the administrative part of advising the newspaper is huge."

Mrs. Phillips must not only take students to out-of-state and in-state conventions but also field phone calls from the community on top of her teaching load of four other English classes for sophomores. Layout takes two days after school until 6 p.m., then one marathon day until midnight each month. Newspaper students are competitive and perfectionistic, but Mrs. Phillips said she is a perfectionist as well. "We have to remind each other to take breaks or be funny or have games, relax a little. At layout at least, I was always making sure the editor in chief [the previous year] was eating."

Carrie, the editor in chief for 2002-2003, said the structure of the journalism program "definitely weeds out some kids, but those who are passionate about it stay. . . It's not easy to juggle your schedule around to stay in journalism. If you care about GPA, it knocks your GPA down because it's a 4.0 class (some advanced classes are weighted and scored on a 4.5 scale)."

The Creekwood Comet is printed 10 times a year using 100 percent advertising revenues, but Mrs. Phillips said the school district often needs to be reminded that the newspaper is a business and not dependent on school funding:

> Just last week, I got an e-mail from the head of our Counseling Department that the assistant principal said that they could have an ad in the newspaper for free. I said, 'He did, did he?' I don't think he understands that it costs $2,500 just to put out the newspaper, for our

printing costs, and that's all made on our advertisements (Interview with Mrs. Phillips, December 23, 2002).

The newspaper program's inspiration is capitalism and unlike other educational endeavors, it has a profit-orientation, rather than solely a service-focused model. Students learn by doing, competing, and succeeding at awards ceremonies. However, they also absorb the journalistic norms and ethics adopted by many professional organizations so the main goals are not financial alone but also educational. Yet at this point in our conversation, Mrs. Phillips reconsidered her complaints about a misguided administration and said, "They are really supportive. They really, really are."

I then asked her whether the school administration ever asked to see the paper before it was printed? "No," she responded, "but then California doesn't live under Hazelwood." Our exchange continued:

> SEA: I know, but it seems like a number of schools don't know that.
> AP: I know. It's always remarkable. When I go to conventions, and I'm hearing other advisors say, 'My principal does prior review,' I say, 'You know that's illegal here, right?'
> SEA: I've interviewed principals who say, 'Look, I'm the publisher of this newspaper, and Hazelwood says that. If they think the Supreme Court agrees, they feel empowered.
> AP: Yeah, but Hazelwood doesn't apply in California because (laughs) well, you know all the laws.
> SEA: Do your students know about Hazelwood?
> AP: It's part of Beginning Journalism
> (Interview with Mrs. Phillips, December 23, 2002).

Mrs. Philips said the journalism program at Creekwood emphasizes student First Amendment rights and tries to get students to apply journalistic standards to everyday situations. Yet it's true the emphasis on rights can be tricky if students do not understand that such freedoms have limits, even in the best of circumstances. Difficulties arise when students write humor, she said. For instance, some students "think anytime you insult somebody, it's funny. . . Satire and sarcasm don't come across in the newspaper very well, and it hasn't been that well-received."

CHAPTER 2: DEMOGRAPICS AND BACKGROUND 73

As they learn, students regularly commit errors in professional judgment, some more egregious than others. One boy included information about a friend's grades, naming him, in a story that was based on an overheard conversation. He knew it was true but needed to get the information on the record, Mrs. Phillips said. Another girl tried to use the newspaper's photography account to develop her personal film. Most stories printed in *The Creeekwood Comet* are sophisticated and mature, exploring such issues as the RU486 abortion pill, a parent's death, intoxication at a Homecoming dance, and online dating. Every issue can contain more than 70 individual stories. Individual editors assign most of the stories, based on what they think readers must know and what they may be interested in. Intrigued by the similarities between this newspaper and those in the professional arena, I asked Mrs. Phillips, "You look at this newspaper as the same as a newspaper out in the community?" She answered with a laugh, "It's better than most of the local papers. They'll call us. Their reporters will comment, 'Wow.'"

Creekwood principal Marla. Hooper avoids cracking down on *The Comet*, in part because of its stellar reputation. She has told the students she values "the relationship of trust" she has with them, and she has been generous with compliments. The editor in chief said she is skeptical about the principal, however, even after the state school press association bestowed her with an award for her service as an outstanding journalism administrator. Carrie scoffed at that. The girl described herself as a conservative Republican, in a class that included other conservative student leaders. This was unusual in that journalists are either liberal or centrist, depending on the study, student journalists at both Coastal and Homestead described themselves as liberal, and both Mrs. Phillips and Mrs. Baker were on the liberal side along with Coastal's Mrs. Thompson.

Still, Carrie's conservatism did not win the principal any points, and the girl described Mrs. Hooper's relationship with the newspaper as an uneasy one. We continued at a table in the journalism classroom. I asked Carrie about a story describing the arrest of some classmates for egging a car, an incident that caused serious injury to the adult driver:

> SEA: If you give her any grief, or cause the parents to give her any grief –
> Carrie: That's the big thing. Pressure is put on her by the parents and if we evoke any negative emotions on the parents' part, their immediate reaction is to call [Mrs. Hooper] and in return, she tries to put pressure on us to minimize those parent calls.

74   CHAPTER 2: DEMOGRAPHICS AND BACKGROUND

> SEA: In that story on the egging, she told the kids, 'Don't run this,' and that must be hard for kids to face because that's the authority of the school --
> Carrie: For me, it's gotten easier with every confrontation (Interview with Carrie, March 31, 2003).

Interestingly, Carrie wanted to become a genetics engineer and considered her skills to be stronger in math and science than in English. There were many other students in the class, in fact, the vast majority, who were not planning to become writers for magazines or newspapers. Among Coastal students, interest in journalism as a career was higher at the start of my study than later, when it dimmed. At Homestead, very few students expressed a desire to become journalists.

When I told Carrie that most students at the other two schools in this study considered journalism to be a class, and their assignments for the newspaper to be homework, she hit on a profound point that seemed to go directly to the issue of the Creekwood students' high motivation:

> Carrie: That's where we differ. It would be interesting for you to go out and ask people whether journalism is a class or an extracurricular because in my mind, there is no question it's an extracurricular.
> SEA: Even though it's a class?
> Carrie: Even though it's a class.
> SEA: You have block schedule, two hours at a time.
> Carrie: It's during class time, but I think the level of commitment is beyond a class. And the fact that it's all student-leader based, that's more extracurricular.
> SEA: There's autonomy that you have here. You feel like you run this paper. It's yours. It's not the teacher's. But the teacher is still at the front of the class and she's still trying to tell you things. Is there a resistance to listening if you feel like this is an extracurricular and not a class?
> Carrie: Definitely not. Even in extracurriculars, you have the advisor. Even on layout nights, if it's a one-three-five day, like it will be tomorrow, we will come in here at noon. It's always a shock when the bell rings at 2:30. It's like, 'wow, we are still in school.' We have this huge area and it's not sitting at the desk constantly. You don't really think about it as a class. As far as the advisor, there's a respect that she's more experienced than we are and we look to her as an

experienced source of knowledge that's looking out for
us and looking out for what we produce.

There was definitely evidence of intrinsic motivation at the other schools, but it usually happened somewhat sporadically. The students' privileged upbringing, their parental income, education and support, helped to advance the college-preparatory aims of this setting, but this upbringing was an incomplete explanation for *The Creekwood Comet*. Students at Coastal High might say their classmates had nowhere near the interest in journalism as existed at Creekwood, but that still begged the question of how such an intense interest in news developed in the first place among some teenagers but not among others. How much of a factor was journalism instruction in this development?

As students talked and ate lunch, inspiration was in the air at Creekwood Canyon. Even the posters on the classroom walls were of slogans from Jack London, Eleanor Roosevelt, and Anna Quindlen. The statement from Eleanor Roosevelt on the back wall read: "No one can make you feel inferior without your consent." Professional-looking newspaper press passes with student photos hung on a side wall. Another slogan on the back wall read, "Work is a SLICE of your life. It's not the entire pizza. - Jacqueline Mitchard." A large classroom, a back meeting room with couches, and a computer lab all were devoted to the newspaper students, who moved fluidly from room to room, confident in the knowledge that all of this belonged to them.

D. Conclusion

In *Theory and Resistance in Education* (2001, xxii), Henry A. Giroux calls upon educators to take sides and extend their reach beyond the classroom by making teaching and learning the instruments of social change. Schools should "provide the conditions for students to learn a range of critical capacities in order to expand the possibilities of human agency and recover the space of the teacher as an oppositional intellectual rather than dutiful technician or de-skilled corporate drone." Thus liberated, teachers would not reject authority, as school officials might fear, but would engage it critically, wrote Giroux. The teachers would "develop pedagogical principles aimed at encouraging students to learn how to govern rather than be governed." Within this reality, teachers would help students take on "the role of active and critical citizens in shaping the most basic and fundamental institutional structures of a vibrant democracy." In fact, as an entry point to his book, Giroux chooses a quote from Bourdieu about the importance of the

critical intellectual. "There is no genuine democracy without genuine opposing critical powers," Bourdieu writes in *Acts of Resistance* (1998).
The teacher at Creekwood Canyon was much closer to achieving this imagined intellectual atmosphere where debate among students was fostered and their divergence of opinion from adults gained them respect, rather than disapproval. The students at Homestead were not expected to contribute to critical debate over how their own education was being handled. However, this was more because of the total atmosphere of the school, where learning was often sacrificed to testing and discipline, than it was because of any one particular classoom. Still, the effects of their learned helplessness were apparent, particularly in a classroom where the project was journalism because of all that was lost. Public writing often can lead to institutional change. However, even notably high-performing schools such as Coastal were adversely affected by teacher turnover, drastic school reform and budgetary cutbacks. Student understanding of journalism may have been sacrificed in this mix.

Giroux is reminiscent of Valenzuela when he argues that schools do not need a standardized curriculum and testing. "On the contrary, they need curricular justice -- forms of teaching that are inclusive, caring, respectful, economically equitable, and whose aim, in part, is to undermine those repressive modes of education that produce social hierarchies and legitimate inequality"(xxvi). At the same time, schools must provide students "with the knowledge and skills needed to become well-rounded critical actors and social agents." A radical pedagogy, Giroux writes, "honors students' diverse experiences by connecting what goes on in classrooms to their everyday lives." In addition, such teaching would "illustrate how knowledge, values, desire, and social relations are always implicated in relations of power and how such an understanding can be used pedagogically and politically by students to further expand and deepen the imperatives of economic and political democracy.'"

In that sense, student tussles with administrative authority at Coastal and Creekwood could become valuable lessons that their voices counted. Creekwood's struggle to connect its stories to student life was just the right approach to get young people engaged with the news. Giroux' theoretical perspective is rooted in that of Bourdieu and his ideas both of cultural capital, discussed earlier, and "habitus," class-based taste, knowledge and action that exists in "body schema and schemes of thought" of every person as each grows. In Bourdieu's view, the schools reproduce the dominant culture, serving elite interests and

CHAPTER 2: DEMOGRAPICS AND BACKGROUND   77

imposing docility and oppression. While they claim to be fair and even-handed they actually promote inequality in subtle ways (Giroux, 87-89).

In *The Schoolhome* (1992), Jane Roland Martin highlights the way school inequality is first constructed in students' homes. "It is a fact too seldom remembered that school and home are partners in the education of a nation's young. Like the housewife's labors that are at once counted on by her husband and discounted by him and his culture, home's continuing contributions to a child's development are both relied on by the school and society and refused public recognition" (6). Lareau examines how this inequality operates through the different ways working-class and middle-upper class parents interact with the school system. While other research has emphasized the importance of the family for providing students with background knowledge that shapes their school experiences, Lareau has looked at the different ways "mothers and fathers oversee the process of their child's schooling." Working-class parents seem to give their children greater autonomy in matters of their education, she writes. "As Pierre Bourdieu would suggest, the standards and criteria for sorting are always changing," Lareau writes (2000). "Elite members of the society, however, comply more quickly and completely to important shifts in standards than do less-privileged groups."

The fact is that students at both Coastal and Creekwood Canyon were being forced to contend with the dehumanizing effects of standardized tests, but it did not seem to eclipse more innovative ways of teaching and learning at those two schools. The upper-income students also appeared to have more reserve energies and cognitive resources to deal with the physically and emotionally draining impact of formal schooling and tests. The negative effects seemed more pronounced at Homestead because of students' more vulnerable state.

It is true that parent influences on schooling are unclear (Stigler 1991.198). There are studies that find children succeeding despite a home environment that does not emphasize achievement (Peak 1989) and those researchers who confirm that academically oriented homes produce children who succeed at school (Bempechat et al. 1989). At the same time, students may fail despite a home environment that encourages them (Ogbu 1989). James W. Stigler points to these conflicting studies and calls the body of research that correlates family to school success or failure "match" theory (Stigler 1991, 199-200). I believe that there is certainly no absolute formula that will guarantee student success, but it is foolhardy to ignore the impact of their upbringing on children's school performance, particularly in circumstances of either hardship or privilege. Privilege can make schooling easier. At the same time, there are cultural resources that Latino families supply their children that should not go unrecognized.

Parental income levels and expectations played a fundamental role in student achievement and motivation levels at the three school newspapers examined in this study, and as such, these elements greatly influenced the quality of the educational experience for students. Lareau points out that this family-school linkage is complicated in that students' parents contribute more than simple expectations and encouragement. They have a distinct way of dealing with school employees and may have the orientation of employers seeking a service. Other factors also contribute in significant ways to the success of journalistic projects, such as the stability of families, the students' English language and literacy skills, the role of authority figures in the journalism program, and each advisor's knowledge of journalism as a subject relevant to the teaching of democratic and professional principles. However, these other factors all have an economic element. Journalism could act, in many ways, as a litmus test for a school, revealing its strengths as well as its weaknesses. Perhaps one could say the same of a number of school activities, but none are so important as the production of the student newspaper because of the ultimate effect the process could have on students' decision-making skills, on their occupational identity formation, and on their later participation in and beliefs about democracy.

Homestead High School often was vexed by its students' poverty-stricken and transient family lives. There was a seemingly intractable disconnection between those young people who were failing their coursework and the official world of school authority figures and teachers. Students did not necessarily have a problem with the postponement of gratification. They were willing to attend school day after day in hopes of graduating.[15] although they did not often enjoy their academic work. Many held different values to those of the school system. Many did not want to go away to college, for instance, because it would mean leaving their families, At times, their families were more important than notions of higher education. Given this fact, not all the teenagers fit the stereotype of self-absorption. But there were those at Homestead who were very affected by the challenges being faced by their families, so much so that they could minimize their own goals for long stretches of time. Sometimes, they did not seem to see a need for making plans at all. On top of this were weak English skills, fear that certain ideas would be viewed negatively by authorities, and lessons

CHAPTER 2: DEMOGRAPICS AND BACKGROUND 79

from an instructor still learning the basics of journalism. With all that in mind, sometimes it was impressive the teacher and her students were able to produce a school newspaper at all.

The high income and test scores at Creekwood Canyon and the school's ability to raise money from parents made its setting entirely distinct from Homestead. Even the physical conditions at Creekwood were different than they were at Homestead. They were closer to the environmental conditions of a college campus than the institutional flavor of a secondary school. The 27-year advisor at Creekwood was able to create something lasting, using a two-part educational program that weeded out those students who might be lacking in seriousness.

The environment also was competitive, with students vying for admission to top colleges and parents pushing them to get ahead. Journalism, an endeavor that required a great deal of labor, was just the task for students looking to distinguish themselves. Of course, the parents also put their money were their hearts were, giving generously to create the kind of environment they wanted for their children. Distrust toward adult authority in this setting might be seen as a positive trait because these students were not ultimately silenced. The students also may have been adopting the adversarial relationship considered so important to the Fourth Estate's watchdog role on those in power.

Coastal students' upper-middle class upbringing and world views helped translate to high test scores and admission to college. However, journalistic excellence would have required greater training and an organizational structure that did not exist. The school's diversity was dwindling but it was still higher than that of Creekwood Canyon. Controversial top-down district educational reform measures led to the school's successful bid for academic autonomy in the 2001-2002 school year. Autonomy meant the school could make its own academic plans but it still had the same pool of dollars from the district with which to do so. Severe budgetary problems were making this more of a challenge, threatening to strip such extras as elective classes. As he was getting ready to graduate, Jamie could not help thinking that the quality of the students was declining. It was obvious to him as he looked at the freshman and sophomore classes and their ability to cope with academically stressful situations. When the staff at *The Coastal Chronicle* received Creekwood's newspaper each month, "We still cry softly in the back room," he said. "It would take a long time to build a program like that because first, you need an advisor to stay longer than a year."

Coastal and Creekwood Canyon students knew they were going on to greater things, whereas Homestead students did not share this confidence, for the most part. Students at Coastal were bound for the Ivy League and other top universities, as were students at Creekwood. At Homestead, fewer youth would go to college. By looking at young people who were more financially insecure and less powerful, alongside those with greater access to financial and social resources, At Creekwood, there was little apathy because the busy and competitive students did not have the time for it. They, too, had many advantages, but used them to investigate events in their school and beyond. At Homestead and to a lesser extent, Coastal, apathy appeared to be rampant. Student journalism should inspire youth and make them less cynical. At Homestead and Coastal, it did just the opposite.

Notes

[1] The student population Lareau studied was elementary school age at schools in the San Francisco Bay area of northern California.
[2] California Department of Education, December 2002.
[3] Public Policy Institute of California, February 2000.
[4] Rand California 2003.
[5] While the student perception was that Latino teachers were rare, they actually were more common at Homestead than elsewhere in the district and state, accounting for just more than 36 percent of faculty compared to the district's 27 percent and the state's mere 13.5 percent. Of course, significantly more teachers were Anglo than Hispanic at Homestead (California Department of Education, January 5, 2004).
[6] Creekwood Canyon's level of Latino faculty was below 8 percent.
[7] Placing limited English proficient students "in a regular program taught in English when they were unable to participate meaningfully . . . constituted discrimination on the basis of national origin in violation of Title VI of the Civil Rights Act," the court ruled.
[8] "Status and Trends in the Education of Hispanics" (April 2003).
[9] Cal. Educ. Code Sec. 48907, February 22, 1977.
[10] Cited in Mehan et. al, 1996, 11.
[11] City News Service, November 13, 2003. Regan, who became Superintendent in 1995, began as a teacher in the 82,000-student district.
[12] Mrs.Thompson was one of only three African-American teachers. There were four Latino faculty at Coastal.
[13] American Factfinder, U.S. Census, 2000.
[14] The attendance rate at Homestead was some 96 percent in 2002,

Why a News Class Resisted News

If there is one class where high school students should be attuned to news, it is the journalism elective. Surely, the sophistication of the upper-middle class staff that produced *The Coastal Chronicle* in 2001-2002 and their eagerness to meet adult expectations for their futures, would win them trust and editorial discretion. After all, Dvorak, Lain and Dickson in the book *Journalism Kids Do Better* (1994), documented the benefits of journalism instruction – improved performance by journalism students in their other writing and English classes and their increased involvement in civic life. Yet my research at Coastal High School in Southern California suggests that secondary school journalism classes often increase student alienation and disempowerment because adults draw upon limited journalism knowledge and inaccurate assumptions about adolescents to direct youth. The acts of school officials, teachers and occasionally parents, bred censorship and self-censorship at Coastal, augmenting students' sense of irrelevance. If journalism should expand knowledge and democratic principles, a school newspaper program also can backfire, multiplying cynicism in adulthood.

Shortsighted approaches to schooling undermine citizenship. In his book, *The Making of Citizens* (2000), education scholar David Buckingham contends that American and British teenagers are apathetic about politics and the media because adults emphasize they should not be concerned with serious issues until later. They do not vote, and he suggests that if they did, they would have more reason to care about political issues. It might seem more convenient to employ censorship with student journalists than allow for experimentation. As Buckingham argues, the adult world too often seeks to protect young people from complicated issues and judgments, instead of preparing them for the future in which they will require critical skills. Students often experience pessimistic media instruction about what journalists do wrong.

Thomas Hine (1999) writes that the meaning of the word teenager is "arbitrary and confusing" because it contains so much individual variation (15):

> Defining a person strictly in terms of age feels natural to contemporary Americans. Our society's commitment to equality seems to demand objective

> classifications. We don't trust people in authority to judge whether, for example this young person is mature enough to drive or to vote, while another one the same age is not. We recognize that such judgments might be correct, but also that they are subject to abuse.

He argues teens are different because they are less experienced and may need advice to reach adulthood safely. The teachers and principal at Coastal faced dissimilar young people and struggled to help but came off as more controlling than supportive.

Media theorist Henry Jenkins contends politicians on the Left and the Right use the teenager as a vehicle to stir adult fears about passing time and the disappearance of tradition. The adult world burdens youth with the mythology of childhood innocence and calls for this innocence to be protected against adult "corruption." As childhood is supposed to represent adult hopes for the future, it is grist for political speeches and raw emotionality. "The innocent child is caught somewhere over the rainbow – between nostalgia and utopian optimism, between the past and the future," Jenkins writes (1999: Introduction, 4-5).

> Children, no less than adults, are active participants in that process of defining their identities, although they join these Interactions from positions of unequal power. When children struggle to reclaim dignity in the face of a schoolyard taunt or confront inequities in their parents' incomes, they are engaged with politics just as surely as adults are when they fight back against homophobia or join a labor union.

Jenkins favors a more complex picture of youth that recognizes their cultural productivity and helps them critically analyze their position in the world (31).

In his book, *Tuned Out: Why Young People Don't Follow the News* (2004), media theorist David Mindich argues that an important reason youth reject news is their "perceived isolation from the political process" (17).

> Many of the young non-readers of news I have spoken with believe that the political process is both morally bankrupt and completely insulated from public pressure. Perhaps political news is only relevant to

people who still believe that the political structure is responsive.

Mindich extends the definition of young people to age 40 because the widespread decline in news consumption began in the 1960s with the parents of today's children. In doing so, he further blurs the already hazy line between youth and adulthood. A range of other thinkers go further to question the very concept of the teenager, saying it fails to grasp the fact that young people actively reject some media and not others.

Mindich, a former CNN assignment editor, examines why youth reject conventional politics. He finds fewer young people watched the debates between Al Gore and George W. Bush than *American Idol*. He points out that just 16.6 percent of 18-to-24 year-olds voted in the 1998 elections. Almost half of 18-24 year olds voted in 1972 (49.6 percent), a year after 18-year-olds won the right to vote, compared with 32.3 percent in the 2000 presidential election. While Mindich admits the media must change to attract youth and finds young people thoughtful and literate, he does not seem ready to accept their cultural forms, fearful they weaken the political process. Young people are more self-interested, more susceptible to advertisers' pandering (81-82):

> We saw it in the 1990s with the explosion of MTV and ESPN. We see it in the marketing of pop star Britney Spears for Pepsi and Tiger Woods for just about everything else. And we see it in the latest TV shows marketed for the 18-34 demographic: *Jackass, The Real World, Survivor,* and *Temptation Island.* The assumption is that what attracts young people has little to do with news and a lot to do with their own wants. Even Jackie Nixon, NPR's thoughtful director of audience research, had this to say about the 18-24 demographic: "When you're an 18 to 24 year old, you're not thinking a whole lot about who's going to be the next president of the United States. You're really trying to think about, Am I going to get married? Am I going to have a successful job? Am I going to be able to afford my apartment? How am I going to pay for my car? And, How cute is the chick or the guy at the end of the bar? And will they go home with me? Their head is in a different place.'

Mindich points to America's declining social capital, such as participation in unions, the Elks club and the PTA.

Similarly, in *Nonvoters* (1999), Jack Doppelt and Ellen Shearer contend that voting is no longer considered a civic duty among the nation's young. Because many parents do not participate in politics or talk to their children about them, both predictors of political participation, the children learn to be less interested (Fetto 1999). Yet there is little to be gained in employing this information to attack youth culture. An alternative, albeit somewhat self-serving approach is "Rock the Vote," a group formed by the recording industry to encourage political participation among the young. The group maintains that young people do not vote because of factors such as frequent residency changes, fewer tax concerns, and the sense politicians ignore them. The Web, where rockthevote.com built its community, serves as an alternative site for young people's political participation.

Media critic Jon Katz pokes fun at the arrogant attitude of adults who cling to traditional journalism even as youth reject it in growing numbers. Youth favor other forms of popular culture, embrace the Internet, and share a belief that the personal is political, he writes, adding (47):

> Journalism has presented this massive shift as an educational problem – look what's keeping the little blockheads from reading now – as well as a menace to society. But the giant communications companies spending billions to get into cable know better. . . . [Young people] take themselves far less seriously than journalism takes itself, define news more broadly than a J-school dean, and are attracted to satire and self-mockery, non-existent in journalism.

Despite Katz' irreverence, these trends are serious for educators and news people, lest they give up on democracy and accept dinosaur status. As much as Mindich seems nostalgic for a past when people allegedly cared about the news media, Katz is naïve if he believes *The Simpsons* or *South Park*, though clever and valuable, can replace reputable news programming and newspapers. Rock the Vote makes some good points about the logistical reasons fewer youth vote but this does not change the fact that Electoral politics for youth are not a priority. They have not been for a long time. In fact, many teenagers find that the biggest attraction of newspapers is the comics, and they do not follow news until late in high school, if at all, write media scholars Kevin G. Barnhurst and Ellen Wartella (1991). As newspaper readership dwindles, conservatives such as Alan Bloom (1987) and E.D. Hirsch (1987), say young people are ignorant of public life.

Barnhurst and Wartella contend that youth "are much more interested in horoscopes, advice columns, fashion features, media news and the like than public affairs. These preferences continue through the young adult years and do not necessarily disappear in adulthood." To understand declining interest in traditional news, they asked undergraduates to write essays about their newspaper experiences. Most subjects were white and upper-middle class, a group also a focus of this study. Youth saw newspapers as awkward to negotiate and aimed at adults. To newspapers, youth were "outsiders." A Simmons Market Research Bureau survey found that from 1967 to 1987, Americans who said they read a newspaper yesterday slipped from 76 to 65 percent with the largest drop, 20 percent, among 18- to 24-year-olds (Barnhurst and Wartella 195).

From Literature to Data

American young people likely never will read the newspaper on a large scale. In fact, to attract a younger crop of readers, partly in imitation of *USA Today*, newspapers began adopting flashier layout styles in the 1980s. A compelling aspect of the study by Barnhurst and Wartella was the way youth often felt guilty about their disinterest in newspapers, an emotion also perpetuated by the high-minded parents of Coastal City who told young people they should read the newspaper to stay informed, whether or not it appealed to them. Behind this advice was parental desire for their children's success and power. Regular newspaper readership has been linked to political participation, with Leo Bogart (1989) concluding that young people who read newspapers have a greater likelihood of voting. "Among youngsters, reading the newspaper goes with understanding and support of freedom of the press," he wrote. Yet newspaper firms find it is almost impossible to alter the way youth see newspapers – more as social objects important to daily ritual, rather than for obtaining discrete facts (Carey 1988). In that way, media education – the actual reading and analysis of stories in the classroom – is crucial to a better understanding of reporting practices and greater comfort with daily newspapers. Also essential is the experience of producing the school newspaper.

Without new ways of socializing the young, journalism cannot single-handedly reverse teen disengagement, a trend also discussed in *Bobos in Paradise* (2000). Of course, David Brooks is more optimistic about the future, contending that the new educated class will bring social peace to America because they have borrowed both from bohemian and bourgeois ideals, '60s rebellion and '80s yuppie enterprise, for a spirit of compromise. Yet if Coastal students also were disinterested in politics, Brooks shows that the educated class generally avoids public service. There is no leadership, he writes, adding, "This is a class of people who grew up with the word potential hanging around their necks and in many ways still, their potential is more striking than their accomplishment" (273).

Journalism at Coastal did little to improve decades of political inertia, but this may have been predictable. Many students were typical in their rejection of the news. Those who regularly produced the Coastal newspaper said they had trouble mustering up the energy to read it for routine critique sessions. While they clung to objectivity as a standard, many also disliked techniques of traditional journalism such as the style of ordering news stories. Censorship only increased their disaffection. Journalism at Coastal was a victim of the school's prestigious, high-performing record (based on an Academic Performance Index that was more than 30 points higher than the statewide goal for all schools in 2000). The API is a controversial 200-to-1000 point measure that charts student achievement on two standardized tests. The focus on high-stakes testing and measurements, grades and college admission, rendered the news of the day beside the point. Student journalists felt they could not cover the world outside school because they were not an integral part of it. The only time of importance was that of the future, but this mentality threatened to leave the students ill prepared for a responsible adulthood. The approach created expert test-takers and schooling sometimes in name only, the "banking education" education theorist Paulo Freire deplored in *Pedagogy of the Oppressed* (1970, 83). Teachers struggled to find a balance between assessment and real learning. Quality reporting and writing are harder skills to teach in a pressure-filled setting, unless one believes that they involve not a search for truth, but a frantic race for facts, then vomiting.

Both the school culture and teenage attitudes toward the news influenced the coverage of every event. There were times when personal prejudice or fear became primary or when each journalist's sense of fairness and balance was in jeopardy or when students' other school demands could not be negotiated easily. This chapter will discuss student handling of three news events. If they claimed to reject the mainstream media, what was their alternative? I examine student coverage of the theft of Advanced Placement tests from the main office, an event the students determined to be "real news," then review students' decision NOT to cover September 11 fully by arguing that it did not directly affect the school. I will then explore a survey about sex and drug use on campus that students wished to conduct because it showed their concern about their social lives, not public affairs. The various intrusions of adult authority changed the nature of the lessons students learned. Restrictions imposed by school officials during the dissemination of the sex survey caused students to censor themselves, taking fewer risks with subsequent coverage.

Because the newspaper was unappealing to other students, my research will describe student views of serving teens wary of news.

Because these journalism students were successful academically, engaged in school and mostly honors students, their attitudes toward the news presented a challenge to any journalism instructor teaching them to produce what many, including the teacher, otherwise discounted. It was revealing that the members of the high school who were supposed to be most devoted to news also were so resistant to it. They could not find much news that interested them, even during the dark moments of September 11, 2001. It may have had something to do with distance or the disbelief many professional reporters were confronting, an outgrowth of the trauma described by Barbie Zelizer and Stuart Allen in *Journalism After September 11* (2002). Professional journalists could not turn away from September 11, but students could, so many did. The youth showed they might fit the categories Buckingham used to divide them in his research (2000, 78-99):

- Cynical chic. This student believed in the corruption of politicians. Such qualities were obvious in my study in copy editor Martin (17) who rejected politics.
- Media critic. Such students claimed to have better critical skills than most. Editor in chief Mary Jo, (17), and reporters Sara (15), and Angel (16) fit this category.
- Disrespectful reader. This student played a subversive role, refused to be "the good citizen" or interview subject, and challenged authority at every turn. The student who fit this category most was co-editor Trevor (17), who at times made fun of the interview process and questioned whether teenagers were worth studying.

However, the realities of newspaper production proved these categories less than ade quate. Jamie (16), Miranda, and Gabe (both 17) all denounced sensationalism, yet they were at odds with Mary Jo (17) about how to deal with it. This made it more difficult to categorize them.

A. The AP Thefts: 'And It Turned Out to Be True, Rejecting Objectivity, News and Authority

Journalism's potential is often found during unexpected events. Stories are fluid, and newspapers must be prepared for change to reflect late-breaking developments. So as students adapt to stories, they react to setbacks and meet challenges during a creative process that involves deciding on story ideas as well as reporting and layout issues. Because nothing earth-shattering may happen every issue, student journalists may come to expect dull regularity. Despite the student talents and interests that could have led to more inventive features, many student journalists viewed news at Coastal High School as boring, overly serious, even mind-numbing to the audience. Students adopted a traditional view that news, like medicine, must be swallowed because it is good for you. They were not usually involved in long-term investigation that called for digging up controversial information. Yet breaking school news in May 2001 would upset any serenity. The story would be a teaching opportunity for the advisor who was on the verge of retirement. The cub editors had been freshly named and were planning their first edition in early May, a yearly tradition for underclassmen. Their plans for the front page and the editorial would have to be scrapped.

As fourth-period journalism began before lunch in the double-sized classroom, which held 40 desks, the editorial board, some members greener than others, appeared eager to proceed. The classroom door opened to the outside world not far from the school's grassy hump of a quad, and its frosted skylights showed hints of the bright sky. Gabe, the new opinions editor, was flirting with Miranda, named news editor with Jamie. Jamie and Miranda had beat out six other candidates for the role. By the end of junior year, both Miranda and Gabe had taken so many Advanced Placement classes, they already could have been in college. They assumed a jaded stance that indicated they had figured high school out long ago. The editors met in a narrow back computer room, 20 feet long and six feet wide, but no one could think of an editorial idea (Field notes, May 9, 2001). The outgoing editor in chief, Ron, would give them tangible inspiration. He arrived at school the next day to ask teacher April Hill, if she had heard the news?

"I said, 'heard what?' and he said 'about the AP exams being stolen.' And I said, 'Are you serious? Get out of here!' And it turned out to be true." Before journalism class had begun that day, Mrs. Hill reflected upon her lack of knowledge about this major school event, something she and most students in the class saw as newsworthy. She probably had been the last to know because "we are so busy in our own worlds," she told me. "Teachers get very insular. *My* room. *My* books. *My* students. And you focus in on that." Mrs. Hill was old-fashioned in her views of what students could do and must be prevented from trying. She had a reputation for being strict, and she sought to stop young people from sensationalizing their news, turning the newspaper into "their own personal soapbox," or being silly. If one asked the students if they or Mrs. Hill were in charge of the paper's content, they always said Mrs. Hill. Students wanted the newspaper to be their own. Mrs. Hill had waged ongoing disputes with Jamie's older brother, Danny, including one in which he described her as Mussolini for giving him a B.

The cheating had momentarily thrown the advisor, who decided to make sure Evan McCormick, the principal, was still coming to speak to the class this morning. He wished to explain to students why he had forbidden them from running a poll of the faculty on the AP thefts and the proper response to them. This was censorship, but the principal viewed his reasoning as valid because the three students involved in the incident had different levels of responsibility. One was expelled for the actual theft of five tests. The other two students only knew about the theft but did not tell authorities. Those students were suspended for five days. The culprit had hidden out in the main office after closing and snatched the AP tests, which were later recovered with seals broken. The exams had been locked up, but the student had gotten the key.

The principal would make an effort to treat students as news reporters and editors grappling with difficult decisions about privacy and fairness. Yet he was not an equal or even the instructor. His very appearance indicated students had taken an inappropriate step and that they faced strict limits. There was to be no poll. In addition, students who wanted to print the names of those involved found they could not.

Students showed obvious anger at the actors in the news story in a way that professional journalists are not supposed to (though as humans, they sometimes do). If objectivity was to be their goal – in fact a central aim of all newspaper journalism -- they were certainly not disinterested parties, ready to relay the unbiased news to a waiting public. Many knew the "guilty" students. Some sought to print the names as punishment of those who stole the tests. About a half-dozen upperclassmen in the journalism class, as many as 100 students at the school, had to take a new version of the multiple-choice section of the English exam. Danny thought this was "ludicrous" and threatened to print the guilty parties' names in big letters on the front page.

As the students waited in class for the arrival of the principal, they prepared to tell him why they thought a poll was important, why the guilty students' names should be published, and why it was their responsibility to report the *full* story as journalists. Before the principal arrived, Jamie objected to his interference in the student poll by saying, "It is our work!" Mrs. Hill (recounting a meeting she had with the principal) said he had valid reasons for banning the poll.

"Are they really valid?" Jamie asked skeptically, and Mrs. Hill was ready:

> Mrs. Hill: He is not against us writing a story. He's not against us writing an editorial and he feels that we definitely should write a very strong editorial condemning this. . . . The repercussions of this event are mind-boggling. But as far as the poll is concerned, he doesn't feel that's a legitimate thing to do at this stage. . . . he brought up the point that how can you say what to do -- I said 'expel' and he said, ' how can you say to expel when they weren't all equal in the participation of the incident. Do you temper justice with mercy, understanding the circumstances behind every single one?
> Ron: My understanding is they were all conspirators in the crime and legally. . .
> Mrs. Hill: The thing is that's rumor and that's your understanding and someone else's understanding is something different, and there are a number of different interpretations out.
> (Field notes, May 11, 2001)

Mrs. Hill's job was to clear the outrage from the classroom and transform these students into "objective" reporters. Perhaps she could only hope to limit the students' outward expressions of prejudice, if not the palpable presence of rage. This may be all that professional journalists do anyway, bury their sentiments inside:

> Ron: The student reaction is very negative.

CHAPTER 3: COASTAL HIGH SCHOOL   91

Mrs. Hill: I said that to him [the principal]. The kids are very upset and a lot of you are very angry, particularly the kids that are taking the AP exam that have worked so hard, to have any aspersions cast upon them, it's really difficult. But one of the things you have to understand in journalism is you cannot write from your anger and show that. That's not good journalism. That's emotionalism and showing your particular slant, and that's not good. What you have to do -- and I mean this -- you guys have to really think about this. You have to rise above this and try to approach it as objectively as possible. Yes, you're angry. I am upset, too. I happen to be very proud of Coastal High School. I think you guys are tremendous kids, most of the time. And I was telling my husband, I said 'I'm so angry to think that this could happen at our school, all those kids, thousands of kids, not just this year . . .' but that's not the way to approach it.

Ron (suspicious that school officials would not tell student reporters the full story): The only way to start is to find out exactly what happened. You have to tell us what happened, or we don't have a story.

Mrs. Hill: OK, well, when Mr. McCormick comes in here and talks to you, that's how you should approach him, to say as journalists, we feel this way, we feel that if you don't answer our questions, you are not being fair with us.

Another senior, Carol (who would be a freshman across the continent at Boston University in the fall): The thing is Mrs. Hill, that Mr. McCormick needs to tell us because we want to write as objectively as possible *exactly everything that happened.*

This effort to apply a civic frame to the news -- to portray journalism as a field providing balance and fairness as it holds a mirror to the world -- was a common way to discuss the production of the news pages at *The Coastal Chronicle*, even though some students could see that their paper was a construction, their own presentation of their school and its students to the rest of the student body. In that way, defenses of their own objectivity largely were disingenuous and reflected professional journalism's use of objectivity as a ritual defense, a contention of sociologist Gaye Tuchman. Jamie saw that despite students' attempts to be unemotional, objective and fair-minded, their fingerprints were indelibly on the news.

There is no such thing as total objectivity, but in high school, the value often is held with intensity by students and teachers Anything experimental on the news pages generally was considered to be against "the rules." These students' view of the world was heavily influenced by mainstream conventions about what news ought to be. The newly appointed news editors also believed in news conventions, so much so, that they only departed from them inadvertently. In particular, their approach to this story about the theft of the AP tests became very serious. They wanted to avoid charges they were being sensationalistic, acting prejudicially, or invading students' privacy, as such issues alarmed adults.

Objectivity is still an important goal of contemporary journalism. It is inextricably tied to morality because of the need to give many different perspectives a fair hearing within news stories. Yet Mindich's *Just the Facts* (1998) quotes journalists who compare it to the North Star, a point journalists say they strive for, knowing that they never can reach; he contends its actual definition is elusive to most of those who claim to practice it. Many journalists are abandoning the assertion of objectivity because they realize that it is an impossible standard.[1] Although Dan Rather defends his objectivity as reality and criticizes other news shows as entertainment-style, Mindich contends he would do better with "the honest admission that he actually does something:"

> What Rather actually does offer is not reality but mediation between out there and in here. . . What we really need Rather to do is explain his filters, to tell us how he interprets reality and why we should buy his interpretation. To do so would mean abandoning the myth of objectivity.

The ex-newsman's objectivity would be questioned again during the 2004 presidential race when he raised doubt about George W. Bush's National Guard service based on materials from a Bush opponent.

If professional journalists wrestle with objectivity, could teens ever become parties disinterested in their own education? Students in the journalism program learned the ideal of objectivity from the teacher, other students and involvement in pre-professional journalism activities, such as camps and conventions. The teacher and principal – as well as the perpetrators of the exam theft – gained a great deal from the teaching of objectivity because it encouraged balance and discouraged aggressive dissent. Just as they do in the outside world, professional news standards employed in high school tended to favor official sources, who made the news by meting out actions in the form of discipline. What they said counted more. The newspaper's problems of coverage could not be attributed to lack of objectivity because reporting takes effort that students may not be willing to expend.

"In matters of controversy, [reporters] attempt to balance sources with conflicting perspectives, if not within a single story then from one story to the next as coverage continues over time," confirms Leon V. Sigal in *Reporters and Officials: The Organization of Politics and Newsmaking* (1973: 15-16). "Keeping the reporter out of the news means relying on sources. Who reporters talk to thus tells a lot about news." However, school officials discouraged journalists from gathering a wide variety of campus opinion. Students succumbed to fears of upsetting adults.

Writing long before Mindich, Sigal defines objectivity as "a set of rhetorical devices and procedures used in composing a news story." Objectivity is no guarantee that a story is correct or unbiased:

> Objective reporting means avoiding as much as possible the overt intrusion of the reporter's personal values into a news story and minimizing explicit interpretation in writing up the story. Reporters do this by eschewing value-laden vocabulary and by writing in the third-person impersonal, not the first-person personal. Above all, they try to attribute the story, and especially any interpretation of what it means, to sources.

The ideal of objectivity also is important to doctors, lawyers and teachers. As it applies to journalists, the concept dates back to the 1920s and was deemed necessary because of disillusionment after World War I, Michael Schudson writes in *Discovering the News: The Ideal of Objectivity* (1978: 6):

> Journalists, like others, lost faith in verities a democratic market society had taken for granted. Their experience of propaganda during the war and public relations thereafter convinced them that the world they reported was one that interested parties had constructed for them to report.

Applying the standard of objectivity has meant that "a person's statements about the world could be trusted if they are submitted to established rules deemed legitimate by a professional community. Facts here are not aspects of the world but consensually validated statements about it." In all professions, objectivity – independence from public sentiment or personal prejudice – helps justify autonomy. It is a concept that critics use both to debunk and glorify journalism, Schudson contends.

In *Time Passages* (1990), George Lipsitz traces the standard of objectivity to the Enlightenment, which "compelled traditional historians to remove their own voice from the text to present evidence as if the facts 'spoke for themselves.' But instead of eliminating subjectivity, this method only disguised it" (28). There is no doubt that journalists have accepted all kinds of injustices and woven them into their work as socially assumed beliefs. The assumptions of professional communities are sometimes wrong and tainted by prejudice so that the objectivity standard is only as good or evil as the society that employs it. As a former reporter, I am hesitant to call for objectivity's abandonment without a sure alternative. Mindich presents an excellent critique of Rather's views, but reporters who do not try for balance assure they will fail to present a variety of views or worse, sentence readers or viewers to one vision, their own. Unlike critics of objectivity including Edward S. Herman and Noam Chomsky, authors of *Manufacturing Consent* (1988), Hendrik Overduin, chairman of the Department of Mass Communication at McNeese State University in Lake Charles, La, is one contemporary defender of the need for objectivity in journalism because without such a standard, "the cause of truth in journalism is doomed." He writes (2003):

> The mere fact that reporters have feelings about the events they cover does not entail that their accounts cannot be objective. The objectivity of their stories would be in jeopardy only if they allowed personal idiosyncrasies, partisan interests, parochialisms, or arbitrary preferences to influence or determine their news judgment.

For the purposes of this study, the more objective student journalists could learn to become, the more respect and independence they received from adults.

There was decidedly not an objective mood in the Coastal classroom. Before Mr. McCormick arrived, Mrs. Hill told the students they must refrain from printing the names of the guilty parties and could not even mention their class years or gender. Besides the standard of

objectivity, she also employed the issue of privacy, which was perhaps an even stronger argument. "No matter what, you know that these are children," she told them. The students were certain they were not children. Indeed, they were more persuaded by appeals to their journalistic integrity and fairness. The argument that the students were minors and thus, needed protection, was not well-received because the students felt they had a similar or higher level of sophistication as adults. Buckingham, Hine and other theorists are sympathetic with this perception as their work questions many of the taken-for-granted distinctions between teens and adults. Buckingham adds about politics,
"It is certainly debatable whether teenagers in general are any more ignorant than the majority of adults, and it is wrong for this to be used as a justification for their perpetual disenfranchisement as a social group" (2000, 219). "Everyone knows who they are anyway," said Jamie, to which Mrs. Hill responded, "Wrong comment, Jamie." When Mr. McCormick arrived, sitting at an empty desk, there was a hush, and all eyes were upon him.
As the students faced Mr. McCormick, he explained his wish to protect all students, both those victimized by the theft and those involved, saying:

> I objected to the poll that I saw come across my e-mail the other day because I felt that that was branding three students without any evidence of them being equally guilty. I don't know once you put that out there among everyone, how an individual would live it down. How do you explain to people that that's not really what took place when everybody has already made up their minds that, 'yeah, you're guilty.' It reminded me of a lynch mentality. We know something happened. Here's these three people. We heard that these are the guys that did it. Let's hang them. . . That crosses the line as journalism students . . . and as a former journalism advisor myself and a member of the newspaper staff myself in high school, you have to be careful that you don't do anything that would do irreparable damage to someone.

The students initially assumed an adversarial stance with the principal. They were supposed to be members of the Fourth Estate and in their view, they had information to report and a job to do. The principal seemed to be getting in the way. Some retained this stance throughout the exchange. By not allowing the students to make these decisions, the principal seemed not to trust them. Perhaps the students had given him reason for this by their arguments to print the perpetrators' names. What students tried to indicate to Mr. McCormick was that students are capable of writing a complex and nuanced story. However, by focusing on the names of the involved students, they may have obscured their point. It was unlikely that the principal would ever allow student journalists to name the guilty parties because even many professional newspapers keep identities of underage "criminals" secret, for all but the most violent offenses.

Some students continued to make their case for printing the names, but Mr. McCormick soon put them off by saying he would ask the district's legal staff, yet Mrs. Hill had been against printing the names from the beginning. Ron was starting to side with her, but he technically no longer had authority as a senior on his way to college. The students' position as members of the newspaper staff gave them the courage they needed to challenge the principal's authority face-to-face. They were not students going up against the powers that be, but student journalists. One senior who was the most set on printing the names also had gone up against the principal before, having written the story about cancerous substances in the bungalows, a story Mr. McCormick questioned during a meeting the two had in his office once the story ran. The role of a journalist gave her immunity to speak out.

Miranda, too, seemed to gain confidence and a giddy sense of power as she designed the front page of the May 18, 2001, issue. The headline read, "AP THEFT STUNS CHS." Mary Jo was the author of the story, which made sense since she had been appointed editor in chief-to-be and was supposed to take on difficult tasks. Her one-source story (only Mr. McCormick was quoted) began and ended on the front page. It was written in an informational style, announcing the actions Mr. McCormick had discussed with the newspaper staff. The lead read, "The theft of five Advanced Placement tests was the cause of substantial concern last week and as a result, two of the AP tests were postponed, the multiple-choice section of one test is being retaken, and one student faces expulsion." Despite the fact that the principal had only prohibited a poll of the faculty -- and did not tell students not to interview them -- there was not a single quote from a faculty member in the article. This was the last issue of the year, and Mary Jo decided no follow-up story was necessary next year. An article might have negatively affected other students involved still attending the school, she said (Interview with Mary Jo, May 5, 2002). "I was stunned to find out this would or could occur," Mr. McCormick said in her story *(The Coastal Chronicle*, May 18, 2001, Page One). "I was very disappointed but also almost immediately concerned for the innocent parties -- the students who studied hard to take these tests."

Though it was this principal's tactic to discuss issues with students so that they could learn from them, he made it very clear that he was in charge of the school newspaper as publisher. This was language that might as well been directly lifted from the Supreme Court's *Hazelwood* decision. Besides giving students the clear message that they must not publish particular items, school authority figures, including the advisor, also could give students explicit instructions that might lead them to act in particular ways. For example, Miranda wrote the editorial on the opinions page, planning to highlight the stress and anxiety of the AP tests, an element of the school pressure cooker that might cause a student to cheat. She was quite familiar with this anxiety as she was living it. Mrs. Hill had gotten herself so involved in the students' editorial that she had to restrain herself from dictating too much. In the back room, as cubs worked on layouts, Mrs. Hill pleaded to Miranda:

> Oh, please don't write an editorial that tries to understand why she did it. Don't do that because for crying out loud, stealing is stealing, whether you steal a dime or you steal $10,000. The basic concept is she took something that does not belong to her. She cast aspersions on the school. She cast doubt on your test. . . Let's say you scored really well. People can say, well, you know we're really not sure. It isn't just for you guys but the people after and the people before. The integrity of Coastal High School could be called into question, which is unfair for all the kids who studied, for all the kids who did what they had to do and put up with the stress, the incredible stress of taking the AP test.

She cautioned that she was not going to write this editorial, but asked Miranda to print her latest version so she could review it.

The advisor and news editor also had a minor dispute over Miranda's plans to take a photo of the locked cabinet that had held the AP tests. The news editor was desperate for art on Page One because it was very gray. The situation prompted Jamie to announce, "This issue is going to suck!" as he began layout of the Front Page (Field notes, Sunday, May 13, 2001).

"You don't want students to get any idea where things are stored," Mrs. Hill warned the students. "That's not necessary." She also directed Miranda not to say that all the students should be expelled, but Miranda called for the expulsion of all three anyway. Miranda wanted to use the word "scandal" in the front-page headline, instead of theft, but Mrs. Hill said the word only would be appropriate if the administration had done something wrong. Miranda used the word scandal in the editorial. Depending on one's point of view, the interventions by the advisor and principal could be seen as censorship. Yet the fact that Miranda was able to go against the advisor in her editorial proved she had latitude.

"The incident also requires us to examine the productivity of our school system's worship of high-stakes testing," she wrote in the unsigned editorial. "When a school's top students are driven to cheat, perhaps more than a flaw in moral character contributes to their decision. Nonetheless, the administration must take firm action to punish this crime, and the immediate expulsion of all three participants in the scandal is absolutely necessary."

After the cub edition came out, Mrs. Hill told me she worried she would get in trouble because Miranda referred to the perpetrator of the AP theft as "she" in the editorial. The principal had warned the newspaper not to reveal the girl's sex. The teacher was known as a my-way-or-the-highway disciplinarian, and much of the newspaper staff both loved and hated her. One problem was that she unabashedly described her decisions involving the newspaper as "censorship," rather than simple editing for journalistic reasons. The word "censorship" caused a great deal of resentment. The two cub news editors were not sure how to view Mr. McCormick. Jamie appreciated his background as a newspaper advisor and thought that underneath, he was "on the students' side" while Miranda called him untrustworthy and "slippery." Below is an exchange we had about the principal's role in another event a year later:

> Miranda: He's slimy. I'm saying he's slippery. He evades questions.
> SEA: OK.
> Miranda: Every time he comes in here, he says, 'You know, I was a journalism teacher, so I really understand where you guys are coming from.'
> SEA: And you don't believe that he does?
> Miranda: "I'm just saying that is what he talks about, instead of answering our questions."

(Field notes, May 15, 2002)

At high schools everywhere, students and teachers often work at cross-purposes. The newspaper can magnify "us" and "them" distinctions, creating bad feelings and situations where students seek information that they believe is improperly denied. The fact that Miranda had used gender in the editorial was a small matter and by no means an identification of any individual. Yet the girl's parents wrote a letter to the editor complaining that the story made their daughter appear guilty and should not have been covered, Jamie said, adding, "It was a really big story." Students learned the names "similar to the way that more than 50 percent of the American population knew that Kennedy was dead within an hour" (Field notes, May 8, 2002). Students who did not read the paper read the front-page story and editorial and remembered them. Other newspaper staff members said such stories -- the "negative" ones -- were an important part of journalism. The principal said if negative news stories might be in one edition, the next one would change the equation. While distrustful of adult authority, the students appreciated freedom because it was recognition of trust and their own worth.

The AP theft incident was controversial at a school where AP results were currency of intellectual prowess. The principal and advisor constrained the students from start to finish, imposing strict limits on every decision, reflecting their own concerns about legal liabilities and invasion of privacy. Students practiced their activism by speaking up. It was meant to be instruction, but the authorities' input was all about what students must not do, rather than what they should.

B. September 11, 2001: Facing and Forgetting the News, Searching for a Personal Stake

That morning, Ellen (16) awoke to her mother's screams. The shouts terrified her. As her mother watched on TV, one airliner and then another struck the World Trade Center, killing thousands. People jumped out of the towers to their deaths. "My mom was just flipping out and trying to call everyone. All the lines to New York were busy. And I was trying to call my friends. Everyone was just really panicky." It had not been long since her family relocated from suburban New York to southern California after a brief move to Atlanta, and the adjustment had not been easy. She found the people she met here at her latest high school to be "fake." Because she liked to write, she had enrolled in journalism for her junior year, and now felt she was watching news unfold. But what should she do about it? Others in the class were upset by the reports but few wanted to write about 9-11. Ellen's New York was burning more than 2,600 miles away

Jeff (16), the only member of the class planning a military career, heard the news on the radio during his car pool ride to school. When he got there, no class was the same as usual. Instead, the students watched TV. People were worried about their friends in New York. One student was "crying all day long because her father was on Manhattan Island." Other parents and relatives were stranded in a variety of locations nationally because airline travel had been suspended. Sitting beside each other at desks in the classroom, Ellen and Jeff looked back in disbelief on the paper's decision to leave coverage of Sept. 11 to the national press. There was a reaction story at the school to tell, they thought. The new editors wrote the first edition, but they were conflicted about what to do. At the time, Ellen and Jeff were mere staff writers, so new, they said, that they were scared to speak up. The newspaper's editors said they had been instructed that past summer at journalism camp that school newspapers should avoid writing about national and international issues, except perhaps for editorials.

This was because professional reporters had more resources and could do a much better job than any mere high school newspaper, or so many believed. But this controversial decision to avoid or downplay Sept. 11 references in stories, made ultimately by editors in chief Mary Jo and Trevor with some of the other editors, had the effect of alienating a significant number of the staff. The ideas they suggested related to Sept. 11 at brainstorming sessions for the October 5 issue and others, such on the reactions of students generally, Muslim students or students with military families, mostly got rejected as irrelevant to the campus, said Ellen and Jeff. Only stories with a specific angle that involved Coastal High School students or alumni were deemed acceptable. Students had to have been there. The paper's relative silence contributed to the staff writers' feelings that they were separate from what was going on in the world. It disempowered them and stamped out their impetus to report and write. This might not have been intended, but it still proved that teens are too often made to feel unimportant, no matter their capabilities. Ellen decided the editors were uncomfortable with what was happening. The easiest step was to downplay or ignore it.

It must be noted that this was not the reaction everywhere. In fact, Mindich writes that students' intense focus on TV news of the 9-11 attacks almost convinced him to change the thesis of his new book about how little young people care about the news (2004). He returned to his bleak diagnosis of their news consumption, however, when a student asked him who would take over if the president was killed by terrorists. A study by the Pew Research Center for the People and the Press (June 9, 2002) found that while there was a spike in attention to the news after September 11, the public's news habits ultimately returned to the levels of spring 2000. "A solid majority of the public (61 percent) continues to track international news only when major developments occur while far fewer (37 percent) are consistently engaged by international news coverage," according to Pew's report "Public's News Habits Little Changed by September 11).

While adults often presume that teenagers cannot cover major international events on the pages of their newspapers, sociologist R.W. Connell (1971) pointed out decades ago that they are fully capable of appreciating complex actions and motives. The notion of the political order, including hierarchy, conflict, elite-mass relationships and political parties is formed during an earlier stage of childhood:

> The construction goes on right through childhood and adolescence, and no doubt into adulthood, as more information comes in, but there is a period, around the ages of 10 or 11, when the work goes on most rapidly and its results show most vividly (38).

Older teens are more able to consider other viewpoints and their own biases, engaging in "ideological thinking (231). Connell found they could discuss complicated concepts using such terms as "democracy," "rights" and "communism," showing that their understanding of the world was well-developed.

Children's political beliefs, Connell contended, are rooted in the ideas of parents and peers, as older teens are less isolated than younger children. However, young people are selective and active as they construct their own identities. If some students feared a new war on terrorism, it may have been because they gained such insecurity from their parents and the overall social worlds in which they moved. "The idea of an external threat to the country thus becomes charged at an early age with personal emotion, with fears of violent intrusion into the "nice and safe places of the child's own life," writes Connell (102). "We will not be far out if we trace the affect-laden threat schemata of later childhood and adolescence to these roots." Although he studied young people's reactions to Vietnam, Connell's work has important implications for their responses to September 11. Life could go on without recognition of the attack because it was possible to move in California circles with scant connection to the tragedy. It is not surprising, then, that some young people had trouble identifying with a highly disturbing event of global import.

Such emotions also were probably behind avoidance of the news event. At the same time, the students admired the coverage of Creekwood Canyon's newspaper *The Comet*, at which students scrambled to employ traditional journalistic practices with success. It might be unfair to blame troubles in the class on September 11. Students also were getting accustomed to new advisor Laura Thompson, who gave the editors much more responsibility than the previous advisor. The students, used to Mrs. Hill, had to learn to work with Mrs. Thompson as well as with each other. Editors were expected to coach writers but often they complained bitterly about them or one another instead. The editors who took the patient approach ended up frustrated when writers did not seem to absorb what they were saying. The editors in chief, who had no experience with classroom discipline, often could not keep the class focused on the newspaper during story idea sessions or post-mortem discussions. September 11 at Coastal only made many teenagers' disaffection with news worse, but these circumstances did not seem to have much to do with censorship by adult authorities, only self-censorship.

As the first big news event they witnessed on TV that year, September 11 seemed unwieldy and far away. Commentary could be found in three opinions stories in the October 5 issue above an inquiring photographer feature about what students thought of portable classrooms. The headlines on Page Three called for more airport security, said that the senior benches showed patriotism, and blasted the media for sensationalism when they should be focusing on positive and patriotic stories. The top editors' decision to apply conventional rules for high school newspapers increased the young people's disconnection. To the extent students felt the newspaper was a meaningless school exercise or reporting a story amounted to homework, the practice of journalism suffered. The first stories on many topics proved to be unfocused with gaping holes. They had been tacked together moments before deadline. It was early in the year, and lack of inspiration hampered progress.

Although Jamie also shared his views with classmates, perhaps the one most affected by September 11 was Steven (17), the Student Focus editor. Student Focus was a section that was supposed to be about important issues in the lives of students. The top editors told him he could not organize a special section about September 11. During the early part of September, he argued relentlessly that the tragedy should be front-page news. Steven felt strongly that there had been time to remake the front page for the Sept. 14 issue to reflect Sept. 11, but when the newspaper was out, the coverage profoundly disappointed him. The top of the front page highlighted the way new students were being welcomed to campus. The right lead story, the spot for the top news, was about the school's plan to construct a new swimming pool and technology center. A story written by Miranda at the bottom of the page carried the headline, "Tragedy delays events. Blast off continues." The lead discussed the postponement of a pep rally and girl's volleyball game due to the tragedy on the East Coast. Next to that story, the students had added the first photo of senior benches that had been painted red, white and blue. "We don't want to give in to terrorist threats that disrupt our way of life," the principal was quoted as saying in the pep rally story. There was no attempt to interview students and faculty about the terrorist attack.

Steven shook his head, reflecting on these facts in the advisor's back office November 19, 2001:

> When the terrorist attack first happened, we covered it very irresponsibly. Everyone needed news about what was going on -- not about the football game. [Creekwood] high school's newspaper had a four-page package with a picture of bin Laden. [Coastal City's] people don't want to go beyond their little realm here. It's something I've learned in the last couple of years, especially on this paper. They don't want to branch out much.

Despite Jeff's observations, one girl (15), complained about some teachers, who also seemed to want to ignore the fact that September 11 was happening. She said a friend's mom had to drive back from St. Louis because all the airports were closed. Another person she knew had a friend aboard one of the planes that crashed into the World Trade Center. In journalism class Sept. 11, students received a lesson from their teacher about TV sensationalism because reporters had mistakenly exaggerated the number of hijacked planes and warned of a non-existent car bomb in front of a major airport. But some students said they were confused about whether there was a "correct" way to cover the news. The new entrants to the journalism class were learning basic news-reporting skills, mostly from the more experienced students. Lessons discouraging sensationalism echoed what authorities wanted in the school press.

Sara, who ultimately would take over for Miranda and Jamie as news editor, wrote the October 5 opinions piece entitled, "Media coverage insensitive." She argued that media outlets were concentrating too much on the negative aspects of September 11 and not the positive displays of patriotism that the attacks had engendered. She conflated TV with print media, painting all journalists with the same broad brush. She wrote:

> News has become a game of ratings as opposed to reporting informative stories. What is aired is a sensationalized half-hour of rubbish. Unnecessary horror stories are printed instead of meaningful news. Is it really necessary to film a helpless person, free-falling hundreds of feet from the World Trade Center and then show it on national television? All over the papers, newscasts and even the Internet are pictures of horror. These articles do not benefit the public. It is merely another way for broadcasts to compete for ratings.

Sara did not discuss how the media *should* have covered one of the most tragic events in American history during its initial hours and days. The news media did not invent these attacks. If tragic images were everywhere on September 11, that was because they were actually taking place. Her final lines called for "a higher level of news, beyond the commotion and uproar of today's media." Sara's attitude proved she had confused media criticism with cynicism. In Buckingham .(2000, 217):

> Cynicism is both more generalized and more distanced than criticism. It implies a wholesale rejection of the text as a text, hence one which does not need to engage with what it actually represents in any detail. At its crudest, it takes the form of popular clichés -- 'the news is all propaganda,' 'everything they tell you is lies' . .

In fact, Sara's commentary did not explore the issue of September 11, probably as an avoidance mechanism. Because the journalism class had a heavy emphasis on the media's flaws, with little discussion of its merits, it intensified student resistance to the news and journalism.

Buckingham argues "there may be limitations in any model of critical viewing that is based merely on a cynical rejection of the medium" (2000, 217).

The other story on the opinions page Oct. 5 was about the senior benches. Ellen was the author, criticizing students who had scrawled, "End xenophobia" on them. "The flag does not represent a fear of strangers in any way," she wrote. "If anything, it represents the melting pot our country truly is." Yet Ellen was dissatisfied with her own coverage Oct. 5 and felt the paper had soft-peddled the attacks, which resulted in the second greatest loss of life in American history after the Civil War Battle of Antietam. By the end of the school year, Ellen was named Student Focus editor and said she planned a retrospective, this time covering all the aspects the newspaper should have covered back then. "I think I would really like to write a first-person article about how September 11 affected people I knew because that might help connect CHS students to something that seems so far away from them," she said. When she could voice opinions openly, Ellen designed a centerfold on the World Trade Center tragedy, writing the major article, "A Student's Perspective: A Personal Account of the September 11 Tragedy." She wrote:

> I know that being on the opposite coast of the tragedy puts a barrier between Californians and the attack. For some, this barrier might provide a sense of security. For others, the distance creates denial or disbelief. This did happen. Real people did die and although it may not have hit close to home for Californians, September 11 still needs to be respected and remembered.
> (*The Coastal Chronicle*, September 20, 2002)

Ellen's retrospective -- which included the old New York skyline and two blackened columns to represent the twin towers, with her story in reverse type -- was starkly different from coverage directly after September 11. How did students see their role then?

Top editors told staff writers that their news story ideas largely had to focus on school events, groups and programs. The front page that issue included the results of a poll on terrorism (80 percent of students said their patriotism had increased since the attack on America, but only 45 percent said they would volunteer for the armed forces in the event of war). That was an interesting fact, yet there was no accompanying story. Polls often were used as a way to dodge difficult issues. They allowed students to avoid the work of reporting and writing while still claiming to have measured student opinion. The main article October 5 or "right lead," positioned on the top right-hand side of the front page, was about homecoming and school spirit while the bottom story focused on changes to University of California admissions standards. The top editors were deeply divided on September 11. Probably more than half the class thought they were doing exactly what they should be doing. The college process often overshadowed other news.

The atmosphere in the classroom September 13 was chaotic even as the two top editors tried to run the brainstorming session for October 5, based on five ideas from each student, some of whom had scribbled down their thoughts seconds before class had begun. For chunks of precious time, the room grew out of control and the noise volume was impossibly loud. One boy read a local newspaper with the Page One headline, "Nation in Anguish," and a girl munched Ruffles potato chips, sneaking them from below her desk. The editor-in-chief Trevor, who said he barely paid attention to the details of the AP thefts in the cub issue, also was having trouble focusing on the news while planning the second issue of the year, one that would involve the entire class. Trevor struggled to keep control as Mrs. Thompson insisted that keeping the class in line was not her job. His attempts to get students to pay attention were uninspiring.

"I know this is boring," he said, "but we have to do it." Later, he added, "Hey everyone, no talking means no talking! I'm really getting ticked off."

When story ideas were low, he said, "Guys we are way under ideas. So think of something. Can you think of anything?"

Trevor and Mary Jo showed they were unsophisticated with classroom, or even newsroom, control, at one point telling students that no stories would mean they would earn no credit. This was a veiled threat against student grades. Trevor's attitude was not representative of all editors or even the entire class, but some of the rowdiest parties that day were editors, which was a problem for morale (Field notes, September 13, 2001).

For the first Student Focus section, Steven included nothing about 9-11 but orchestrated a 75th anniversary retrospective of the student newspaper, decade by decade. Working on that section with his co-editor Courtney made him think about the weight of history, how embarrassing it might be 50, or even 10, years in the future when someone writing a similar historical piece searched the archives to learn what high school students of today were thinking about the biggest event that happened to their generation thus far. "The editors wrote an

CHAPTER 3: COASTAL HIGH SCHOOL

opinions article about how September 11 affected the football game. Come on! If that's all people go back and find, what does that say about this event? It says, yeah they knew about it, but they didn't want to address it." His second Student Focus section on fine-dining appeared in the October 5 issue. There was no criticism of any restaurant in the reviews so as not to cause problems. It was still difficult for him to hide his simmering dissatisfaction. The editors in chief "would have been very, very mad" if Steven had put together any Student Focus Section on 9-11, he said, "and they probably wouldn't have printed it." The situation did not change for the rest of the academic year. When students heard at summer journalism camp that they should avoid world news, Steven said, it was the right general approach. School newspapers should focus on school events. Yet in the case of September 11, the students had used this idea too rigidly, he said.

Mrs. Thompson said she would have allowed the editors to cover September 11 more thoroughly if they wanted. But at the time of the tragedy, the students were oversaturated with the constant press reports on the subject so that they had grown weary of hearing about it, she said, adding that Steven did not voice his opinion to the news editors as they prepared their September 14 edition, disputing his account.

"I told him he needed to take his position up with the editors. That's part of what being an editor is all about. He felt it was newsworthy, but he also did not want to go against what the newspaper was traditionally about" -- local and school issues, not national ones. (Field notes, September 26, 2001).

While Steven continued to express his point of view, at least after the fact, Courtney (16), Steven's co-editor, was much less ardent about the need for Sept. 11 coverage. She was planning on becoming a lawyer, although she thought it would be important to gain a familiarity with the news business through summer internships during college. "I'm sure we were all thinking this is the biggest news story we could ever publish," she said while class was winding to a close at the end of her senior year:

> But the entire news media of America and probably most of the world was covering this, and I don't think we needed to do it here. We showed our concern obviously, but I don't think we needed to -- I don't want to say waste the Student Focus pages on it -- but we didn't need to say what had already been said.
> (Field notes, May 22, 2002).

It would not have been possible to reconstruct the September 14 issue in time ("we didn't even have the facts straight by then"), and by the time the next edition came out, "of course, it's never going to be old news, but at that point, three weeks later, people were in the stage of moving on and reparations and not dwelling on the buildings and planes having crashed into them."

Mrs. Thompson tried to motivate students Oct. 10, 2003 by holding up the high school newspaper from across town, *The Creekwood Comet*. "I want this," she said. "We don't have this." The bell rang. "This newspaper is really good, the only one [there were a pile of other newspapers nearby] that is better than ours," she continued. "They get a lot of money. There are at least 40 ads, and it's full color. We had seven ads... We had to scrape together money for the blue box on the front (the paper otherwise used only red). That's a sad thing for just needing a blue box." The staff of 31 at the other school was around the same size. "Besides the flash of it, the articles are really good."

The "competing" paper was 24 pages to *The Coastal Chronicle's* 12. "I just get mad when I see other schools that are better than us," said Mrs. Thompson. One other difference was the fact that the other school had two journalism classes, and no one got to write until they were trained and recommended for the second class. The paper was dated September 27, meaning it was late but did not lack depth. Perhaps Coastal High could have done more serious work had the editors not rushed and involved the entire staff. The students also noticed that the other school had one editor per section, as opposed to two. One editor meant less diffusion of responsibility, but Mrs. Hill used to say that students benefited from sharing the load because they had heavy schedules. Journalism was not previously considered an advanced class, but it had become one, students said. Miranda's initial reaction was to call the other paper very professional but point out that it writes about national and international news, which *The Coastal Chronicle* did not. "I think we should be allowed to do that. It makes things a lot more interesting," she said.

The Creekwood paper's section on September 11 was four pages long. There was a big story interviewing relatives of students who had family in the World Trade Center. The pictures were borrowed from *The Associated Press*, with permission. The student reporters interviewed teachers about their memories of Pearl Harbor and put together an inquiring photographer feature on the perspectives of students who had grown up in foreign countries. There were alumni interviewed who were attending New York colleges. A student wrote a news analysis about

CHAPTER 3: COASTAL HIGH SCHOOL 109

religious fanaticism, another wrote about the history of the Middle Eastern conflict, and a third examined the definition of terrorism. There was a timeline of terrorist events along with a photo of Osama bin Laden and the headline, "When Terror Strikes Home." The other newspaper proved that the topic of September 11 was useful to teaching a wide array of academic subjects. Its coverage also showed the students read other press coverage.

Miranda's comment about *The Coastal Chronicle* not being able to cover world events aside, Mrs. Thompson said she did not mean to emphasize the other high school's coverage of September 11, just to point out that the Creekwood paper's staff had a work ethic, a dedication to the news that this staff lacked. Yet the news staff's lack of dedication was determined by what the other students permitted them to cover. The advisor also was not dedicated to the news. In contrast, *The Comet* found creative ways to link global turmoil to its own community. Her students covered what they needed to cover, reflected Mrs. Thompson (Interview May 31, 2002). They wrote a story about an alumnus killed in the World Trade Center, the cancellation of the pep rally, the painting of the senior benches, and problems with SAT tests getting lost in transit. They wrote a few opinions articles. They also covered a youth peace rally in late October. In other media, "it was everywhere, and rightfully so, but I think at some point, there comes over-saturation and not just over-saturation, but I think at times you tend to get callous to it when you see, you know, when on many news stations, everywhere on TV, you see the planes crashing into the buildings over and over again. It becomes too much, and we become desensitized to it."

The front-page article Jack (17) had written about a local peace rally in the Oct. 26 issue was significant because the decision to display it prominently answered the pro-war direction of the mainstream media. His story only obliquely mentioned September 11 but also reflected the students' desire for stability. The story asked that all attacks end, no matter who was behind them, and that discrimination against Muslims, Middle Easterners and immigrants stop. "An eye for an eye makes the world go blind" was the statement issued by the city youths who had organized the rally, which a few Coastal High students attended. One student was quoted as saying that the search for peace is "unpopular because it's true. It's unpopular because it's hidden." There was no attempt at a balanced presentation that would have analyzed the U.S. government or Bush administration's position or included any other views *(The Coastal Chronicle*, October 26, 2001). The front page had a very leftist bias on that day, one that might not have been far from

Jack's own orientation. His story also showed that he might not have seen the attacks on America in anything but a philosophical way. The coverage of the peace rally was a statement against retaliation.

Staff writer Deborah (16) also sought to express herself more in the student newspaper. Before she entered the class, she published a story about the Outward Bound program that was a personal reflection. It was available on an Internet web site dedicated to the environment. She thought the school newspaper would also print it, but was surprised when she had to make it less personal and much shorter. The version that ran on the features page with Jamie's alumnus story Oct. 5 was shorter and drier, devoid of its power. It ran next to the retirement announcement for a teacher. Deborah had grown cynical about what had happened. "Most of the things I do or am interested in outside of school, I really don't bring into here -- mostly because when I take something seriously, I take it to heart personally. When I write about it and they totally tear it apart, it crushes me." She was correct that these disappointments are a routine part of journalism. It led her to reject the profession. She said she was never thrilled about news as the class defined it. She wrote one story on a water pipe bursting and said it was the most "boring" thing she had ever written. "You didn't have to have any creative thoughts to put that together. If I was anyone, I wouldn't read it. I would have looked at the picture and said, 'Wow.'"

Paul (15), a quiet boy who planned to go out for football, sat near Deborah, and I asked, "What are your thoughts about this newspaper and whether it meets the kids' needs at school?"

> I have talked to many of my friends and they said that it wasn't that great. The newspaper needs to have better ideas that relate more to students and make it interesting for them. So when we do our seven ideas (increased from five), we should have an assignment where we actually have to ask students what they want to see in the paper.

Sitting beside Paul, Johnny (16) interpreted the decision to downplay Sept. 11 as a way to avoid bad news. With fewer restrictions on what types of stories were acceptable, he said:

> I'm sure we'd be able to write more catchy articles and stuff because no one wants to read about like, 'blah, blah, blah, this club is doing this' or 'tomorrow is hat day,' just like crap. In a way, bad news is good news,

CHAPTER 3: COASTAL HIGH SCHOOL 111

you know? We can't write about horrible stuff that's happened, and as much as people don't want to admit it, that's what they'll read. Like on the news, you see more plane crashes and car accidents than positive stuff. Why don't they show on the news every time someone has a baby or something? It doesn't happen. No one cares. They just care about bad stuff. (Field notes, April 5, 2002)

Far from addressing the newspaper's flaws, Mary Jo blamed reader apathy on laziness, also the reason many reporters preferred to do minimal work. "They look the subject up on the Internet, ask a couple of people, 'Can you give me a quote?' and turn it in." She planned to study broadcasting in college. In photography, she said, one has to keep a camera ready at all times, just in case. "It's the same with stories. You have to be constantly looking. They don't just fall into your lap. And I don't think students do that. Journalism, for them, starts at the beginning of fifth period and then it ends."

Jeff was already in flight training to be a pilot. Perhaps, I thought, his way of life was elsewhere. Maybe he, too, struggled to write about what he had no personal stake in. The students in Buckingham's study also were more interested in issues in which they had a personal stake. Students he interviewed struggled to connect "'political' dimensions of their everyday experiences with the official discourse of politics encountered through the media" (2000, 203). At a layout session, students bantered about their love for "ER," Dateline and MTV's "the Osbournes," about the way real-life had merged with entertainment so that sometimes the two were indistinguishable. Mary Jo said it was a sad commentary that many people could not believe their own eyes that planes had crashed into the World Trade Center on 9-11 because the sight looked like something out of a Hollywood movie.

I talked about the newspaper with Jamie and Miranda, how it might compete with real life for students so accustomed to visual technology. The students on The Coastal Chronicle had divided their sections quite rigidly, and there was little chance a story slated for features or Student Focus or sports could run on Page One. At professional papers, I told them, section editors sometimes compete for their reporters' work to go out front at daily news meetings. Courtney said she preferred to focus on those who read the newspaper, not try to attract or please the ones who did not. Just running a story on Page One was no guarantee anyone would read it, especially in high school. The newly appointed news editor for the 2002-2003 year, Sara, would eventually decide the readers did not matter. Student editors knew better. The argument rang familiar.

It is not unusual for a newspaper to claim it serves readers' best interests and never ask any reader what those interests are. Public journalism, the idea that readers can play a significant role in deciding what issues are important to the community, is becoming more common, but it is still hardly universal. In *Putting Reality Together* (1978) about the BBC News, sociologist Philip Schlesinger discusses the distance that exists between the news organization and its audience. He quotes a newsman who says that it is highly hypocritical for broadcasters to claim they consider the listeners as they construct stories. It also simply is inconsistent with news routines.

"The only thing you think about is what other journalists are going to think about it," a newsman says. "And anyway you write stories for the editor, not the audience." In fact, Schlesinger contends that journalists rely on their work setting for meaning and actually may devalue views held by the audience. People who contact journalists to discuss stories are viewed as "cranks." Most audience reaction is actually assumed to be from hysterical, sick or unstable people, he argues

"The broad picture available from production studies is one in which the mass communicator enjoys little 'feedback' from his audience, a feature of the work-situation which necessarily creates a heavy reliance on occupational knowledge and the cognitive support of the organization." Despite rhetoric to the contrary, journalists have a long history of prejudice and resistance to reader input.

Journalists' inability to connect with their audiences does not contribute readily to citizen involvement or pressroom advocacy. In fact, some student journalists questioned whether they had a readership to serve at all. After school in mid-April, I had this discussion with the copy editor Martin:

> SEA: I'm coming to the distinct understanding that you are saying there are a lot of people in this class who aren't interested in the news, in general.
> Martin: Yes.
> SEA: Why?
> Martin: It's a cultural thing. Even my siblings, they don't care about the news.
> SEA: It's teenagers' culture?

CHAPTER 3: COASTAL HIGH SCHOOL 113

> Martin: I'd say teenagers in general. It's just not pertinent to their daily lives, and they are more worried about what they are going to wear, things like that.
> SEA: Is it hard to operate a newspaper in that environment? Where people aren't reading the news, don't care about the news?
> Martin: It gives us more flexibility as to what to write. We don't have to give real news because they don't want real news.
> Trevor (breaking in): The average teenager today doesn't care about much, except for what's he having for dinner, how high the waves are today, and who's got the best-looking girlfriend, Students today are so amazingly immature. .

Yet Trevor exemplified the problems he identified. He said that he did not believe "in a lot of stuff. All the local news, I refuse to watch because it's sensationalism." In this way, he dismissed the news media, acting the part of cynical chic or the disrespectful viewer Buckingham describes in *The Making of Citizens*. He was cynical, as opposed to critical. Martin, too, was cynical, adding, "I don't care for politics. I don't care at all."

The same disinterest plagued student government because there were so few candidates for office that academic year. They had to be cajoled into running "Maybe it's just this school, or maybe it's just high schoolers in general, but they tend to be very much self-involved," said Mary Jo. " If it doesn't affect them, they don't care. People want things quicker and quicker. You look it up on the Internet or on TV and it's quick. No one reads anything anymore."

Courtney said that it was unlikely her involvement in the newspaper would make her a better citizen, though the newspaper forced her to become more aware, which was an essential first step. Directly outside the classroom on benches, across from the soda and snack machines, Angel (16) and I discussed her dissatisfaction with local and school news. The long gap between publications limits the relevance of the school newspaper -- and those who produce it, she said, adding:

> By the time we find out about it and we start writing a story, by the time the story comes out in the paper, it's old and it's not as interesting. It's just so much different to compare political and world news to high school. Because high school is just your little playground, and the world is so much more different.

> In high school, you don't really change lives. I mean, you don't really change government policies and stuff like that. In high school, that's not going to happen, so students think, 'Why worry about it?'

Angel was the sole Hispanic student in class. She was being bused to Coastal to get a good education.

She applied to be news editor and did not get the post, so she decided to drop the class, then changed her mind. She had no plans to enter journalism:

> Angel: [Journalism's] about getting what I want done accomplished so I can have a good grade.
> SEA: So you are just focusing on the grade in the class and not on the larger questions?
> Angel: I don't feel a sense of responsibility to this school at all.
> SEA: Do you feel like a journalist at all, like a student journalist?
> Angel: No, because I feel that high school is so minor that this is really not important.
> SEA: It's not important?
> Angel: Because high school is so small. It doesn't encompass other issues. It leaves out so many other issues that it's like basically worthless. The newspaper is so focused on this school, on school events, they are so insular. That's why I feel it's minor. It doesn't focus on anything else than what is happening in this school.
> (Field notes, April 29, 2002)

The idea that world events could be skimmed over in the newspaper or not mentioned at all was a factor in Angel's thinking. Why care about a newspaper that is going out of its way to limit coverage of what many in the adult world are talking -- and worrying-- about? When she looked back at the year, all the stories she had written, everything that had happened, she said she could remember none of it. The newspaper contributed to Angel's sense of futility and she stayed only to improve her college chances.

Rebecca, (16), one of the two new editors in chief, said making news for high-schoolers is a challenge:

> What they want to read, they don't really care about what's current. They just want to read funny stuff,

something humorous. And they don't want to take us seriously, so we kind of don't take ourselves seriously. I think our audience, our demographic, is what shapes our feelings of inferiority. Even when we do a decent issue, there's still the same response. And nobody wants to seem interested in the school anyway because that's just uncool. What they do is they just throw the paper aside and say, 'Oh, whatever. I don't care.' (Field notes, May 28, 2002)

Rebecca's use of the terminology "our demographic" showed she was comfortable with wording appropriate to the media business. She admired her mother, an ex-daily newspaper reporter and hoped to write for magazines. Her assessment may have let students on the newspaper staff off too easily. If they found a way to write more compelling news, perhaps the audience would respond. Despite Rebecca's philosophy and journalism students' own malaise, both news and the Front Page were treated with exaggerated reverence. Trevor called the newspaper's front page "the place for seriousness -- for serious facts pertaining to our high school that students should know." It was viewed as inadequate but holy. Students protected themselves when they put heavy restrictions on the Front Page -- if it was above reproach, then so were they.

C. Sex Survey: 'What is the Point of News?'
Persistence and 'Actual Meaning'

Steven took himself very seriously, working 40 hours a week as a manager at a bakery and restaurant. Dropping 9-11 as a personal crusade, he toiled on a student poll about alcohol, drugs and student sexual behavior. This was an endeavor that might irritate any administrator, but it also was necessary in Steven's view to document problems many students had in their personal lives.

At first, the poll was in the hands of two other staff members, including co-editor Mary Jo, and the newspaper's effort incited controversy. Below are the proposed questions:

1. Are you: Male   Female
2. What grade are you in? 9   10   11   12
3. Have you ever had sex?   Yes   No
4. Have you ever taken drugs?   Yes   No
5. How often do you drink alcohol?   Never   Sometimes   Often
6. Have you ever gotten drunk at a party?   Yes   No
7. Have you ever taken drugs at a party?   Yes   No

8. Have you ever attended a school function under the influence of drugs or alcohol? Yes   No
9. Have you ever had sex under the influence of drugs or alcohol? Yes   No

The day students returned from their first attempt to distribute the poll, Mrs. Thompson announced that there had been "an incident" that Mary Jo would like to speak with everyone about. "We had good intentions – to find out what effect drugs and alcohol are having at our school," Mary Jo told the class haltingly. "[The vice principal] got calls from teachers saying they did not want to distribute the poll, so she put out a notice saying, 'do not hand out to students.'" At this, there were audible gasps in the classroom at what appeared to be a violation of students' free speech rights. At this point, no one knew the School Board had a regulation on the distribution of surveys. Even if one interprets the rule to only be applicable to school staff, the students had wanted English teachers to distribute the poll in their classes. Perhaps this was their largest error. In class on this day, students could not see a legitimate reason for the action taken by the teachers and a school official. There was not a student in the classroom sympathetic to the administration's decision to withhold the survey:

> Mary Jo: My name is on the back of these polls. Now the teachers all must think I'm a freak! I thought I should apologize and say we only meant this to go out to juniors and seniors. So there went the poll.
> Gabe, (with a measure of disgust): You shouldn't apologize! Why do you care what the teachers think? Put *my* name on the polls!
> Students also worried about the administration changing the writing of the Student Focus section.
> Gabe: It's changing. Some of your articles will not be used. (This statement caused a stir, but Mary Jo explained that some of the articles were not placed because of space considerations and nothing else. Yet the students did not appear to believe her, making cynical comments, such as "Yeah, right"). There was a lot of talking.
> Mary Jo: Listen up! All we did was add some phone numbers and the names of drugs, so students would be more aware. This makes me happy. We are not censoring articles.
> (Field notes, October 17, 2001)

CHAPTER 3: COASTAL HIGH SCHOOL 117

Despite Mary Jo's assessment about censorship, Student Focus editor Steven was not pleased. *The Coastal Chronicle* added contact boxes to the pages to give students phone numbers to call if they need help with drug or alcohol problems. This change came at the suggestion of Mrs. Thompson. She said she thought the boxes were a small revision that might mollify the administration because they added a prevention aim to the section. This teacher interference could be called censorship, but newspapers where I have worked often considered it a "community-friendly act" to include boxes giving people self-help information and phone numbers of places to turn for assistance. "I think it's the right direction to take," Mrs. Thompson said. "I want to know what you think."

"The focus has gone from telling students what happens to preventing it," said Steven. "That's a big change."

There was enough change to prompt spontaneous debate about the nature of news:

Mary Jo: Can we write about whatever we want? No. You have to do what's tasteful.
Jamie: The administration has control. Can we hand it out after
school? There was laughter (although this alternative made sense legally).
Mary Jo: Personally, I think the fact that the administration did not want to admit that students at their school engage in this type of behavior is bad. We have sex, drugs and alcohol at our school. (Students asked whether they could use the classrooms of teachers who approved of the poll, or maybe each student in the class could ask 10 people to fill it out? But Mary Jo said she told the vice principal she would come to the administration with any poll, so these ideas were out.)
Mary Jo: What is the point of news? We are not just writing articles to say there are drugs on campus.
Some students object at once: Yes we are!
Gabe: I am saying we are an objective newspaper, not the school propaganda sheet. When Gabe started to speak again, Mary Jo told him to "shut up."
A girl expressed the general sentiment of the class: I'm mad. I wish I had stronger words to express it.
The advisor told me after class: I didn't see a problem with the poll, and I think the majority of teachers

didn't have a problem with it. There were three teachers that did. Sex was their main objection. I don't think [the vice principal] has even seen the poll. It is not graphic. We have a meeting with her tomorrow.
(Field notes, October 17, 2001)

There would never be a meeting with the vice principal. Instead, Mr. McCormick and the vice principal Mrs. Thomas showed up in class the next day to discuss the poll with all students, something the principal said he enjoys doing because of the debate that results. The problem was the intimidation factor. It also reduced the negotiation power of the individual editors. Because Coastal was a publicly funded high school, the principal told me he needed to make sure it was not imposing any particular view on a captive audience and also that it was "not going into certain areas that the Legislature has deemed inappropriate, including sexual behavior." The school district's guidelines indicated that the student newspaper's poll could only be circulated with parental permission, which is what the principal told students. Mr. McCormick blamed himself for not telling Mrs. Thompson about the rule in the educational code after Mrs. Hill, retired. "I like to not only tell the teacher but I like to go down and discuss it with the students why things are happening. I think we owe students that in the educational process."

The school district interpreted the state educational code 49074, 5 15 13 to mean:

> No test, questionnaire, survey or examination containing any questions about the pupil's personal beliefs or practices in sex, family life, morality and religion or any questions about his parents' or guardians' beliefs and practices in sex, family life, morality and religion, shall be administered to any pupil in kindergarten or grade 1 through grade 12, inclusive, unless the parent or guardian of the pupil is notified in writing that such test, questionnaire, survey or examination is to be administered and the parent or guardian of the pupil gives written permission for the pupil to take such test, questionnaire, survey or examination. (Administrative procedure 4934)

Despite these words, Steven was determined to press on. Mr. McCormick said he left the classroom expecting the poll to be dropped. Steven decided to figure out a way to send permission slips home. He wanted to satisfy Mr. McCormick's other perennial complaint about student polls, that results were inaccurate and unscientific.

Even before Mr. McCormick came to the classroom, students were prepared to discuss with him how the poll might be conducted. This showed some restraint on the principal's part because he did not stop the students from continuing their poll as long as they adhered to the district policy. According to the Student Press Law Center's executive director Goodman, the principal might have been within his rights to stop the poll, as long as students used teachers to distribute it, but the principal said:

> What I appreciated on the students' part was they had done a little bit of their own legwork. They got the procedure out, read it closely, and they had come up with alternatives. And I'm always willing to listen to that. (McCormick interview, November 26, 2001)

The obstacles Mr. McCormick put in Steven's path would have given anyone else pause, but Steven continued to approach Mr. McCormick daily and finally, he was able to get a letter to parents about the poll approved by him and by the school district. Steven also received help from a statistics teacher to run a computer program that selected at random a group of 430 from the student body. All parents would not receive letters. Steven said:

> We numbered all the students from 1 to 1,600 and we took 430 of those students out (using the statistics teacher's random equation). We made a separate list, then we had to go and look up their first period classes to distribute these permission slips. It's a two-sided slip. On one side, it asks the student if they will participate in it, and what it will be about, and on the other side is a parent permission slip. Also it says when they are going to take the poll. The poll is going to be controlled. So they are going to come through the door at lunch, hopefully from Monday to Friday next week, and take the poll.

Steven's dogged persistence was admirable. The seriousness of the poll was doubtful at first because Steven originally had entitled his project, "[Coastal City's] Wild Side, but ultimately the poll was handled with greater maturity than that name suggested. Why had this poll had become something of a mission for him? "Because there is no relevance to writing about sex and drugs if you can't prove that they are issues at the school," he said. "There are questions that if they are answered honestly, I know from personal experience and my associates, that we will find there are a lot of moral issues going on. I could name 100 people who have gotten drunk at a school dance."

Mrs. Thompson said she did not want to be a censor, but she became much more strict as the year progressed. At this early stage, there was still the optimism she had harbored before she began the class. She wanted students to experience as much as they could and to learn to cope with whatever reaction their work generated. "They really want to do this," she told me Oct. 24 and laughed. "I think Mr. McCormick, for sure, is surprised that they are still doing it because he told them a lot of things that they would have to do" (Interview, Mrs. Thompson, October 24, 2001). I was present when Steven returned to tell her his permission slip had been approved and now he needed her help to make 430 copies. The advisor and student smiled at each other. "I don't know how it got done, but it did," Steven said. He also said, "Mr. McCormick kind of doesn't want us to do it, but he respects the reason behind it. We are not going to publish a paper of smut that says, 'Eighty percent of CHS students are having sex. Oh my God!' The pages are going to be very controversial pages, yes, but we are hoping to print the facts."

Despite his successes, Steven underestimated the number of parents unwilling to sign the permission slip and the controversy the poll would cause. The side of the permission slip directed at students included a copy of the poll so parents could review the questions, but this turned out to be confusing to parents and students, who thought participants had to fill out the copy being sent home. Some parents read their children's responses, then signed the permission slip. The letter to parents read:

> Dear Parent/Guardian:
> As the primary student publication of Coastal High School, *The Coastal Chronicle* has made a consistent effort to cover topics that affect the school community. Our staff has become increasingly aware of prevalent issues that concern the welfare of the student body. In response to these issues, which include but are not limited to alcohol abuse, drug abuse, all and any form of addiction, sexual behavior and other illegal activities that take place, we as a staff seek to publish newsworthy articles to bring about

awareness of the fact that these problems exist. Along with this, we will be publishing resource information for those who need help. In order to do this accurately and professionally, and to give factual substance to information we obtain, it is necessary that we include interviews and polls of students. We request permission to have your student participate in this poll, simply to gain enough information to produce a representative sample of all CHS students. We ensure that polls will be conducted in an organized and scientific fashion, using a random sampling of students. Student privacy and safety are of great concern; as such all polls will be anonymous. Thank you in advance for your cooperation.
(*The Coastal Chronicle* staff, October 24, 2001)

In order to conduct this poll, Steven had to delay the Student Focus section, which was already finished and about to be printed, and quickly enlist staff writers to put together a section on Halloween. The Student Focus section on alcohol and drug abuse would run in the next edition, theoretically giving students time to get the permission slips back and conduct the poll. "The [Halloween] articles are poorly written, and they don't have much relevance to anything," he said. A good part of the class wanted to run their drug and alcohol stories without a poll, but not Steven. Even Courtney, Steven's co-editor, was ready to ditch the poll. " She was in the back making some changes. I got in front of the class and I read the ed code. And I told the class there has to be a change.

"Has this all been worth it?" I asked Steven.

"I wanted the pages to have actual meaning," he explained.

The next section, in which the articles on drug and alcohol abuse would run, was planned for 16 pages on Nov. 24, a major feat for the students which they planned to continue for the rest of the year, so they were hoping the newspaper's content would be special. Scheduling had improved substantially for students, and it seemed they were using their layout time more efficiently, which may have been the reason Mrs. Thompson allowed the expansion. Mary Jo believed students had learned from this experience that news cannot be printed without good reason. "We have the paper not just to print stuff and get it out to the students. Our stories have to have some sort of purpose:"

"A positive purpose?" I asked her.

> "Yes," she answered. "Some things can be neutral, but I think the purpose of news should be positive or have a positive purpose, like give some perspective. We have an editorial this issue about how parents and faculty can be naive about what their children are doing. So it wasn't just our purpose to say there are drinks at our school. I thought that was taking the wrong direction."
> "I don't really have that much of a problem with it anymore because they [school officials] really weren't controlling what we could print in the paper," agreed Gabe. "They were just controlling how we could distribute the poll. That was kind of their right. We could have written anything, I guess."
> The lesson was about professionalism, added Jamie. "I think Mr. McCormick is a really good principal because he's not censoring us. He is not saying you absolutely cannot do this."
> (Field notes, October 24, 2001)

It was true that Mr. McCormick was not necessarily censoring the students this time, but he was making their jobs almost impossible – even if he did it with a smile. Still, at this juncture, it looked like the labor put in by Steven and the rest of the class might pay off, though Courtney was starting to worry. She said that the newspaper should have sent out more polls because she guessed more than 30 people were not going to return them. Steven's prediction had not been realistic. What had essentially been one young man's Holy Grail ended when he got pneumonia. He was absent from class when only 150 surveys were returned, not enough for representativeness. Before the surveys came back Oct. 29, Steven, like Courtney, had been worried about the confused student reactions to the permission slips. "I'll be happy when this is over," he told me, exhausted.

After class, a few editors gathered for an impromptu discussion on the poll and how they could best explain the newspaper's goals when teachers would question them. Miranda was worried that the newspaper was not addressing the underlying problems for social ills, such as poor communication between parents and teens:

> Miranda: I think the question is not just how many people are doing it [using drugs or alcohol, having premature sex] but why are they doing it? Or why are so many people doing it? I think the answer has to do with a lot of factors... because my parents don't love me, they don't pay attention to me, or I don't feel good about the way I look, but if you are not asking why, it's kind of superficial.

CHAPTER 3: COASTAL HIGH SCHOOL

> Gabe, a press rights advocate, said he believed the newspaper was being questioned simply because the issues involved are controversial. But other students told him that they need to be able to explain why they are conducting their poll.
> Mary Jo: Is it just because we can?
> Gabe: No. We are doing it because we are a newspaper, and a newspaper needs to report facts, and we are writing about the subject.
> Then he went on to question other stories and why they were in the paper, especially because they didn't interest him.
> Mrs. Thompson: I think you will have a backlash, and I don't see a problem with having a backlash, but you need to have something to say when people question why are you doing this.
> (Field notes, October 29, 2001)

The poll was dead. Parental discontent was obvious from comments recipients wrote on polls and sent to an English class. While there were positive comments, most were negative. The reactions appeared on the back page of the Nov. 24 issue with a note:

> Last month, *The Coastal Chronicle* attempted to poll a randomly selected portion of the student body about sex, and drug and alcohol abuse. Regretfully, we did not receive enough responses to publish statistically accurate results – we therefore chose not to print the information gathered. Some parents responded to *The Coastal Chronicle* in regards to the poll. To depict their views, we are printing comments from parents with their consent:
>
> A student newspaper cannot conduct a scientific poll. Students don't take these seriously and tend to exaggerate or outright fib. Publishing this false information serves no purpose other than to illustrate how little truth this kind of poll provides.
>
> I think it is necessary to keep students informed how bad drug use is. I'm for it.
>
> Aside from the simple bias, there is a question of language. Are the questions biased or ambiguous? Is the meaning clear and generally shared by

respondents? For example, will the students be Clintonesque and define sex as involving only coitus or copulation? Or do hand jobs (from either sex) get included, not to mention oral sex? This is such a difficult area that unless some common definition is used, you can't really know what to make of a response indicating yes or no to the question of whether a respondent had sex.

This kind of survey is not appropriate for high school kids. I am very concerned to have the administration sanction this kind of work.

I think these questions are inappropriate! I do not believe kids will answer them honestly, which will result in inconclusive findings. I certainly do not want to know the results and worry that kids that are not doing these things may feel encouraged to because they are in the minority.

I have read *The Coastal Chronicle* many times, and this is not the place for a serious discussion of anything. (Coming attractions/movies/ bands might be the exception). I applaud their interest in student welfare but NO, I do not wish for my student to participate.
(The Coastal Chronicle, November 21, 2001, 16)

The attempt to conduct this poll not only showed students the difficulty of such an enterprise, it gave them a window into parents' attitudes. If the students, namely Steven, were so persistent with this poll, I asked Mr. McCormick, couldn't they just have sent more random parental permission slips out? Eventually, they might have gotten the 400 students they needed. But Mr. McCormick questioned whether the poll's sample would be representative at that point because so many initially had refused to participate. At the same time, he claimed to be "thinking of the Woodwards and Bernsteins of the world:"

We would never have had the Watergate expose if they had been faint of heart and not determined in their own minds that they needed to keep at it when it looked like it was a losing cause. So I'd be the last person to tell a student after you skin your knees a couple of times, you ought to get off the path and go somewhere else

CHAPTER 3: COASTAL HIGH SCHOOL 125

but at some point in time, I would have urged, well I would have suggested, 'you're putting a lot of hours into this and not too many people seem interested. Are you sure you want to do it?'
(Interview, Mr. McCormick, November 26, 2001)

The students learned from their survey, yet there was no intellectual awakening in the journalism classroom. Many students still appeared to be milling around aimlessly.

Despite this, Mrs. Thompson ranked the wrangling over the poll as one of the best lessons learned in journalism – it taught students patience and persistence as well as planning, ethical conduct, and deft negotiation skills. Granted, the poll never materialized, but the process is more important to an educator than the product, she said. Her actions belied these sentiments to some extent. Behavior problems in the class and a lack of responsibility among some students, including editors, caused her to change her teaching style from one who supported press freedom in high school to a realist ready to restrict student journalists. Disputes arose between Mrs. Thompson and the editorial board. Some students wanted to stay with the methods Mrs. Hill had used to run the class, which caused a meeting with vice principal Thomas.

By the time students began a new quarter January 27, Mrs. Thompson – uncomfortable with chaos in the classroom – sought to strengthen her own, and the school's, control over the class. Discussion by students had already taken place about what they thought a "Class Constitution" should entail. Mrs. Thompson's syllabus was different and much tougher than the students' version. The teacher wrote:

> 1. The advisor has the responsibility to ensure that all content of *The Coastal Chronicle* is acceptable for publication. Controversial topics including but not limited to sex, illegal substances, violence, etc., may require the approval of the [Coastal] High School administration.
> 2. The advisor and administration of Coastal High School observe [sic] the right to postpone or cease publication under certain circumstances. Discussions will be held with all involved parties before such action is to be taken.

To some students, the language appeared threatening. The syllabus said nothing of the press freedoms students were supposed to enjoy. They wanted to know if it was final, and Mrs. Thompson told him it was. Jamie had worked on his own version of a constitution that prohibited the advisor and the administration from ever suspending the newspaper. Mrs. Thompson had taken that step briefly after students did not seem to be observing the rules of conduct she had established. The rules had little to do with journalism but were more about matters such as eating in the classroom and signing out for interviews.

Students angered Mrs. Thompson when they spilled water on one computer, so she had Trevor physically remove the computers and lock students out of the back room. They came to appreciate the newspaper more once it was gone, yet there was a question whether such a harsh move could have been avoided. Not all students agreed immediately to the time limits she had set for layout because Mrs. Hill used to stay with them until the late hours. This was not something Mrs. Thompson was willing to do. Students eventually adapted their schedules to meet the advisor's demands. Editors viewed the editors in chief as ineffectual so the newspaper hierarchy had broken down. Yet by the spring, these issues had lost their momentum The upperclassmen and underclassmen were working on separate editions, the senior and cub issues again, when the principal took a stance that reminded many of his intervention with the 'wild side' poll.

This was the moment Miranda characterized Mr. McCormick as "slippery." A Latino acting group, which performed at other area schools, was supposed to visit campus to perform skits, including one that named the superintendent and suggested he was racist. The principal would not allow that skit to be performed unless the superintendent's name was removed. Because the principal had said nothing when Jamie wrote a highly critical editorial of the superintendent, students said they did not understand why he was censoring this play group. Angel, the organizer of the event at Coastal, also said there was something about Mr. McCormick she did not trust.

Mrs. Thompson said the visiting play should not have been censored and Mr. McCormick was showing the students that he could be very inconsistent:

> In many ways, when he talks to the journalism class as individuals, he is very much for them being journalists and doing the hard stories. He says, 'Yeah, you're a journalist. This is what you do.' Then he turns around and he'll censor things. But I think part of that comes from being an administrator. It's not an easy thing to be a principal because every day, you are making

CHAPTER 3: COASTAL HIGH SCHOOL 127

difficult decisions. And he was a journalism advisor. So I'm sure at least part of him wants to say 'yes, go do do do.' But then you are an administrator with pressures from parents, teachers and students, too, so you make the best decision you think at the time.
(Interview with Mrs. Thompson, May 31, 2002)

There was inconsistency on the part of not only Mr. McCormick but also Mrs. Thompson, who was frustrated by the class structure and how much autonomy to give students for most of the year. At times, her frustration was obvious to the class. In retrospect, Mrs. Thompson said, students in the journalism class viewed both the school's teachers and the administration as "authoritarian" and "trying to block them. We were a force to be overcome." Just as real journalists play an adversarial role with government officials, student journalists often saw the school authorities in a similar light. In many cases, this perception was warranted. Yet students, particularly Mary Jo but also some of the staff writers, were their own censors. One newly appointed news editor admitted that the high school newspaper does a lot of "glorification" of the rest of the school, a description no professional newspaper would want to have of itself.

That was why seniors working on their final edition were sensitive when Mary Jo and Trevor let Mr. McCormick view the final goodbye notes seniors were writing for the newspaper and their poll results naming each other to positions, like "most cynical" or "most stressed" or "most likely to be ditching class." The categories were already ones that the principal had seen and approved or scratched out. A conversation I saw in late May confirmed that students and adults lived in different worlds they wished to protect from one other. An argument broke out after class when Mary Jo and Miranda discussed the administration reviewing the senior issue material. Miranda had seen Mary Jo with the pile of results, and she suspected where the editor in chief was going, given that she judged so many things in the newspaper "inappropriate:"

Miranda (sarcastically)· I think it is ridiculous that you are asking McCormick! Why don't we just run all our articles by him, too? Maybe he should have copies of the paper right before every issue. We'll change anything he says.
(Mary Jo (she said because there was no sense talking to Miranda) listened to her silently, then stomped out of the classroom.)

The seniors, gathered together in a corner of the back room, were quiet.
SEA: He wants to see the answers?
Miranda: I don't think he actually asked to see them. I think Mary Jo said, 'Oh, let's see if the answers are any good.' That's not her job as editor in chief.
Courtney: "She grabbed the answers out of our hands and ran to the office with them."
Gabe (imitating Mary Jo): 'My goal is to censor us.' That's what she said.
Miranda: These are seniors' inside personal things -- half of them you won't understand.
Gabe: She is taking all of the personality out of the senior edition.
Courtney: Yeah, you can't censor everything. Most of it's implied anyway. It's not like: 'My best memory -- I smoked pot.' It's like, 'When I was in the wrong state of mind . . .' They know how to word it.
Trevor who was present when Mary Jo brought the results to McCormick (at an earlier point than everyone thought): She went through and handed him a few.
Gabe: I bet she went through and handed him her personal favorites. She is such a bitch.
Miranda: That's not her call at all. Guess what? There are five people working on the poll. Why did she think she got to take all these polls to McCormick? She didn't even talk to anybody.
Trevor: One of McCormick's major concerns –
Courtney: We don't want anything that will make people feel bad but --
Trevor: That was the major thing from the get-go. One of McCormick's major concerns is that he wants 'to save these people from themselves.' Quote, unquote.
(Field notes, May 20, 2002)

The notion that high school seniors somehow needed to be rescued from their own immaturity raised everyone's ire, and they grew defensive. No statement I heard so aptly captured student journalists' reasons for frustration with adults. The students had often felt they were in an ongoing battle to prove their own worth as fully reasonable people. They knew they had additional press rights in California, but Courtney felt there was little difference between censorship at this school and one subject to the restrictions of *Hazelwood*. The standards in *Hazelwood* still reflected the way adults viewed young people in secondary school. Young people understood intuitively they could not act as journalists. The societal beliefs of adults about young people cause young people's alienation as a rational response to the limits of their social position and "a growing awareness of their own powerlessness," argues Buckingham (2000, 202).

In fact, Hine contends that without high schools – complete with school officials and instructors -- to define and restrict them, there would be no such thing as teenagers. Now high schools have achieved such societal acceptance they are invisible –except when a disturbed youth brings a gun to class -- and high school newspapers have become as ineffectual as preschool scrawl. According to Hine (139):

> Well into the twentieth century, some young people – those with clear vision, strong ambition and little patience – were able to bypass high school and move directly into making a living. Now young people who wish to succeed in any sort of legitimate enterprise must make it through high school. To reject your family is one thing; there may be very good reasons.To reject high school is to reject society as a whole.

The aim of recognizing teenagers as capable and listening to them, according to Jenkins, is "to create the conditions through which they develop a political consciousness, to defend their access to the information they need to frame their own judgments, and to build the technologies that enable them to exchange their ideas with others of their generation" (32). The protection of students' free speech rights was not a goal of the Coastal journalism program. If it were, relevant student press law would have been made explicit to them as part of the curriculum, as it was at Creekwood.

Courtney might have liked the newspaper better as an extracurricular activity. She hated having to come up with seven ideas for brainstorming sessions, some for each section, and believed ideas should be submitted as they came up or they were dull and forced. "A lot of things have been bothering me that we don't have enough chance to explain ourselves. We don't have enough freedom. It's always so regimented." School officials wielded too much control so that student autonomy was false freedom that could mean the newspaper was a "pretend" newspaper, just as high school was a pretend life. The poll of student use of alcohol and drugs and of their sexual behavior was highly controversial, in part because premature sex, maybe any sex, is not something adults like to discuss with their children, particularly in public. The administration skillfully made it appear to students that it was assisting them, but the poll was doomed to failure from the moment the administrators applied the guidelines under which the teens could publish it.

The article about Mr. McCormick censoring the visiting student skit never was printed. The cubs decided to scrap their edition so the senior issue could be expanded. That way, they would start out the next year with $1,000, the same amount as last year. Some students were enraged they had worked for a newspaper that would never be published. Rebecca thought the decision was right because "people actually keep it. My mom told me she kept her senior issue from like 30-40 years ago." Yet the view of a school newspaper as a keepsake, similar to a yearbook, reduced its value as a First Amendment tool. High school was to be viewed with nostalgia years later, with little effect on the contemporary adult world.

D. Conclusion – An Invaluable Beginning?

Censorship, both subtle and not-so-subtle, was damaging to the journalism program at Coastal. It was practiced by well-meaning educators sure it was in the best interest of the vulnerable population they served. Sometimes, it seemed to conflict directly with Cal. Educ. Code Sec. 48907, a provision that a number of students could rattle off from memory, although some had never heard of it. It prohibited prior restraint of student expression unless it was obscene, libelous or slanderous or incited students to disruption, unlawful acts or the violation of school rules. Censorship occurred despite this law in the guise of discretion or a way to defeat sensationalism.

The decision to downplay September 11 reflected the paper's general approach to news coverage. In some ways, it could not be viewed as unusual in that regional newspapers all across the nation, papers that had prided themselves on local coverage, now found a need to pay more attention to foreign news:

> While the (*St. Louis*) *Post-Dispatch* has, in its 124-year history, often had a broader outlook than many regional papers, it seemed that almost any decent local story could keep virtually any foreign news off page one. September 11 changed that -- to some extent. (Seplow, July/August 2002, 19).

A survey by the Pew International Journalism Program found that 95 percent of editors reported reader interest in international news had increased since the attacks on the World Trade Center and the Pentagon (Seplow, 28). In October 2001, the Pew Research Center reported that Americans had adopted "a new internationalist sentiment," but by June 2002, news habits were "not markedly different than the spring of 2000," the center said.

There was no doubt that student interest in foreign news also had increased at Coastal, based on the perceptions of journalism students as they attended other classes and discussed events with friends after school. Yet some students felt that *The Coastal Chronicle* was not the best place for reports about the conflict overseas -- it should not even try to be such a place for news. The school's sensitivity about the issues that teenagers confronted daily bothered many students. One boy described the climate for high school journalism as one where students thought "you can't do that," even if it was a legitimate topic. "It seems like they dismiss things not for the right reasons, just because they don't want to cause a controversy or make someone upset," he said. He was assigned to write about students wearing green ribbons for marijuana legalization:

> I was going to write a full article on it, but they did not want a full article because it was about marijuana, so they ended up having me write a news brief. But it's something that's happening at this school, and it's news. . . It seems stupid to me that just because it's about an issue we shouldn't condone, we are not writing about it. It's like someone saying we are not going to write about Russia or China because we don't believe in communism.

The desire not to make anyone uncomfortable seemed to be a major consideration during the handling of both the AP theft story and to a greater degree, the poll on sex and drugs. It was behind September 11 coverage, but this was mainly a self-protective move. Students may not have wanted to make themselves uncomfortable, or even upset their academic schedules. Some saw they practiced a stunted journalism and hoped for better conditions after high school. Others had no such illusions.

Besides being hyper-aware of the sensitive nature of the school setting, students were told to avoid anything resembling sensationalism. Students did not have a clear understanding of how to write about the effect of September 11 without crossing an invisible line that would have constituted overkill. As a former Gannett Co. newspaper reporter, I could not help thinking that their description of what counted as news seemed to take a page directly from Alan Neuharth's concept of the "Journalism of Hope." The idea, which the newspaper mogul introduced in 1983, was that a newspaper's voice should advocate "understanding and unity rather than disdain and divisiveness." Media theorist Ben Badikian, criticized Neuharth's "Journalism of Hope" as the "Journalism of Joy." In *The Making of McPaper* (Pritchard, 1987, 316), he said:

> At best, I think that's a meaningless phrase for journalism. It's just an inappropriate way to look at the news, as it would be to say that we should have the journalism of doom and gloom. News tends to accentuate conflict. Some of that is inevitably negative.

It was Badikian's notion of news that high school journalism, as practiced at *The Coastal Chronicle,* could not -- and likely would not be permitted to -- accept. Students thought they were being traditional and avoiding sensationalism on their front page, but they did not cover many news stories that were covered elsewhere.

This was, in part, because many students seemed to label any bad news as sensationalism. If they did cover news events, they did not cover them deeply in most cases. This was viewed as responsible, but it also could be seen as superficial. It was probably no coincidence that Student Focus editor Courtney said she got the bulk of her format and story ideas from *USA Today*. She read it daily "by accident" -- because her father brought it home from the office. It was a choice between that and *The Wall Street Journal.* There was no contest. She loved the "Life" section about movie stars, giving her the idea of contacting famous graduates of her high school. The Student Focus section actually seemed to be the most thoughtful part of the paper. The prevailing attitude about September 11 coverage made me recall Gannett's emphasis on "chicken dinner journalism" as being most essential to readers -- the small local stories in which readers figure prominently and could see their own names, their children's names, and their communities. Neuharth's overall idea about journalism turned out to be the journalism that often gets practiced in high school, and indeed, high school is open to charges of insularity, as if only what happened in the school hallways, cafeteria

CHAPTER 3: COASTAL HIGH SCHOOL

and classrooms had any value. This insularity was more obvious after September 11.
It often could lead to an irritating "good news" philosophy. Prichard wrote:

> In its early days, *USA Today* may have carried the 'good news' philosophy too far. In a *Washington Journalism Review* article assessing the newspaper after four years, Barbara Matusow wrote, 'Many journalists were particularly disturbed by the paper's relentlessly upbeat tone -- a reflection of Neuharth's philosophy that news is something more than a recital of hurricanes and other calamities. . . the early *USA Today* sounded mindlessly breezy at times; one headline following a plane crash proclaimed: 'Miracle, 327 survive, 55 die.'

At times, co-editor Mary Jo could have been Neuharth. There was something about her blanket skepticism of the news media that begged the question of what the young people might offer in its place? If it turned out to be the news that *The Coastal Chronicle* was producing, they were dissatisfied with that answer as well. If news was the serious section of the paper, if the newspaper was a good representation of what was going on around them, student editors wanted to know why readers were so uninterested in it?

The lack of September 11 coverage also appeared to be dependent upon weariness. A *USA Today* story about the anniversary carried the headline, "Enough. As the anniversary of the terror attacks approaches, some say they can't bear to see it again." The words covered at least half the cover of the *Life* section. The story described a study of 2,273 Americans by North Carolina's Research Triangle Institute, which found a link between hours spent watching TV following September 11 and post-traumatic stress disorder. Even the students who wanted to write about September 11 found its images very troubling. But weariness was only one factor in a complex cocktail that kept September 11 news from "interfering" with the school newspaper.

The problem with high school journalism programs are the limits they face, including direction from school officials and the teacher that can chill expression, intentionally or unintentionally. These limits caused students to impose more limits on themselves. Although research shows professional journalism instruction is generally lacking (about 25 percent of teachers have college or professional media experience, according to Dvorak, Lain and Dickson, 1994: 97). Mrs. Thompson had minored in college journalism. The case of Mrs. Hill, who had eight years' experience advising but no journalism background, might justify intervention by the principal, but he knew as little as she about the press. As a potential solution to the alienation of youth, Buckingham calls for schools to encourage children's "critical participation as cultural producers." He wants new forms of journalism and politics to emerge from the education system (Buckingham, 2000, 222-223). The best way to accomplish this aim may be journalism programs, as long as they offer serious instruction in news-writing and standards such as fairness, balance, and accuracy. Yet such a vision is far from becoming a reality.

Notes

[1] Mindich divides objectivity into five components: 1) detachment, a reporter's biases are to be kept out of the news; 2) nonpartisanship, reporters need to get all angles of the story; 3) the inverted pyramid, the style of writing that places the most important news elements at the top of a story and the least at the bottom; 4) naïve empiricism or reliance on facts to report the reality or truth of events; and 5) balance, the goal of undistorted reporting through even-handedness.

Make It a Great Day – Or Not

Working-class teens in the journalism class at Homestead High School had given up on changing their circumstances, having mostly surrendered to school testing, schedules and rules. The journalism class at Homestead was not revolutionary and did not alter the formula that leaves Latino youth with low participation rates in politics and civic life. Students were practicing disengagement early. The issue is significant because a student newspaper is a form of early participation and may be a site of social change. In addition, early disaffection with the news media could contribute to reduce minority participation in newsrooms (Dvorak 2003). The teacher did not emphasize student rights, discuss definitions of news, reinforce rules of newsgathering and writing, or go over delicacies of journalistic ethics. This may have been because she was unfamiliar with them or did not think such sophisticated concepts were relevant. More so than might be the case in an affluent school, *The Homestead Herald* was, in the words of one student, "a kiddie newspaper." The Latino youth had little reason to be concerned about official interference, which had a recent history at the school, because their journalism was not usually controversial.

Students' silence during story idea sessions did not necessarily equal approval. Complaints about story selection by the teacher would erupt at rare moments Mrs. Webb deemed inappropriate. Students resented teacher control of the newspaper at times, but they also were unwilling to take on more responsibility. Often, they accepted whatever assignments the teacher imposed, doing their duty in an unimaginative way, as if little mattered. Teachers blamed student disinterest on lack of motivation, but students also were reacting to low expectations teachers had set, in a familiar pattern of failure. The cause of this was complex: School and life prospects alienated the youth, but they also disengaged themselves.

Students in this study were aware of their social position as poor, and their parents mainly worked in service-sector jobs, received government benefits, or were unemployed. One girl who called herself "ghetto" said her mother referred to her jokingly as "my ghetto child." They were largely the children of bakers, mechanics, maids, landscapers, and lower-paid office staff. Most came from large families. They were uncertain of their options and greeted the slogan on the announcements, "Make it a great day or not. The choice is yours" with some derision. It was as if school officials believed they could reverse the factors causing student defeat by reciting a catch phrase. Students knew those at a competing high school had wealthier families and posh cars. They considered me rich, too, because I usually could make change when they asked. They knew I was there to observe, ask about journalism, and help out as an ex-newspaper reporter. They did not seem to connect their condition with a grander social scheme. Typical adolescent classifications that mask class distinctions were more salient to them, such as jocks or "school boys," gangsters, and punkers.

Students felt their options were limited. Numerous scholars have pointed to the way schools reproduce the inequalities of the outside society (Eckert 1989; Heath 1982; Everhart 1983; Bourdieu and Passeron 1977; Willis 1977) even while claiming they do the opposite. For instance, students' use of social categories was a way they identified those who accepted the middle-class ideology of mostly white teachers, wrote Penelope Eckert (1989) in an ethnography of affiliation in schools. Like Eckert, Robert Everhart concludes in *Reading, Writing and Resistance* (1983) that "students have a propensity to coalesce into friendship groups that provide, for many, the real meaning of their daily lives in the school." The consequence of this is that all schoolwork, including lessons about journalism and news, becomes a sidelight to other imperatives. My research is part of a literature of reproduction and resistance that dates back to the 1950s and 1960s. It includes Willard Waller's 1965 research about the conflicting cultures of adults and students in schools. Informal groups set up by students flout school norms by privileging clothes, athletics and popularity over academics, found C. Wayne Gordon (1957) and J.S. Coleman (1961). The fault for schools that do not succeed must rest with adults, but students at Homestead were complicit in their own undoing by rejecting their schooling. Mehan, Villanueva, Hubbard and Lintz (1996), contend that teachers, through an untracked, college prep program with social supports, can offset what working-class students lack for pursuing college. Would a newspaper offer another alternative peer group setting – reporters in a newsroom?

Ostensibly, those who aspired to school norms were the nerds and to a lesser extent, the jocks and schoolboys, versus "the gangsters" who were deemed more marginal to school life. The gangsters in this school were equivalent to the burnouts of Eckert's research. Yet in this working-class environment, the categories were more complex than first thought. Even when they chose to be silent, students seen as gangsters practiced a self-defensive form of resistance to schooling. According to Angela Valenzuela (1999), "What looks to teachers and administrators

CHAPTER 4: HOMESTEAD HIGH SCHOOL 137

like opposition and lack of caring feels to students like powerlessness and alienation. Some students' clear perception of the weakness of their position politicizes them into deliberately conveying an uncaring attitude as a form of resistance not to education, but to the irrelevant, uncaring and controlling aspects of schooling" (94). Students' use of categorical references was another direct commentary on their attitudes toward school and their place in the world. They employed cultural categories like *pocho*, the Spanish word for a Mexican-American student, born here, who speaks only English. One boy said a classmate called him "beaner," a slur for Mexican that can be as offensive as "nigger" unless it is used lightly by friends. Most students considered themselves "normal," the in-betweens Eckert cites that did not choose to align themselves with any particular group.

In *Growing Up Girl* (2001), Valerie Walkerdine, Helen Lucey and June Melody argue that young people perform their class in everything they do:

From house to dress, from accent to appearance, Eliza Doolittle is as present in the early twenty-first century as she was in the nineteenth. And more than this, the living out of these marks of difference is filled with desire, longing, anxiety, pain, defense. Class is at once profoundly social and profoundly emotional and lived in its specificity in particular cultural and geographic locations (53).

Students in this journalism class were very resistant to the subject of journalism and often rejected it as the province of boring adults, yet they did not realize that this very act of rejection might limit their social mobility, which can depend on access to information and confident self-assertion. They did not grasp the larger purposes of the media or their part in it. As they often do in other settings, the young people had difficulty connecting their own lives to world events. Some associated the news with homes they were trying to avoid, places where pessimism played incessantly on TV. They did not want to reproduce the same material. Much success within middle-class instruction involves being able to endure what one initially rejects, or in journalism parlance, "to make the assignment your own." Many students, again more than in suburban schools, had genuine difficulty accepting this concept as it seemed to collide with their cultural values.

It is a rarity for teachers to use journalism to help youth break out of the blue-collar cycle and enter the white-collar world. Thus, Mrs. Webb did not recognize a need to know her students' life circumstances or goals. For many students, home already was an unstable location because they faced frequent relocation. Many students had single mothers. Some could not rely on their family makeup to stay constant, as boyfriends, stepsiblings and death led to more complex arrangements. Students often did not have their own rooms or quiet places to study. Maria, 16, had to sleep on the couch. They could not depend on their parents having money. However, these issues were not discussed in journalism class. While a teacher is not a social worker, Mrs. Webb's lack of knowledge increased some students' perceptions that the school did not care about them, contributing to poor academic performance. As Mehan et. al write, "The actions that educators take everyday in school settings constitute students' educational careers, indeed their identities. Depending on the vector of their actions, the prospect for more equitable education is increased or prevailing inequities are reinforced" (229).

As an example, the Latino students Valenzuela studied in Houston were particularly affected by uncaring attitudes of teachers and school officials. Valenzuela attributed this to the Mexican cultural concept of "*educacion*," a broader term than in English. *Educacion* refers to "the family's role of inculcating in children a sense of moral, social and personal responsibility" that acts as "the foundation for all other learning," Valenzuela wrote (23). While some journalism students told me they had experienced rudeness from teachers, Mrs. Webb was more palatable to them than most. Yet she described herself as conservative and traditional. Her approach was more authoritarian than relaxed. She expected to inject knowledge and assign work to students and she did not successfully generate story ideas through discussion of students' school and family lives. Her expectations for quality work were minimal, and she would inflict so-called "book-work" on anyone who appeared to be dawdling.

Despite this, many students missed Mrs. Webb when she went on maternity leave twice, in fall 2001 and spring 2003. She could not speak Spanish, and her lack of knowledge of student lives may have sent the message that their culture was not significant or mattered only during yearly events covered in the newspaper, such as Cinco de Mayo. While many teach without knowing what prior experiences students bring to the classroom, this lack of knowledge places the journalism educator at a greater disadvantage because many story ideas spring from experience. New to the school and the subject of journalism, Mrs. Webb started out by bringing controversial material written by the student editor to the principal for approval. With her current students, there was no need.

CHAPTER 4: HOMESTEAD HIGH SCHOOL 139

Students said they avoided subjects they thought could get the teacher in trouble.

Teacher caring was what Valenzuela called more "aesthetic" than "authentic," and many Homestead teachers looked only for a superficial relationship with students. Instead of attributing the pro-school ethic of Mexican-born youth to the cultural precept of *educacion*, teachers simply praised their positive outlook. "When teachers withhold social ties from Mexican-American youth, they confirm this group's belief that schooling is impersonal, irrelevant and lifeless," found Valenzuela. Rather than view students as having limitless futures, many teachers at Homestead saw their students as a problem population who would graduate from high school to sit at home and fritter away their lives, or as Valenzuela wrote, as "hapless, disengaged individuals who act out their defiance through their strut-and-swagger attitude toward school rules" (32).

This bias explains verbal abuse students said they experienced in other classes. Maria, a girl that the substitute teacher described as having difficulties at home, pointed to her tattered World History book as proof students were mistreated:

Maria: The classrooms are overcrowded. There are teachers [some of them Asian] teaching English and math who don't even speak English. They are disrespectful to the students. The teachers can be rude and insulting. Even if it's unintentional, they make you feel stupid.
Tony (also 16, seated nearby): People have laughed and said, 'You are never going to go to college.'
    SEA: Teachers have said that to you?
Tony: They said that to my friend. They put us down instead of encouraging us.
SEA: Could students write about that in the school newspaper?
Tony: We don't say anything about it. No one would listen. They don't care what we say because they already have their things planned. And they are not going to change plans for us.
Maria: They don't take the students into consideration. It's how it feels at times. I am so bothered by the whole school and its rules and regulations that I don't even want to come to school anymore.
               (Field notes, May 13, 2003)

This sense of alienation from the official world of school and a dearth of trustworthy adults further reduced educational chances for students. At the same time, many were experiencing disruptive changes

140 CHAPTER 4: HOMESTEAD HIGH SCHOOL

in family composition, housing or both. In contrast, research on upper-middle class neighborhoods, shows they are often more stable with greater mechanisms for adult-child social exchange (Sampson 20001: 3-30). Sampson described the "collective efficacy" of Chicago neighborhoods as "the ability of a community structure to realize the common values of its residents and maintain effective social controls" (8). In stable neighborhoods, parents look out for each other's children, a phenomenon similar to the parent networks that sociologist Lareau identified in upper-middle income communities -- ties that benefit children's schoolwork.

Lareau delved into the psychology of working-class parents whose attitudes toward schooling often cause them to distance themselves from their children's schools. She argued they are intimidated by teachers because of the parents' own lack of education and self-esteem. Their belief in the separation between home and school meant working class parents were unlikely to help their children with academic work at home while upper-middle-class families sought to supply whatever was needed through private tutoring or their own coaching. To a great extent, Lareau wrote, "parents' activities shaped the degree to which children received a 'generic' or a 'customized' educational experience within schools" (123). Homestead parents usually did not supervise their children's homework or ask about the newspaper. This may point to the importance of parental support to all school activities, even those thought supplemental.[1] Similarly, Valenzuela's study found that 18 percent of parents had completed high school. Most had little educational "advantage" to offer youth (9).

Teenagers at Homestead described their parents as not intervening when they were placed in tracked classes above or below their abilities and not necessarily questioning it when the students rejected college. In both areas, upper-middle class parents may be more aggressively involved as they recognize these issues – teacher and student predictions about the future -- contribute to young people's educational and career attainment. Upper-middle class parents often viewed involvement in the newspaper as beneficial for college admission. The parents of Homestead students encouraged their children verbally but frowned upon them spending time after-school for layout. They needed them for other household chores.

Both Lali (17), a senior and the editor in chief, and Lupita (16) the student who hoped to be editor in chief the next year, said their parents blamed them for poor grades and almost never phoned teachers. Both girls' parents had dropped out of high school, with Lupita's guardians returning for their General Education Development diplomas. "Mine don't call really but she [my guardian] talks to me and tells me, 'You need to bring up your grades or because whatever you're graduating and stuff like that.," said Lupita. "She'll tell me to ask the teacher if there's anything I can do to still pass." Many parents had no higher standard for their children than to pass or earn Cs and graduate from high school. In many cases, the students would be the first in their families to graduate. In what would be heresy in many upper-middle class households, Lali said: "My parents are not really pushing me to go to college. They said that it's my choice. " Nearby, another journalism student added, "My parents don't really push me at all because they're not familiar with college, so they have no clue and they really don't talk about it with me."

A. Terrorism, Sniper Shootings, the War on Iraq:
'Let it slide': Facing and Forgetting the News,
Rejection of Journalism as Resistance to 'Schooling'

Because journalism teacher Stacey Webb wanted her students to take an interest in politics and world events, she asked me to address the class about terrorism. I had spoken with the class on occasion. She left me with them to do other work in the next room. This time, I read them a web-based story I had written about a young newlywed who had lost her husband, a bond trader, on the 104th floor of the World Trade Center. The students were moved by the details, evident in one remark: "When you are reading it, you can actually picture what's happening -- what the people are seeing and how they are feeling."

Mrs. Webb had once told me that her students were "not journalists, but riff-raff I rounded together." This was harsh, and I knew there was more to them than that. Yet my own discussion of September 11 showed me they were not an easy group to teach. Instead of talking about the tragedy or the idea of writing about terrorism, they remained silent, even sullen, about the news. Beyond the one comment, there was not much energy in the classroom, mostly blank faces. I wanted to know why.

I would discover later in focus group discussions that the subject matter was disturbing to them, both distant and frightening, perhaps somewhat like the disappointments of their own schooling. During my talk in September 2002, the students said they had never been to New York or known anyone from there, with the possible exception of me. "It's sad," one girl commented about the story. "She [the widowed bride] had all these plans." The others left it at that. The teacher later would talk about the fact that the city in which they lived might be a prime terrorist target, an attempt to bring the news closer to them. They did not want it closer. This was cause for more apprehension, not inspiration to report and write. A few boys morosely discussed what option they would have chosen if they were high in one of the towers when the jets struck -- burning or jumping to their oblivion.

Interviewed later, Carlos (16) remembered being afraid when he came to school the morning of September 11, 2001. He expressed cynicism about Homestead's awkward reaction, which treated students as though they were a threat or in need of protection:

Carlos: They said we were on lock-down schedule and we should be alert. We were not allowed to go to the bathroom because they were bombing New York City.
SEA: You were not allowed to go the bathroom?
Carlos: I was like why? We are so far away. Why should we not be allowed to go to the bathroom? They locked the classrooms. We couldn't go out.
(Field notes, January 27, 2003)

Carlos' family also was on edge because his mother supervised maid service at a hotel that was over a bridge named as a target. Other students either remembered being glued to the news or turning their TVs off in disgust. Adults showed the same reactions, but may have had an easier time seeing the link between news reports and their community. They also might have had more experience dealing with reports of human suffering.

The newspaper could have been an outlet for expressing these emotions, but the timing was not right, said Mrs. Webb. The staff had just sent an issue for printing and was not about to remake it. The year-round school, which began a new year each July, was about to go on break and Mrs. Webb was almost ready to begin the first of two maternity leaves. September 11 went uncovered. The students had little prior experience in thinking as journalists so no one was particularly concerned. This was a bit like the decision against covering September 11 at Coastal High School, but much more extreme. Homestead students barely acknowledged in the class that September 11 happened while Coastal students may have discarded them but were more familiar with journalistic norms and practices. Creekwood Canyon had finished its center spread already but made a different choice than Homestead, readily scrapping it to make a four-page pullout. This showed an understanding that news would not bend to student schedules.

CHAPTER 4: HOMESTEAD HIGH SCHOOL 143

Jessica (17), who joined the class much later in January 2003, gave me insight into teenage weariness of outside news reports about terrorism. She said she hoped to use the newspaper to write about what actually interested teenagers because no one could make anyone else care about world events:

Honestly, the shuttle crashing, the whole 9-11, everything going on, all these tragedies, it affects us, the war and everything, it affects us. But no one wants to talk about it. No one really wants to listen to it. They just want to go on with their lives and say, 'You know what? When it affects me, it will affect me,' but at this point, they are just like 'talk about something else. Don't hang on this depressing stuff because no one likes it.' I hate this depressing stuff. After September 11, I turned off the TV. . . I didn't watch TV that whole month. I'd go upstairs and they'd have the TV on. I'd say, 'Turn it off. It's so depressing.' It's like, 'Get over it.' I mean, don't get over it. Move on. Remember it, but move on. It's time. OK, it's almost two years later. Let it slide.
(Field notes, Tuesday February 4, 2003)

In September 2002, a year after the terrorist attacks and days after the first edition of the year – when little else was in the outside media but stories about the terrorist threat -- the students decided to make "body image" the theme of the next edition, hair, makeup, clothes, tattoos. My field notes reflect that I helped them with their Internet research during classes in mid-September. I encouraged them to interview other students in the school because the Internet often was their main choice for research. Unlike other similarly situated schools, Homestead was well equipped with close to 500 computers through a state grant. The journalism classroom had at least 15, enough for every student, and the use of 20 additional laptops from the reading program. Yet nowhere was it more apparent that the latest technology does not make a journalism class. They had spent almost a month working on the stories when Mrs. Webb decided she would switch their theme to terrorism. They were not too happy about this, but did not say much – at least not openly. Instead, they each signed up for at least two required stories, listed on a white board, as they were supposed to. Mrs. Webb was trying to get students interested in what other journalists in the nation were covering at a time when most of her students were routinely discouraged and disengaged. Because I had addressed the class, I understood her plight more deeply. The students were well practiced in keeping quiet. Was journalism about teaching students to follow traditional standards of news judgment or about allowing them to develop their own ideas of what was important to their peers?

When Mrs. Webb tried to shift the students' vision to include world news, the students ironically had come dressed in their sleepwear for pajama day. Enrique (16) had dyed his hair maroon-red. They all watched the litany of daily announcements on the TV monitor: The Columbus Day parade. The computer lab schedule. College deadlines. Students presented a quick TV skit about the fear of never graduating high school. Ds and Fs had decreased by 2 percent throughout Homestead. Tomorrow, everyone needed to wear red for a Homecoming Week assembly. Then the students, teacher and I listened to the ritual motto – "Make it a great day – or not. The choice is yours." There were a few groans in the classroom. Before instruction began, the teacher told me she wanted the class to "branch out" and consider the subject of terrorism. "Hopefully, we can do it with them," she told me. "I think so. They need to consider the role of politics."

Teaching to strengths, not deficits?

Hearing the word "we," I knew she wanted to enlist me in her effort to change student mindsets, specifically what the students had already planned for their next edition. This would be risky. She turned to address the students. "Make sure you do a good job and pass your classes. You guys aren't getting Fs are you? Tomorrow you need to wear red for Assembly Day. The next paper is coming out in a couple of weeks. There's an assignment list on the board." Her statements positioned her as an authority figure that reinforced official school interests and was fully in charge of the student newspaper and its contents. She told me it was not possible to let the students run the newspaper because they would sit there and do nothing. The students were largely dependent on the teacher's decision-making. "I think with all of my classes, including this one, if I came in and let them sit without giving them any short-term goals, I don't think anything would ever happen."

The idea that students do not take their educations seriously ignores the reality of an unequal education system that actually subtracts cultural resources from Latino youth, contends Valenzuela, also citing Kozol. School spirit and effort might lag among some youth because they feel disrespected by those in power. Teachers often focus on superficial factors such as the way students dress rather than trying to figure out who students are. She was hardly the worst offender, but Mrs. Webb

CHAPTER 4: HOMESTEAD HIGH SCHOOL

was part of a much more widespread affliction of urban schools intended for working-class, minority youth. "Research has shown that instruction in inner-city schools is often based on cognitively low-level, unchallenging, rote material," wrote education theorist Jean Anyon in Ghetto Schooling (1997: 7). Her ethnographic study of Newark, NJ schools found the relations between teachers and students to be poor, with students subject to routine verbal abuse from teachers who assumed the worst about their capabilities (also see Darling-Hammond 1996; Delpit 1995; Oakes 1990).

Anyon quotes an outside evaluation of the Newark school district that found few instances in any classroom, regardless of the subject or grade level of students being encouraged to generate their own ideas, to collaborate in problem-solving activities, to write in class, to read widely and independently, or to use skills and facts in context.

Even when journalism assignments required such activities, Mrs. Webb often found herself reverting to less independent measures out of frustration or the concern that students were indifferent. She had trouble getting them to take initiative, saying they enjoyed writing news most because the listing of facts was simple. This ignored the potential creativity of news writing. Besides my guest lecture, she did not introduce any outside journalistic writing, whether local or national. Even if she was not rude to her students, they came from a greater school setting that assumed they were defective, so they were usually unreceptive to Mrs. Webb's efforts to motivate them. She also had trouble seeing the error of her own assumptions about students' inadequacies as well as the invisible classroom structures and values that might have worked to stimulate them.

Citing other scholarly research, in particular Michelle Fine (1991), Olga Vasquez (2003) discusses the way Latino students face nagging stereotypes in school (also see Oakes, Mehan and Vasquez' own work):

how a constellation of administrative and ideological practices and beliefs – what [Fine] called 'intuitional fetishes' – unintentionally lead to the expulsion and exclusion of low-status students. Of particular relevance to these processes are the unquestioned adherence to notions of universal access to public education, the 'good intentions' of educational professionals, and the distinctions that exist between public and private spheres for some populations. As Fine aptly concluded, these factors lead institutions to 'construct and legitimate a set of beliefs about equal opportunity, the inevitability of failure, and the immutability of home problems that undermine academic achievement' (20).

Perhaps the greatest hardship Latino students face is suspect educational beliefs about their capabilities, and this may lead to self-fulfilling prophesies of failure. Along similar lines, education theorist Lisa Delpit points to teacher education as largely responsible for spreading the concepts that socioeconomic status, cultural difference and single-parent households inevitably lead to academic failure. "It is hard to believe that these children can possibly be successful after their teachers have been so thoroughly exposed to so much negative indoctrination," she writes in *Other People's Children* (1995: 172). "When teachers receive that kind of education, there is a tendency to assume deficits in students rather than to locate and teach to strengths." Again, the key to countering this dilemma is learning about students' lives outside of school, she writes. Even when they meet the requirements for college and gain admission, Latino students feel disconnected and isolated from middle-class norms, suggests Vasquez.

Whose War Is It Anyway?

The school newspaper was more challenging than Mrs. Webb's other classes. Structuring the class to write about school events was difficult enough, but world events proved very intimidating. The class in which Mrs. Webb informed the students they now would be discussing terrorism went this way:

Mrs.Webb: What's going on in the world? (Students responded with vacant looks). What happened over in Bali?
Students (exchanging puzzled glances): Bali? What's Bali?
Mrs. Webb: There was a bomb set off at a club. Was it two clubs, Ms. Amster? (She looked at me).
SEA: It was two clubs where a lot of Westerners go on vacation.
Mrs. Webb (nodding): One of the things I want you to think about is to think more global what's going on as we work on our articles for our next publication. Our last publication we had a small article on September 11, but I wish that I would have brought it up to you that maybe we should have done something a little bigger on September 11, you know, a year later, what was going on in our world and how people were dealing with it. But I didn't so we just have that one part (a photograph and caption in the Sept. 11, 2002 edition). But there are a lot of things that are going on in our world that affect us, especially right here [in this city]. We have the sniper back East, the

CHAPTER 4: HOMESTEAD HIGH SCHOOL

bombing in Bali, we have everything that went on in New York and Pennsylvania and D.C. with the terrorism, but right here, living in [this city]. We are very close to the base. You guys see the base every time you go down Highway 5. . . . And on the news yesterday – I don't know if you watch the news ---
Enrique: There was a report about a unit of the United States Navy. They came from here.
Mrs. Webb: [This city] to terrorists could be an ideal place for an attack because they would try to hurt our strength and our strength would be in our military. We are very close to the bases here. Something could happen – and we hope that nothing would ever happen -- but something could happen right here on the bases and we would feel the effects of it. So on the news yesterday, they were talking about how this city, the bay, the bases could be targets. So that's something we need to be aware of. So what I am getting at is we talked about a body image theme for this paper, and I wanted to share this with you to see what you think. I was thinking we could hold that, and address the issues that are going on right now. Because this is hot. Any day now, we could be at war with Iraq. They [the school] might say, 'Turn on the television. This is what's happening.' Any day now, we could be on lockdown because something could be happening. So I want you to think about that. How do you guys feel about addressing the news globally? What's going on here and back East, the war with Iraq, different forms of terror. . . I think it would give our class a lot of credibility addressing issues like that because body image is pretty much timeless. We could come back to it. That would allow you to do a bit more research. So comments, questions, feedback? What do you think?
    Students: (Total silence, numb faces).
    Mrs. Webb: C'mon!
    Enrique (reluctantly): It's a good idea.
Other students remained quiet. One student mentioned that her dad is ex-Navy and her brother is in the Army. Mrs. Webb talked about the draft and how that might affect students turning 18. No boy was turning 18. I asked them if there were Islamic students on campus and some of them nodded. What does anyone know about them?
    A few students responded: Nothing.
Mrs. Webb: How much do our students know? How much do you know about the conflict in the Middle East? What do you know about Osama bin Laden? What do you know about Saddam Hussein? What do you know about al Qaeda? That's information that may or may not be interesting to you, but that's information that some students don't know about. And your

history teachers may touch on this information or they may not. Being high school students, you are going to be out there on your own. You're going to be able to vote. It all ties in together. *This is a big deal.*
(Field notes, October 15, 2002)

It was apparent that the teacher thought these issues more important, a bigger deal to the newspaper, than the students did. Her effort to inject the news into the class worked partially, on some students, such as Delia, who was excited because of her front-page story in the Sept. 11, 2002, edition for which she attended a press conference. She had been the only student journalist present. Lupita, too, was softening her resistance toward journalism, a class that she did not want initially. Yet because changing the theme had not been their idea, opposition to a special section on terrorism simmered below the surface. Mrs. Webb's attempts to elicit student participation failed, probably because of classroom discontent mixed with apathy. The teacher's desire to relate national and global issues to students and address the issues in the school newspaper was understandable, yet so was the students' wish NOT to write about the subject. The teacher also had no knowledge of student lives from which to form a link for students. Enrique was probably the most conflicted about the terrorism section because he recognized the stories' importance yet also wanted to run the body image theme. He was a boy experimenting with his identity every day – evident in the fact that he always seemed to have his hair dyed a new color. How did the military fit into his worldview?

The teacher said the body image issue needed to be postponed because war with Iraq was looming, but this was tantamount to her telling the teens that *they* needed to be postponed. Although the students needed to learn how journalism was practiced professionally, they had a difficult time adjusting to definitions of the news that were different from their own. What were their own? Students wanted the class to be pleasurable and use the newspaper to build their personal identities, such as through styles of clothing or music. In fact, in *Cultural Studies Goes to School* (1994), Buckingham and co-author Julian Sefton-Green find that such topics as popular music are uncomfortable for teachers because they draw direct attention to the ways in which teens and adults differ – "the tensions" between what "belongs" to students and what adults enjoy (62). For students, these distinctions – as well as the growing bureaucratic pressures of school – amounted to the real defining conflict of their young lives, not Iraq. For

CHAPTER 4: HOMESTEAD HIGH SCHOOL 149

the class, the media were personal, and they actively appropriated popular cultural forms to make and remake themselves. This is not to say that there was no space for teaching, but the teacher needed to work collaboratively with students consistent with a student-run newspaper. This seemed unfeasible to her.

To be fair, it was hard within the school culture of disengagement. Particularly, it was difficult for Mrs. Webb to relax the distrust the official school world had of popular cultural products loved by students. Buckingham and Green note:

> The collective reading of girls' magazines or the informal discussion of computer games that take place outside lessons, in the playground or during registration at the beginning of the day, are familiar aspects of school life. Indeed, such activities might partly be seen as a form of resistance to the institutional constraints of the school: having a quick blast on your Walkman between classes, or surreptitiously reading *Just Seventeen* in the middle of a boring lesson, may serve as a kind of 'escape attempt,' albeit one which runs the risk of official censure or temporary confiscation.

Mrs. Webb periodically focused on Enrique's guitar or Roberto's walkman, threatening discipline, and she also used these instances to reinforce the fact that journalism, while distinct because of newspaper production, was "still a class" that required the same standards of behavior as other classes.

Mrs. Webb felt a sense of urgency about the potential war in Iraq and thought the class should feel the same way: The centerfold for November 18, 2002 was devoted to terrorism with the headline, "Terrorism in America. Students Express Opinions on War." A boy had added a photo of the Statue of Liberty with the American flag on one side, and on the other side, an American flag with the motto, "God Bless America." Two columns gave arguments for and against war with Iraq. Maria's piece opposing war was hastily researched (for example, it did not mention the U.S. administration's central justification for the war, that Iraq had weapons of mass destruction). Her story reflected many teens' discomfort with a military solution, and it indicated alienation as they stood outside the prevailing consensus:

> With everything that has happened since September 11, the possibility of the U.S. going to war with Iraq for their involvement with the terrorist attacks is still hanging in the air.

The problem is how does the public feel about this? Is war the answer to our problems or just a means of vengeance? I am completely against the thought of going to war.

The opposing viewpoint said, "I believe that we should go to war with Iraq because Saddam Hussein is threatening us with acts of terrorism and the use of chemical weapons on America and other countries." The columns also revealed the murky and confused justifications Americans were hearing for war from the Bush Administration. This was supposed to be a pre-emptive war rather than a response that came after an attack, the way most wars had previously begun. It also was interesting that Mexico, like Canada, was opposed to the war in Iraq.

Most stories were not tailored to the class population of predominantly Mexican-American youth, although some of this was because students would not sign up for assignments, such as one about family members serving in the military. They appeared to look for the easier tasks that did not require much labor beyond Internet research. Enrique and Roberto (15) co-authored an article discussing Osama bin Laden, his past and history of terrorist attacks. The lead mentions bin Laden's upbringing in a wealthy family and the fact that he left home at 22. The story is otherwise a litany of horrific events that bin Laden caused, according to the terrorist, "because the U.S. government is unjust, criminal and tyrannical." In the last paragraph:

Osama bin Laden is currently said to be hiding in the caves of the mountain regions of Afghanistan. But no one knows for sure exactly where Osama is hiding or what he looks like now but rest assure (sic) we will find him.

Lupita interviewed a single Muslim student who commented on Sept. 11 by saying, "The terrorists had no reason killing all those people. They didn't give them life so they have no reason to take it away." She said Islam is "not about how people act. It's against the religion to kill." The headline was "Muslim Student Speaks Out." The fact that the story was short with no other students quoted did not show much effort.

The work appeared superficial, but Delia may have done the best she could, given time constraints, when she wrote about a letter by 9-11 families to President Bush that she took from a website. A truncated, one-source story was about local ports being terrorist targets. A creative idea, also teacher-orchestrated, involved contacting a girl via e-mail whose school was in the vicinity of the sniper shootings. Tony wrote the story about the sniper attacks from information he gleaned off the

CHAPTER 4: HOMESTEAD HIGH SCHOOL 151

Internet. The problem was that the snipers were caught by the time the paper came out and mention of this did not come until the final paragraphs of either story. The paper ran a photo of 17-year-old John Lee Malvo and John Allen Muhammad, almost as an afterthought. A piece about the draft had no sources but the Selective Service web site.

I was not sure that most students were just going through the motions with these stories on terrorism until that winter during a discussion between Enrique and his classmate, Roberto. Enrique said he had not wanted to write about terrorism at the time and neither had his classmates. Students may not have appreciated the section, but it represented something distinct from the stories that had run in the newspaper in recent memory. Still, Enrique criticized Mrs. Webb's change in plans as unnecessary because The Homestead Herald was supposed to be the students' newspaper:

Enrique: Every time she left the room before the last paper we had to write on terrorism, when she left the room, we'd be like, 'Do you want to do this? [to each other]. A lot of people said, 'Yeah, I don't want to do it either.' A lot of us didn't want to do it! I think everybody didn't.
Roberto: But me and him we're the only ones complaining about it. Everyone else took it as it came.
SEA: Just because it was a class and it was assigned?
Roberto: Yeah.
Enrique: I wanted this class to be fun. I was trying to make it fun. Because for me, if I find school fun, then I want to come here. Roberto: You are more interested to do better when you're proud of something.
(Field notes, January 14, 2003)

The body image stories were scrapped and never resurrected. This was despite the fact that Mrs. Webb told them, "We're going to hold what you have because it's still going to work. We are still going to use the research that you've done."

When the terrorism issue was distributed, other students in the school complained to Enrique and Roberto, saying, "Why would you want to write about that? They pound us outside of school with that. We really don't want to hear about it." Students hear too much about terrorism from parents and grandparents, Roberto said. "When you pound them with the school newspaper, it's like there's no escaping it." "Is the news at home?" I asked them, then documented this exchange:

Enrique: Well, it's on TV. It's always on TV. If you want to hear about the terrorist attacks or anything about Osama bin Laden, you just turn on CNN and you can watch it if you want. But most people don't really want to hear about that right now. It's not that it's old news – it's just –
Roberto: It's bad enough they have to worry about pimples and girls and then when they are trying to give you the whole thing about –
Enrique: That they could come bomb here. It scares them and they don't want to hear about it. They want to hear about stuff that they like. Like that's why we try to write about video games and bands that form outside of school, music, anything we can that's entertaining. We don't really try to go on to actual news – news about the school, yeah, events at school, sports, that's what we should be writing about, not terrorist attacks. Sometimes, every once in a while, one or two articles in the paper, it's OK because some people may be interested. Maybe even a quarter of the student body may be interested, but most students are not."
SEA: So you think you should make an effort to keep it out, more than make an effort to cover it?
Roberto: Well, most of the time me and him go against the grain, so I don't know.
Enrique: She told us at the beginning of the semester that this was our paper, that we could put whatever we want in here, then all of a sudden she said we have to write about terrorist attacks. If we don't, our grade goes down, so she kind of threatened our grade so we had no choice. (Field notes, January 14, 2003)

As Roberto saw it, the teacher thought he and Enrique were rowdy because they were "more independent-minded. Them [others in the class], they do what they're told. Us, we basically do what we really want to do so she is watching us more closely. We get more unwanted attention. It's kind of cool because it seems like we're rebels." Because they did not get to do what they wanted, Enrique and Roberto said they planned to do the minimum in response to the teacher's assignments.

Oppositional Culture of Working-Class and Latino Youth

The boys were building an oppositional culture designed to frustrate the teacher's goals just below the level of a disciplinary response. In the battleground that was school, they had become the enemies of Mrs. Webb – and the enemies of the "unthinking" classmates perceived to follow her -- much like the working-class white youth of Paul Willis' classic study examining the schools' complicity in maintaining the

CHAPTER 4: HOMESTEAD HIGH SCHOOL 153

British class system (1977). The more they rebelled against her assignments, the more students limited their options for the future, one way the schools unknowingly promulgate inequity – with students' consent. Willis, too, found the boys he studied essentially chose their own working-class fate – they rejected both the teacher and pro-school students, "the ear'oles" -- in part because of cultural prescriptions that emphasized physicality and masculinity over mental prowess. The idea of individual choice – the rebelliousness Roberto so favored – only has currency for the choices of upper-middle class youth, Willis wrote:

> The whole ideology and language of developmental psychology with its centrality of the individual and the meaningful choices open to him makes its entrance. "Personal development,' 'self-concept,' 'occupational choice,'all gain a currency where they are only really a tautological and individualised distortion of the cultural level turning on the pivot of spurious difference – in individuals and in the jobs available (188).

In this respect, the rejection of news and news careers in the unlikely figure of Mrs. Webb, also meant the rejection of power in the world, a reality which the boys, still struggling in school, did not consciously recognize.

This is not to say that young people at Homestead would never overcome their circumstances – that would be cynical in the extreme -- but it was strikingly apparent that the school, or anyone who wielded control, held low expectations of boys like Enrique and Roberto, probably out of the fear that they would become disruptive. The boys ended up finding unofficial ways of obtaining power and solidarity. In her study of Latino youth, Valenzuela found that their self-representations and resistance to school intensify teachers' assumptions that students are troublemakers (61):

> From these adults' perspective, the way youth dress, talk and generally deport themselves 'proves' that they do not care about school. For their part, students argue that they should be assessed, valued and engaged as whole people, not as automatons in baggy pants. . . they prefer a model of schooling premised on respectful, caring relations.

English-speaking teachers see language and cultural differences in students but dismiss them and any responsibility they have to make their instruction culturally relevant, Valenzuela argued. Teachers and counselors "more often lament their students' linguistic limitations than they do their own" (66).

Mexican-American students' rejection of the pro-school ethos was a way the school actually divided Mexican-born and U.S. born youth. Valenzuela identified a cultural need for students to discuss openly the differences in social identities among them, as it appeared critical to self-awareness about their visions of school and school performance. "When immigrant youth become unavailable either as friends or potential sources of academic support, U.S.-born youth are shut off from the pro-school, achievement-oriented ethos that prevails among so many of them," she writes. While American-born students expressed respect for parents who were Mexican-born, they did not always consider themselves members of the same social circles at Homestead as the more recent Mexican immigrants. In journalism class at Homestead, the students usually sat apart. Immigrants such as Delia and Ana expressed shock at some of the behavior of their American-born classmates, particularly at open disrespect for authority.

There were plenty of ways in which Mrs. Webb discredited students' views and cultural heritage in her wish to uphold American traditions. One of Roberto's assignments was supposed to be about Lincoln's Birthday, and I could see that it was not very newsworthy. The next question for a journalist would be, "What about Lincoln's birthday?" He said angrily, "It's not news. I am going to put my name on that article, and I don't think it's worth my name. I feel it's not worth me putting my effort into it." What was news? The imposition of an exit exam on the junior class, he said. "That would be like a terrorist attack on us within the [school] community. That would be something students would want to see." Yet even if Mrs. Webb could allow more latitude to journalism students, the climate of the school was very much one in which adults kept strict control and students had little. The student newspaper had become more of a class project than a forum for student expression. It was questionable whether Roberto would have done the story about the exit exam had Mrs. Webb given him permission. In many ways, journalism, perhaps the news itself, had become a point of separation between teenagers and adults, a way of defining each other, particularly where students like Enrique and Roberto were concerned. A recent 60 Minutes edition (January 8, 2004) demonstrated the way adults in the heavily Latino Houston school system sharply underestimated the number of dropouts so that they could win recognition and money. This was similar to the way Homestead pushed

CHAPTER 4: HOMESTEAD HIGH SCHOOL 155

testing on its students, whether it was beneficial for their learning or not. In fairness, the school had little choice.

Roberto compared news of terrorism to "an ex-girlfriend who won't leave you alone and they keep stalking you even if you got a girlfriend already and they can't realize it." He had no desire to write about the issue and could not grasp why Mrs. Webb kept pressing the class to do it. I found a plausible explanation for student reluctance to deal with the Iraq War in the work of ethnic studies scholar George Lipsitz. Lipsitz argues in *The Possesive Investment in Whiteness* (1998) that the patriotism that surfaced during the Gulf War was disingenuous in a nation so dedicated – in subtle and not-so-subtle ways -- to the advancement of white people's education, jobs, housing, even environmental health. "In times of crisis, the illusion that all contradictions and differences would be solved if we would only agree to one kind of culture, one kind of education, one kind of patriotism, one kind of sexuality, and one kind of family can be comforting." But this comfort is mainly in the interest of white privilege. The book presents the argument that whites have benefited from systemic efforts from colonial times to the present to create economic advantage for European-Americans. It makes sense, then, that there could be, among disenfranchised Mexican-American students, frustration, even an outpouring of doubt at the worth and purpose of a war directed at an enemy which was dark and foreign. Perhaps the war was not in the best economic interests of working-class kids, who actually might have to fight and die in larger numbers because of the ease of accessing college aid through military service.

In *The Ethnic Eye* (1996), Chon Noriega details the hard-fought Chicano Civil Rights Movement and the difficulty film and TV writers experienced securing chances to produce their own media and create "our own institutions." He discusses the unification of four student groups under a single organization – El Movimiento Estudiantil Chicano de Azlan (the Chicano Student Movement of Azlan or M.E.Ch.A.). "The rejection of the self-designation 'Mexican-American' in favor of 'Chicano' and the fact that mecha is vernacular Spanish for "match," underscored the student movement's militant nationalism.," he writes. The newspaper covered the campus M.E.Ch.A. chapter but not in any great detail. An article in the February 13, 2003 edition about the group's annual retreat emphasized that the organization would help students "come through with all their plans," learn about the history of Chicanos in the U.S., maintain their grades and expand brotherhood or sisterhood. Although its roots were highly political, the Homestead group seemed more social in nature. The group may have taken the least controversial direction it could with students, which was to foster their individual goals while upholding their heritage. However, MECh.A.'s influence was unclear. The story had been assigned to the least experienced and newest writer on the newspaper staff.

Primacy of the local?

What role did a single classroom, led by a white, conservative teacher, play in these teenagers' rejection of conventional journalism and politics, particularly when the professional media were focused on terrorism? The teacher was not openly cynical about the media in front of them, but she did not give them much reason to like journalistic practices either. There was no discussion of the war as anything deeper than a threatening event. Perhaps she could have been more open about her own feelings regarding Iraq and presented other views –if students were willing to listen. It may be true, as Neil Hollander suggested after Vietnam (1971), that "today's politics are the politics of war" (the subject of terrorism seemed to dominate the media after September 11, 2001 so that there was no journalism without considering the issue). Yet student exploration of political decisions was more complicated because of their fear and other emotional responses to terror. Mrs. Webb faced a class disinclined toward American politics to begin with, They were even more dismissive when it became clear that war had become the central preoccupation of political life. Perhaps they were more political than a narrow definition of politics would indicate and needed to grasp the true impact of the news on them. An introduction to Lipsitz' ideas might have politicized the class or at least made them less complacent. If young people could only succeed in school by accepting a white, middle class vision of themselves, what was lost in the process?

The youth of the Vietnam era faced the question of the draft. Their friends were dying. In some ways, the contemporary threat of terrorism for California students only could fuel a sense of fatalism about the future that did not advance their motivation to achieve. Students might have been able to get help from parents, but their participation in Electoral politics also was low. Rosemarie Moser, editor of *Shocking Violence II: Violent Disaster, War, and Terrorism Affecting Our Youth* (2002, 5-9), suggests that reason and reassurance can help young people cope with crises. In fact, this study might suggest that journalism – with its emphasis on the collection of divergent views and their organized presentation -- could be an effective tool to deal with the incomprehensible. Through a newspaper, students also might explore

CHAPTER 4: HOMESTEAD HIGH SCHOOL 157

questions of racism and dispossession, why certain groups andindividuals hate Americans and whether the criminal justice system can ever make a democratic society safe from terrorism (McCauley 2003).

The problem is that such discussions integrating and processing what has happened to the nation require "an atmosphere of connectedness," which did not exist in Mrs. Webb's classroom. So-called normal adolescence in which teenagers may feel omnipotent, as though nothing tragic can happen to them, might take a different form among these youth, who certainly had experienced disappointment, tragedy and most probably violence. An authentic conversation needed to give students a chance to voice their own experiences. They would care about politics if they could more easily see how it mattered to them. For example, perhaps they could have read the story of a Mexican-born soldier, killed in action, and discussed the downsides of taking the military option for poor youth. The tie-in to school and students in the class was very important so that students probably only should have included stories on terror with a Homestead angle.

Demonstrating the immediacy of the issue elsewhere in the nation, Nikki Atkinson, a high school student in Fairfax, Va., much closer to the attacks, told a Congressional hearing that life was different because her classmates were "worried about anthrax and another possible attack. Many of us are rethinking our career options:"

> At school, teachers were willing to take time out of class to let us talk about our feelings. They never pretended that they had the answers, and they never told us that our feelings were wrong or invalid. They just listened. This helped us to gradually assimilate back into our daily routines. But all the while, there is still the gnawing fear in the back of our minds – what will the terrorists do next? S(Senate Subcomittee on Children and Families, November 2, 2001)

Distance did not mean Homestead students were incapable of an intellectual discussion about the attacks. They needed to speak without the sense that judgment or an assignment would come immediately after the talk. They needed to know they were in a safe place to talk. The newspaper was theirs, whether or not they wanted to cover terrorism.

Fear about the war again depended on whether friends and family were afraid, and young people's apparent apathetic nature when it came to news had much to do with the uninvolved roles they were encouraged to assume in school. For Mexican-American young people, in particular, the family probably played a more primary role than Hollander suggested when he called the mass media "the new parent."

Most of the class was Latino and even Jessica had been raised since age 4 by a Mexican-American stepmother. This ethnic group might resist the media and politics with greater persistence than others. In the Journal of Broadcasting & Electronic Media (1993), Erica Weintraub Austin and C. Leigh Nelson write that previous research supports "lower efficacy for Hispanics, reflecting a fatalistic attitude, less skepticism, knowledge and political communication as a result of less interest in politics for Hispanics" (422). Students generally showed more interest in local issues than distant or national ones and demonstrated greater facility discussing more culturally relevant topics affecting the Hispanic community. Because family and community are so important to these young people's development, efforts to improve students' civic involvement should encompass entire households, not only individuals (McDevitt and Chaffee 2002).

After Terrorism

The Homestead Herald after the terrorism issue was devoted to the holidays, with stories about New Year's resolutions and the meaning of Christmas so that the body image idea was sacrificed, then lost out to Valentine's Day. The topics seemed to get lighter as the year went on. The first issue of the year had contained Delia's story on a local press conference about child molestation. A later issue focused on the dangers substance abuse but treated it more as a lifestyle magazine might. These were teacher-directed themes. They were not too far a field from the *Cosmo Girl* approach, and perhaps they carried greater student interest. Mrs. Webb did not pursue world issues for the rest of the year. The school calendar was her main source of ideas. Enrique ended up transferring to an alternative program so that he would earn enough credits to graduate with his class next year, and Roberto decided to switch electives to drama. Roberto's decision came shortly after the story assignment about Lincoln's Birthday. In her own defense, Mrs. Webb said the two boys were only interested in writing about arts and entertainment and thought what was important to them was important to everyone. "I want them to have ownership," she insisted when we discussed the complaints about the body image section. "I want it to be their paper. I don't want it to be my paper." Yet Lincoln's Birthday wasn't the only holiday Mrs. Webb assigned to students as a story.

The news editor wrote a story in the terrorism edition called "Remembering Columbus." Despite a spate of criticism directed at

Columbus and his negative legacy for native populations, there was no mention of anything critical about the holiday:
This year the holiday parade was called 'Columbus Day Parade of Patriotism'. .Thousand [sic] of people attended the event to show the spirit of freedom, appreciation and support to the men and women of our military (2).

This report came despite the fact that activists in at least 20 cities nationally had protested the holiday including in San Diego and Tijuana, Mexico. "The holiday, once an optimistic celebration of America's discovery, has been condemned by some as an archaic, "Euro-centric" holiday that demeans indigenous Americans," wrote Jennifer Harper of *The Washington Times* (October 14, 2003). " – and the Spanish, Italian and Portuguese explorers who followed – were 'worse than Hitler,' said Venezuelan President Hugo Chavez in Caracas on Saturday, noting that they triggered 'the biggest invasion and genocide ever seen in the history of humanity.'" Pacifica radio covered the issue extensively on its program Democracy Now! (October 14, 2003), interviewing American Indian Movement protesters in Washington, D.C. and others.

The teacher did not challenge the news editor's story, and students accepted this unquestioningly. There was no denying that students appeared more interested in rejecting the news than using it to learn. The teacher awkwardly tried to change this at times but could not. When she told students that terrorism was "hot," justifying their need to cover it, she sounded like a tabloid editor or talk show producer rather than a journalism educator. In other words, she was not very convincing. Delia was among the few in the class who professed an interest in news. While a couple of students said they watched local TV news, she managed to read the local daily newspaper. When I asked her how she decided to write her story on the child molestation press conference, Delia said: "[Mrs. Webb] told me what to do." This was instruction but needed to be combined with stories the students actually chose and wrote.

On the face of it, Delia had accomplished a feat just to attend Homestead High School because her family was living in two places, with her aunt nearby and with her grandfather in Tijuana. She was hardly in a position to make more independent decisions. She was assistant editor but the long commutes made it impossible for her to stay after school. Delia was proud of the front-page story she wrote, "Officials Address Sex Offenders in National City," but an important element of the lead was buried in a photo caption saying that 141 registered sex offenders lived in the community around the school. However, a news-feature is difficult to write and could be written in many ways. The actual lead was: "People across the nation have tuned into the trial about [a local child] who was kidnapped and murdered in [a nearby community] on February 1. . . ." The story goes on to mention another man in the local area who exposed himself to female students and then quotes principal Mr. Frank warning students to be careful.

Delia forfeited the assistant editor post to Lupita. This might have bothered her more if the school was more interested in its newspaper. There was not much of an enthusiastic audience, Delia said, as students at the upper-middle class Coastal High also said. There was no reaction to the child molestation story. During Delia's sixth-period history class, the day the newspapers with the terrorism theme were delivered, she noticed some newspapers left over:

Like a lot. I was telling everyone, 'read my article, read my article.' Some of them did. . . And then my teacher threw all of them away! I said to him, 'Do you know how long we have to work on that newspaper? We spend all this time so that you guys will read it. He said, 'Well, nobody wants the newspaper. Do you guys? Do you want them?' I was like, 'Oh, my God.' Nobody raised their hands. They didn't. He threw them away.

B. Forging Identities in Newspaper Class: Why Body Image?

Enrique was seven years old, and his little brother, 2, when his father, a mechanic, died on the freeway. A police officer had impounded the car but did not take him off Interstate 5. He made it across the lanes but was struck as he tried to use an emergency telephone. A lawyer told his mother she did not have a case, and she believed him, although the family has been told since that this may have been a mistake. Since his death, money has been scarce. The family has relied on the mother's disability check plus $500 in monthly government assistance for the two boys. Yet there are moments when poverty does not seem to matter. Enrique said he was surprised when his mother got him the guitar he had always wanted. The salesman cut the price from $500 to $222 "so my mom said.. 'We might as well get it then.' I was surprised . . . I had only about $100." The way his father had been killed and the family's subsequent deprivation may have sent a message to Enrique about their importance. He no longer trusted the police, yet this early trauma would not be the only cause. He carried the guitar everywhere, treasuring it as his most prized possession, cradling it like gold. It was an extension of his body.

He and Roberto, the band's lead singer, practiced with friends, including a third journalism student, in Enrique's garage. "If I'm going anywhere, I ask mom if she can give me a ride because I don't want to walk, I don't want to get the guitar stolen." Enrique had much greater interest in music than journalism, although he liked to write and was impressed by the teenage journalist in the movie "Almost Famous." Toward his band, he showed the kind of motivation that Mrs. Webb said she sought toward the newspaper. Enrique said:

I've been practicing. I do that as much as I can so that when we do have a session, I play well. I don't play the notes wrong or nothing, So I already know the timing. I also like it because when I come to school during lunch, I play and all my friends, if they know the songs, they start singing them.

The boys all dreamed of a record contract. What Enrique wanted to do with their songs was to make people feel happy and understood, to play songs young people could relate to, that encouraged them not to give up. The band played punk and hard rock but did not want to be lumped into a single category. While his mother encouraged him with the guitar, she did not press him to get good grades. "As long as I have a C, my mom says I'm OK, as long as I'm passing." When neighbors complain about the noise and the police show up, threatening to confiscate instruments, his mother tells him "just keep playing. She'd rather have us in the house practicing instead of on the street."

The garage band's heavy use of punk sounds was political, their way of expressing frustration with working-class lives and the educational system. Their musical tastes – such "new punk" bands as *Blink 182* and *Good Charlotte* – were made up of white, not Chicano artists (Blink 182 originated not far away in Southern California, but *Good Charlotte* came from Waldorf, Maryland). They had broad appeal for young people of many different ethnicities, evidenced by the Good Charlotte hits that blasted daily at my gym for largely white suburbanites in Orange County, Ca. In *Dangerous Crossroads* (1994), Lipsitz argues that the global accessibility of many musical forms is a way capitalism both corrupts local meaning and provides a chance for "a new public sphere with emancipatory potential:"

The cross-cultural communication carried on within today's contemporary popular music retains residual contradictions of centuries of colonialism, class domination and racism. But it also speaks to currents of culture and politics emerging from fundamentally new geopolitical and economic realities. The rapid mobility of capital and populations across the globe has problematized traditional understandings of place and made displacement a widely shared experience (5).

Lipsitz demonstrates that urban identity -- long rooted in particular struggles within cities and states --- now has become more a matter of connections between places, with musicians building their identities by borrowing from cultures throughout the world. Enrique's seeming lack of identification with his ethnic identity in his music, too, was not unusual, Lipsitz' research demonstrates (84-90).

Young Chicanos launched punk bands in the late 1970s and early 1980s with East Los Angeles groups including *Lost Illegals, Odd Squad, the Bags and the Brat.* The Eastside revival "seemed remarkable mostly for its distance from Mexican-American culture," Lipsitz writes. "Chicano punk rockers adopted the simple chord structures, driving rhythms, energetic amateurism, and 'pogo' dancing first made popular by working-class dropouts and art school bohemians in England and appropriated by alienated suburban youth in the U.S.A." Lipsitz contends, "the appropriation of punk rock music by young Chicanos was a means of making visible aspects of their lives and culture that would otherwise be ignored." He cites Therese Covarrubias of *the Brat* who was raised in an English-speaking home, learning Spanish only in school. "Her father liked listening to the big-band sound of the Benny Goodman orchestra, while her older brothers and sisters introduced her to Bob Dylan, *the Rolling Stones*, and *the Who*. Covarrubias listed British pop and rock performers David Bowie and Bryan Ferry as her own favorites; nowhere in her genealogy of musical influences did she recall any Chicano artists." This would seem as though Covarrubias is part of a generation for whom ethnicity is irrelevant, but she feared being labeled a Chicana artist might cut her off from mainstream radio. In another case, an East Los Angeles Chicano band, *Los Lobos*, mixes "surrealism, jazz and Japanese instruments with rock n'roll on their album *Kiko* – not as a way of denying their Mexican heritage but rather as a way of claiming citizenship in a larger artistic and political world as *part* of the Chicano experience" (90).

Enrique's mother agreed to his pierced ears -- with hesitation. He dyed his hair a different color every two weeks or so, from blond to blue to maroon to pink, and he wore a hoop in his lips. Otherwise, his school clothes were not outrageous, usually khaki pants and T-shirts. I asked about the way he presented himself:

SEA: OK, you have earrings. You have a hoop in your lips. This kind of stuff, why do you do it?
Enrique: I do it for a number of reasons. It's for the band because it makes a good image for the band. Another reason is because I like it, and I also like to

CHAPTER 4: HOMESTEAD HIGH SCHOOL 163

look different. Somebody looks around on campus and they see a pink head. They know it's me. I like it because everybody can point me out no matter what. The lip ring. I don't know. My favorite guitarist is Tom Delonge. He's from Blink 182. He's really, really funny, and he only has his lip pierced and his ears pierced and he used to have his eyebrow [pierced]. I'm planning on getting my eyebrow soon, but I don't know, I'm kind of scared.

Punk began in the 1970s in Britain as "an attempt to use fashion and clothing to challenge class identities and positions," wrote Malcolm Barnard in *Fashion as Communication* (2001, 1996, 136-138). The movement also was a statement against the predictable fashions offered to the young by large corporations. With punk styles, "the rules and norms of conventional attractiveness were generally broken, flouted and ignored" using do-it-yourself styles that were supposed to be more representative of the working classes. "In this sense then punk may be seen as reversing the privilege accorded to styles, fabrics and colors. What was considered good taste by the dominant classes is opposed by using what was considered poor taste by those classes." In the Homestead classroom, the appropriation of Punk styles was viewed as personal, a way of setting oneself apart from everyone else in high school and being tenaciously different. This was so important to Enrique and Roberto that if they saw anyone at school trying to be like them, they changed colors or the pants they wore. Originality was a political statement, yet the boys did not define it this way.

A Military Future?

If the band idea did not succeed, Enrique said he planned to enter the Marines, something that surprised me given his other inclinations. "Won't that be kind of hard for you?" I asked him, " somebody who is kind of funky and likes to be an individual. It seems like the military would take all of your individuality away." He struggled to explain the inconsistency, but his limited choices probably boiled down to finances:
Enrique: They would, but I was in ROTC a while so I already know how to do that. But I got out – barely.

SEA: Barely?
Enrique: They weren't going to let me out because I was a really good cadet, they said, and they really needed me. But I didn't want to be in it because I needed to work on my personality more. . . ROTC was bringing the band down kind of because people would say it doesn't really look like he's actually in a rock band.

The work of ethnic studies scholar Jorge Mariscal sheds light on Enrique's conflict. Enrique told me he liked both the Marines – the uniform, marching, rifles and combat – and his punk band. How was this possible?

In an article for the political newsletter *Counterpunch* on the militarization of U.S. culture (May 5, 2003), Mariscal points to the story of Jesus Gonzalez who during high school organized against the anti-immigrant Proposition 187 and in support of Native American environmental causes. "Despite his early childhood formation within progressive circles, Gonzalez surprised everyone he knew when he decided to drop out of college because he had to be a Marine," wrote Mariscal:

Drawing upon distorted notions of masculinity, the glamour of the uniform, and the myth of rugged individualism, military recruitment ads – a solitary Marine scaling the face of a mountain, for example – cast a spell to which working class youth are especially susceptible. A relative lack of economic and educational opportunies seals the ideological deal. In Gonzalez's case, the fantasy of military service overwhelmed the humanistic values with which he had been raised.

Gonzelez was killed in action in Iraq April 12, 2003. Mariscal criticizes as destructive the incursion of JROTC units in American schools since the 1990s, saying they attract youths unsure of their future to the military. He suggests the messages of the Marines on an official website that youths will be treated as family if they join and 'you are special, you are a fighter, we will take care of you' are especially seductive "for young men and women without economic privilege and who often do not enjoy stability at home."

Both boys were juniors, but Roberto had no future plans other than the band, saying, "I am just hoping we make it because school-wise, I don't think I have a long shot at going to college. I would have to go to community college. So basically my life is riding on this band." He earned side money by piercing other students' bodies. He explained one technique that involved making a hole and then stretching it, "making it bigger with certain tools so it hurts." He pointed to his ears, which had small metallic cups embedded in the lobes. "It's basically like an addiction because once you have something, you want it again," said Enrique. "Even though you know it hurts, you say, 'OK it'll go away.' It hurts but you feel you need it," Roberto said of his piercing business, "It's mostly a hobby. It relaxes me, I guess. Like I just pierced my lip

yesterday. I did it last night. My mom was looking at me and she said, 'You must like pain or something.'"
"It probably did hurt," I said, wincing.
"Yeah, and I did it really slow. But it's weird. If I don't have something throbbing or something sore, then I feel weird."
The popularity of piercing was directly related to pain. The piercing also came because young people wanted control, particularly in the school environment where everything was proscribed. The only things Homestead students may have felt they had control over were their bodies. At Homestead, it also was a way to make them feel something beyond the numbness they exhibited in the classroom. Piercing among teenagers was not necessarily related to socioeconomic status. To adults, such behavior could appear less like self-expression and more like self-destruction, perhaps indicating depression or even suicidal ideation. In fact, many forms of popular culture among teens involve self-mutilation, the act of deliberately hurting one's skin with pins, staples, cuts, burns and tattoos. Examples of pop icons who commit bodily harm, depending on one's point of view, are Marilyn Manson, who has rubbed broken glass on his body on MTV and basketball star Dennis Rodman, who dyes his hair many colors, has multiple piercings and wears tattoos.
By making themselves bizarre, youth sometimes identify their culture with the homeless, drug users, drifters. This could be social commentary through style or an indication that they are dissatisfied with their own lives. In *A Bright Red Scream* (1999), Marlilee Strong describes one young man whose acts to harm himself were a way of managing a sense of internal chaos in his life (1999). Self-harm has become accepted in contemporary youth culture, but there is no definitive answer as to why.
Enrique decided to take journalism when he heard the teacher was looking for people. He had Mrs. Webb in the beginning of sophomore year and liked her but transferred out after half the semester because of scheduling problems. He was pretty sure she did not remember him from that time. He appeared to wish she did. Mrs. Webb made him assistant news editor, a title that did not mean much to him except more work. Roberto, too, was honored to be in the class because he had not thought he was good enough, something I had also heard others say about themselves. As one of their first stories, Roberto and Enrique wrote an article on a teenage band. I was impressed by the fact that they interviewed the members, attended a concert, and listened to the music. It was a first-hand research effort not often seen in the class. "We consider ourselves a starting band and the advice we would give to other bands is practice, practice, practice," the band's vocalist, also a guitarist,

remarked in the article. The group's web site is included at the end of the story, and so is a photo (*The Homestead Herald*, September 11, 2002). The third member of the class, also in Enrique's band, had enough dedication to music he would go to the public library to download songs on a zip disk, burning CDs at a friend's house. Their love of music gave students incentive to learn and use new technology. Without money for the latest gadgets, students adopted strategies for access.

The students' band, "Nothing in Common," is about "doing what you feel and singing what you think," said Roberto. "You just don't want to be a trend." But in some ways, the boys were becoming a part of a trend by buying into what had become a media-driven fad, even as they tried to avoid it. Enrique's hero punk rocker Tom Delonge of *Blink 182* attended but never graduated high school.

It may have inspired them that Good Charlotte's twin brothers, Benji and Joel, who launched the group, came from a working-class background. They had little money or equipment and no industry connections, according to the band's official web site (GoodCharlotterocks.com, July 15, 2003). Opportunity came when their song, "Can't Go On," won a local contest and the band was offered a supporting role in a series of already-sold-out East Coast concerts. "We had no money, no transportation and no way to do the gigs," Benji said (Sony Music Entertainment July 2003.) "Our mom was living in like a shed on our neighbor's property, and the only thing she really owned was a mini-van. She said, 'You guys take the mini-van to play the shows and I'll catch rides or walk to work.' That just shows you how she's been there for us the whole time." Enrique had to be struck by similarities between the twins' mother and his own. The twins did not think of starting a band until age 16, shortly after their father walked out on them. Teens could sympathize with their songs of home disruption.

Students defined themselves and peer groups by what music they enjoyed. In fact, sociologist and rock critic Simon Frith writes that leisure is a serious issue for youth and an outlet for working-class tensions:

> Leisure has become the only setting for the experience of self, for the exploration of one's own skills and capacities, for the development of creative relations with other people. But this experience is, by its very nature, fleeting; and rock n'roll began as American working class music – the music of a class that has rarely been symbolized as a class. American class experience is mediated through historical images of individual achievement and failure;

workers remember their past in terms of mobility rather than solidarity, self-sufficiency rather than socialism. Rock 'n' roll accounts of loneliness and rebellion *celebrate* the conditions that produce them; rock's dominant value has always been tolerance.

The words of Good Charlotte spoke to high school students and did not preach to them in a way that they hated in school. The band's words also were political in that they discussed powerlessness as well as the dangers of materialism. The music was personal, and the teens associated politics not with themselves but adulthood and staid old men in suits. Teens use rock music, but uses and interpretations vary. As media scholarship since the rejected hypodermic models of the 1970s have argued, rock lyrics do not cause guaranteed reactions in listeners. They are personal; people are attracted to popular music based on how it seems to represent their own experiences and beliefs.

The lyrics to Good Charlotte's song "The Anthem" were testament to student resistance to their schooling and an overwhelming sense of boredom:

It's a new day, but it all feels old/
   It's a good life that's what I'm told/
But everything it all feels the same
   And my high school it felt more to me
      like a jail cell a penitentiary

"The Story of My Old Man" is about a father who is drunk and leaves his family, and it rails against teens repeating the mistakes of adults around them. The band tells listeners, "This is the story of my old man/ Just like his father before him./ I'm telling you to do anything you can/ So you don't end up just like them." "Hold On" may inspire teens who are close to giving up. "We all bleed the same way you do/ We all have the same things to go thru/ Hold on/ If you feel like letting go/ Hold on/ It gets better than you know." The teens applied the band's lyrics to their own lives. The words spoke to their hopes for success, control and freedom. "If I stumble and I fall, should I get up and carry on, or will it all just be the same? "Cause I'm young and hopeless, I'm lost and I know this. I'm going nowhere fast that's what they say."

Good Charlotte serves as an example of the way hegemony can function because the band's oppositional songs have been appropriated by mainstream capitalism and sold to young people, rich and poor, thus rendering their original rebellion less menacing to dominant interests. The appeal to mainstream youth is part of the marketing strategy of popular bands. Dick Hebdige, building on the theories of Stuart Hall and Antonio Gramsci, attempts to capture the complexity of the process by which some social groups retain their power over others -- with their consent -- by making their own authority appear commonsensical. The process of incorporation – the acceptance of marginal forms by the mainstream – is never automatic but always contested. He writes,

> Style in subculture is, then, pregnant with significance. Its transformations go 'against nature,' interrupting the process of 'normalization.' As such, they are gestures, movements towards a speech which offends the 'silent majority,' which challenges the principles of unity and cohesion, which contradicts the myth of consensus.

His work lends support to the notion that pop music can still be very valuable for youth resistance, despite its manipulation on the marketplace. Hebdige contends that working class youth "in part contest and in part agree with the dominant definitions of who and what they are, and there is a substantial amount of shared ideological ground" between them and the adult working class and the dominant culture in its more accessible forms (86). Songs carry powerful meaning for youth, even if they do not erase class inequity.

Indeed, Frith writes that "rock operates as counterculture only at moments. There are creative breakthroughs, when the music does express the needs of real communities, but it never takes the industry long to control and corrupt the results. Indeed, the record companies' task has been made easier by the confusion of countercultural ideology within the ideology of youth." The importance of rock in the creation of identity for working class young people cannot be overstated, however, according to Frith, and this probably made the teacher's goals unattainable without a recognition of the value of teen music and styles: Music appeared to welcome the students without judgment so that journalism could better compete when it made space for music.

Because arts and entertainment appealed to the students more than the adults around them, Mrs. Webb might have been better off encouraging them to pursue this topic deeply. A guitar and CD player in the classroom seemed more like a potential disruption to her than an opportunity. Instead of writing about Abraham Lincoln Day, what if Roberto had been assigned to write about the history of punk rock or to interview teens about why it was popular locally? As Jessica had stated earlier, no one could make anyone else care about world events. In professional newspapers, writers do specialize. Of course, this could not be the only issue students explored. Mrs. Webb's self-described conservatism and allegiance to the school's authoritarian style made it difficult for her to listen to students' voices or help them find story ideas in what they said. Mostly it was me who tried to do that in my long conversations with them. Roberto originally wanted to write for the school newspaper because it would be his "chance to complain," he said. Mrs. Webb was finding it difficult to give students more responsibility, but it seemed as though she had a chance with them, particularly at the beginning of the course.

The two newest students in January 2003, Jessica and Kimberly, both white, who said they had a serious interest in politics, also took their music very seriously. Their interest probably would help the class the following year, Mrs. Webb said. For them, politics was personal. Kimberly wrote on a question sheet for the study (March 13, 2003):

My favorite activity out of school is going to music shows. The whole environment is so much fun. Everyone there has a different perspective on life other than the cookie-cutter version other people do. Protests are great, too, for the same reasons.

Unlike others in the class, Jessica was less enamored with the punk bands appealing to teenagers. She called *Blink 182* and *Good Charlotte* "happy bands" and said "what we listen to kind of goes more to what we believe in." These bands included *Anti-Flag* and *Crass* (a band that sounded more like screaming and noise when this researcher sampled its album "Yes Sir, I Will"). "It doesn't mean anti-the American Flag," Kimberly said of Anti-Flag. "It means what you believe in." Kimberly authored an unusual front-page story on an all-day workshop training student activists at a local university cafe. The article was an advertisement for the left-leaning group that organized the event. It began:

For students who know that there are injustices in the world and would like to help rid the world of these injustices there are many people that would welcome you and help you become active in the struggle for the constant betterment of all.

Breakout sessions voiced opposition to war, opposed military entry into high schools, and favored vegetarian cooking (The Homestead Herald, March 20, 2003). The appearance of the story showed that students who wanted to write on specific political topics could do so under circumstances that the teacher approved. However, the story was about something Kimberly enjoyed doing, and it did not reflect the interests of the rest of campus. No Homestead students were quoted. The event was at least a half-hour's drive away. The story below it was more typical, about Black History Month.

Yet her story showed Kimberly's interest in using the paper for advocacy. Anarchy was a misunderstood movement and more peaceful than most people thought, she told me. "The people today who are anarchists just don't think you should have one set of rules. If they don't like it, they go live on their own." Just as Mrs. Webb did not know the depth of the boys' interest in punk rock, she had little idea that she had invited two girls investigating anarchy into the journalism classroom either. Jessica said her style created a stir whenever she made trips to rural Ohio to visit her mother, who was remarried with a new family. "I show up and I wear all black on Sunday. They might as well have stoned me. I got looks from little old ladies and it was terrible. And I'm like, 'at home, that's normal.' I was wearing fishnet stockings and the black skirt and a black sweater because it was cold." The identity of the two girls was wrapped up in "pushing the envelope," as Jessica put it, and her oppositional style of black dress also was an attempt to make a statement. Her hero was Henry David Thoreau. Kimberly, the sole AP student in the class, wore '50s preppy clothes that looked like they came from second-hand stores but also a lip ring. Kimberly led protests against the Iraq War, met with students on campus for a political organizing session and said she and Jessica wanted to start a political page of the newspaper. Kimberly said she became political because of what she ate. She became a vegetarian after reading more about it.

When the two girls first entered the class, Jessica said, Mrs. Webb:

gave us rules, guidelines to go by so I want to be able to express my opinion, but I am going to have that fear that one of the administrators will get mad. She says when it comes down to it, she'll tell us if it's too risqué, but I'm not afraid to go to that point. A good writer is not afraid to take a chance. That's what gets you noticed.

Mrs. Webb did not attach these guidelines to professional journalistic ethics. Although Jessica and Kimberly had musical tastes that they associated with distinct world views, the ideas of Enrique and Roberto were not so different from them as they might have thought. All the teenagers shared desire for originality. Mrs. Webb might have been able to capitalize on this desire as she continued to teach journalism. Instead, her claims that students would gain credibility by writing about terrorism did not seem to have an effect. Most students did not want credibility. Unlike students who wrote for an award-winning high school paper across town (discussed in the next chapter), those at Homestead did not perceive themselves to be journalists.

Recalling the newspaper's tepid nature, I asked Jessica and Kimberly if they had ever read it before they joined the class? They both said they had. "What are your thoughts on it?" I asked.

Jessica; Bland.
Kimberly: There's nothing in there. It needs some spice.
SEA: There's nothing in there?
Jessica: There's stuff in there, but I don't want to offend anybody, when you think about it, it's kind of like ditzy stuff, like sweethearts is coming up and let's talk about the pep rally and the football game. You can't get involved in the pep rally.
SEA: In a political way? You want to add politics to the class?
Kimberly: I do have this fear that I will be sharing things that are real personal, and you don't want to put your music out there to be a trend. We want people to like it because that's what they believe in.
Jessica: I was a little bummed out when I went into Hot Topic, and I saw anarchy stuff everywhere. It's a trend now. It's supposed to be a belief. You don't go in there and see Bibles everywhere.
(Field notes, January 14, 2003)

They hated trends and looked for the real meaning beneath the surface. *Hot Topic* is a mall-based chain of retail stores with commodities that appeal to teenagers looking to be part of the latest fashion. They can buy underground club, punk, or gothic clothing, band t-shirts and other items. For the girls, it was hard to see their interests marketed and sold as products when the ideas behind them were so important. It reminded me of the first time I heard an editor refer to the newspaper as a product. I thought it reduced the First Amendment value of the press if a newspaper was no more important than, say, chewing gum. Yet for other teens, commercialism fired the desire for fame.

Career Paths

Many teens were unsure what career path they might take. Maria wanted to be a writer but not a reporter. The only way she expressed her views was if she was forced. Most students were resistant to the idea of being journalists because as Tony said, "you'd be in a rush your whole life." Said another student: "I have a different kind of mind of what a journalist should be. The media are so pushy about a story, about getting a story done and stuff. And for me, I don't want to be like that." I asked her, "You don't think people like journalists?"

"Yeah, exactly," she responded. "Because sometimes, they don't have their permission. They are just getting too nosey. They don't have a limit. For me, I have a limit to what I write."

There are limits, of course, but this student appeared to be accepting the conventional wisdom that the media were not to be trusted, which fed into the idea that she, too, should be strictly controlled in what she wrote. I had seen this before. The media should exercise good judgment, but students needed to learn how to do that themselves. Maria echoed this adult vision of the high school press.

At most times, Maria blended into the background of the class. Most females were more quiet and reserved. They tended to defer tthe males during class discussions. Delpit writes that most teachers are unaware of this as a cultural issue among Latinas and routinely hold activities in gender-mixed groups, although the girls would be less reticent in single-sex arrangements (170). This tendency may have contributed to a lack of productivity during story idea sessions in journalism class. The girls probably had even greater obsessions than males when it came to music, style, and their bodies. Their favorite magazines were *Seventeen, YM, Cosmo Girl* and *J14*. Ironically after her comments about journalists, Maria said her dream for adulthood was to become a writer for *Cosmo Girl*. Although her father spoke primarily Spanish, Maria considered herself literate only in English, a fact that sometimes estranged the two of them.

She shared an interest with other Latina girls in romance, and women's magazines – mainly in English – fulfilled an important need for her and classmates as they have focused on the formation of female identity since the 1900s.

Today's publishers have vigorously pursued the Hispanic market. However, Arlene Davila (2001) contends that advertisements attempt not only to sell products but also suggest buying them will enable consumers to take part in democracy. Such falsehoods may give girls an inaccuratepicture of what political participation means. In addition, the magazines may encourage inaccurate self-concepts because several girls, already malnourished, claimed they were on diets. Maria defended <u>Cosmo Girl</u> by saying it not only explored hair, makeup and boys but contained articles on such issues as sexual discrimination, harassment and assault. The main headlines in a recent edition (August 2003) were typical, including, "Get a Better Body in Two Weeks!" "Find Your True Love," and ""Why Don't You Have a Boyfriend?"

CHAPTER 4: HOMESTEAD HIGH SCHOOL 173

Susana, a girl who was thinking of college or joining the Coast Guard after school, was news editor and seemed to understand what the role entailed. Unfortunately, she had to transfer out after a semester. "You have to think what if I was the reader?" she told me. "What do I want to read about and then get other people's perspectives." Susana said students in journalism class needed to step beyond themselves to get the opinions of others. This was true, but ideas also could begin with their own knowledge. Journalists learn to keep their eyes open and think of everything that happens to them in their own lives as a potential story. This approach also may cause the media to have an upper-middle class bias, but that was not a danger at Homestead. I asked why Enrique and Roberto did not write about the process of forming a band, but Susana cut in:

> Susana: Because it's probably not about us that's why!
> SEA: The paper's not about you?
> Susana: It's about people and stories.
> Tony: I think we have to give people what they want to read. You have to really try and get into their minds more than what you are thinking about, so it's kind of hard if you want to write and you have ideas about yourself. There's two different types of writing. You have to get more focused on what they are doing.

Tony learned, however, that he could use his own knowledge of an injustice, something that had happened to him, to write a column about an unfair library practice. The column resulted in the library changing its practice, albeit not immediately. This taught him one person with the power of a newspaper could make an impact. When I told Mrs. Webb he showed promise as a journalist, she said, "He's just so aggressive about it."

The comment about Tony's aggression again hinted at a bias against Latino males. His spirited attitude would be admired in an upper-middle class student. The main issue about which Tony seemed to feel strongly was school uniforms, which the students had been required to wear in middle school. He never wanted to go back to them. Control of student dress was a divisive political issue between adults and teens:

> Tony: They think something is going to happen when something really isn't. They'll be like, 'If you wear that, then there's going to be a fight.' But there won't. There won't. It's just a hat. How is a hat going to provoke a fight? Unless you're starting it. Unless you're doing something.
> Susana: The thing with adults. They think everything's gang-like.
> Tony: Your clothes, your hair.

Susana: It's just style.   (Field notes, November 12, 2002)

But Lupita said there had been gang-related fights at school, including a week earlier (Field notes, May 8, 2002). She wrote a feature about a group to help gang members.
This issue extended to gym uniforms and helped teens form negative opinions about authorities that wanted to control their dress. Tony felt the newspaper could not write an editorial critical of something the principal had done or said. The teacher probably would not allow it, Susana said "because she doesn't want the principal ragging on her case about how to run the newspaper." I helped them work on a general editorial about why hats should be allowed in class. Then teens extended this perception of unfair control to all adults who could not understand youth. "Older people have a different view," Tony said. During a focus group discussion about Mr. Frank, the central authority figure in the school, students said he was self-interested and thought he was doing a good job as principal if the physical look of the school and students was in order:

Tony: He's a punk. I don't like him.
SEA: OK, so you don't trust him?
Tony: No.
Susana: Uh huh. I mean, he's good with restricting things, restricting everything.
Tony: Yeah. On Fridays, the football players wear our jerseys, and we used to wear our practice socks, just kind of to be comfortable in school and relax. And he did not let us wear that anymore because the shorts were too long or whatever. I was like, 'They are just shorts.' He said, 'no you have to look better, to represent whatever. They are too long.' It was just a bunch of dumb things. He says, 'Oh, the students look good so I'm a good principal.'
SEA: You could come up with a list of ways you though he was being self-interested and
Tony: All kinds of ways.
Susana: All kinds of ways
SEA: And you could write something that said that. But you don't think there's any way it would ever be printed?
Tony: It wouldn't get printed in the newspaper, but if we made print-outs and hand them out at school maybe. That's the only way.
SEA: You mean like an underground newspaper?
Susana: Yeah.
Tony: It's kind of a way to back the newspaper up. Just print them out and hand them out to people, but I don't think people would read them, and if they would, it wouldn't really matter because they would say, 'What can we do about it? You are just telling us this when we already know it.'

CHAPTER 4: HOMESTEAD HIGH SCHOOL 175

While he was one of the more articulate teenagers, Tony seemed to be floating in life without much direction; He referred to his family's voice constantly in the back of his mind. "In our family, there's some people who didn't do anything after high school, and they say, 'you don't want to end up like them. Be something. Do something. You don't want to be stuck in one place forever." But Tony had little idea how to be somebody, how not to be stuck. He was failing two classes.

C. Political Beliefs, the Media and Self-Assertion

When substitute teacher Dave Perez, 29, one of the rare Latino men in training to teach, took over for Mrs. Webb in the spring of 2003, he was shocked by the nature of the journalism students. He struggled to describe them for an interviewer:

> I found this journalism class to be somehow, somewhat – and this may be an unfair criticism, maybe too hash of a word – but I found it to be somewhat anemic in its energy, and I pictured a class full of kids, maybe an AP class full of kids, who were really proud and embracing the fact that they had a voice and they had an audience and they were, they were going to have a vehicle to express themselves, and it hasn't really turned out [that way].

Instead, Mr. Perez found himself having to push the students to do the minimum, much more than he would have to in another journalism elective, in a different setting.

Having spent the fall working on a grassroots campaign for mayor of the local city, Mr. Perez said he would enter many homes in the area to obtain support, noticing that there were always TVs but not a single bookshelf or any reading material in the living rooms. He saw this as proof that families were not aware of the importance of being "educated citizens." If education was not a priority, then political life also was devalued, he said. "I think these are all things that make it difficult for these kids to steer toward a career, toward taking pride in their academics here at [Homestead] High School" (Interview with Mr. Perez, May 13, 2003).

Most students in the journalism class not only were turned off to journalism but they appeared to be even less interested in Electoral politics, sometimes to a remarkable degree, although this appearance could be deceptive. For example, in one conversation, two journalism students were unsure George W. Bush was president. Their lack of knowledge caused them to reject political talk:

> SEA: I'd like to talk to you about politics.

Linda: Like the president?
Roberto: Politics? I could care less about politics.
Linda: Well, I can't vote so I'm not concerned. Yeah, I really don't care about 'that guy.' Once I get to vote, then I'll start caring.
Roberto: It's weird because sometimes I'll forget who is even the president.
Linda: I don't know who our president is. I thought it was George Bush? Then I thought, 'Oh, he's old news. Never mind.'
Roberto: Isn't . . . it . . . George Bush?
Linda: Oh, it is?
SEA (nodding): Yes. So it's just totally irrelevant when he gets up and makes a speech?
Roberto: It gets on my nerves how people like adults are always saying, 'Oh, you should care what happens to your country. If you don't vote, then you can't complain' and stuff like that. I say, 'I really don't care. Why are you going to try and tell me what to do with my life? I do what I want. And I hate when they try and sit there and change your mind. They say, 'Well, you have to vote because if you don't vote, you can't complain.'
SEA: But you can't vote.
Roberto: True, I can't vote yet. It doesn't matter. But sometimes I say I don't even think I'm going to vote when I get older. I don't know. I could change my mind by the time I'm able to. (Field notes, September 3, 2002)

I include this exchange not to mirror other studies that have declared teenagers incompetent with a very minimal conception of government and history, but to show the extent of the disengagement of some youth who do not feel necessary to the political process. The upper-middle class students were tough on politicians and suspicious of their motives, but they never would have had such a tentative conversation. Such facts as knowledge of the President's name, the day of the week, the month and year, are basic questions a neurologist might use to gauge one's cognitive ability after a traumatic accident. It could not have been true that young people were so unaware as this. Learning about the students' actual knowledge and beliefs required more investigation.

According to Buckingham (2000), young people's lack of knowledge about the news or politics reflects not ignorance or immaturity but disenfranchisement – their purposeful exclusion from such arenas. This is despite the fact that youth clearly are capable of grasping political concepts by the time they are teenagers, as this dissertation has previously confirmed. This disenfranchisement is greater for working class youth, Buckingham contends in *After the Death of Childhood* (178):

CHAPTER 4: HOMESTEAD HIGH SCHOOL 177

Broadly speaking, the middle class or upwardly mobile children were more likely to express a positive interest in and/or knowledge about political issues (as conventionally defined); and there was some evidence that this reflected their own perceptions of their potential futures or at least as 'stakeholders' in society. By contrast, the working-class children, particularly in the U.S. schools, appeared to be less well-informed and more comprehensively alienated.

For a more accurate idea of children's political sense, Buckingham defines the meaning of political thinking as "a view of the political self in collective or social terms."

This is a very broad view that might not be accepted by many journalists, but Buckingham also is critical of the conservative and narrow nature of most news. News must invite skepticism and active engagement, he writes, adding, "News can no longer afford to confine itself to the words and actions of the powerful or to the narrow and exclusive discourses which currently dominate the public sphere of social and political debate." He includes in his definition of politics, "the choice available at school lunches, the attempt to introduce compulsory uniforms, or even the organization of the school playground." It is possible to include as political issues the success of Tiger Woods and the Spice Girls, he contends. He also believes young people would be more engaged in politics if they could vote.

In his book, *Tuned Out: Why Young People Don't Follow the News* (2004), Mindich also argues that journalism must change to attract youths. Traditional news shows do not bother appealing to young people because they know that young people do not watch, an instance of circular logic. At the same time, he is less accepting of today's "entertainment glut," contending it is inconsistent with "quality journalism." He writes that "journalists need to ask whether adding Britney, and perhaps a few young readers, justifies making democracy poorer by the subtraction of serious news" (183). Instead, he advocates initiating children's interest in news early through short breaks during Saturday morning cartoons. " One of the easiest ways to introduce news into a child's diet is to throw it in with the sugary stuff," he maintains. "We should insist that every network (including the Cartoon Network) carry news as a fixed percentage (let's say 5 percent) of its children's programming" (171).

What teens knew

At the same time, teens' political alienation should not be overstated. Teenagers at Homestead were less political than most adults, to be sure, and they suffered from greater apathy than adults. Yet they were concerned about those issues that they felt affected them, either locally or in the school. Because Mexico was not too distant and many close relatives still lived there, it was much easier to get them talking, even in an animated way, about Mexican than U.S. politics. And their knowledge of Mexican elected officials gave them much greater faith in U.S. government officials and politicians than the average white voter. During one focus group discussion with Tony, Lupita and Carlos, all Mexican-Americans, as well as a new Central American student, Mariana, they not only discussed the current president of Mexico, Vincente Fox, but also compared him to the former president, Carlos Salinas Gotari. They were sharply critical of Mexican police, telling stories from personal experience about corruption and police bribe-taking.

Carlos and Lupita had witnessed Lupita's guardian successfully offer $40 to a Mexican cop at a quincenerra to release a friend caught with a marijuana pipe. Tony said he knew the public works department in Mexico was incompetent because the street in front of his grandmother's house remained unpaved perpetually. "When they finally did put [pavement] in, it was a thin layer of concrete and the rocks have started popping up already. It doesn't work. It's not good at all. If they are going to do something, do it right the first time."

Tony: All I know is it's corrupt, from when you watch the news. They are all corrupt. Like that president they had – the bald guy – a few years ago, Salinas. He was corrupt. He took so much money from them and then took off. I've heard that the president they have right now, he's not a good president supposedly.
Marisa: I've heard that, too.
Lupita: When I went to TJ, he was there and the people were all around. I heard a taxi driver say, 'Why does anyone even go? He's just stealing money from us.'
Tony: Some people don't want him to be president because they wanted other parties to win. But I don't know. None of them do nothing. TJ is always going to be TJ, and Mexico is always going to be Mexico.

The attitude of resignation seemed pervasive in the journalism class. Mindich's focus on getting youth to tune back in to the news – at all levels from ages 11 to 40 -- would appear less urgent if interest in news on TV, radio and in newspapers was not connected to interest in democracy. Worries about teenage apathy in the political system have existed since the 1950s and 1960s, but the problem is greater now because their parents, too, have proven disinterested in news, Mindich demonstrates with research.

Many white teachers lack sufficient cultural knowledge to motivate their students (Delpit 1995). For example, she cites Jaime Escalante, the legendary math teacher, who taught poor Latino youth "ganas" or the desire to learn and Calculus skills (164). In a quote from the movie, *Stand and Deliver*, Escalante says, "You have to learn math. The Mayans discovered zero. Math is in your blood!" (164) Mrs. Webb could learn from Escalante, but Escalante possessed high math skills as compared with Mrs. Webb's low journalistic knowledge. In addition, there is the issue of approach. Freire explains that the teacher cannot take full power with the notion that *later* students will become revolutionary and take action to recast their lives. They must empower students. "The world – no longer something to be described with deceptive words – becomes the object of that transforming action by men and women which results in their humanization," he writes in *Pedagogy of the Oppressed* (1970: 86).

Mrs. Webb worked in a school that was unlikely to adopt change. Lipsitz shows that inequality is not primarily a function of students' or teachers' own faults. "Inadequate funding to inner-city schools means that minority youths frequently encounter larger classes, fewer counselors, more inexperienced teachers and more poorly equipped laboratories and libraries than their white counterparts" (1998, 38). Even where equipment issues largely have been remedied, other systemic handicaps highlight differences between campuses.

These teenagers could be brought out of their apparent apathy for issues they felt mattered, something Buckingham also noted in his research. It just depended on what was being asked of them and how relevant they perceived it to be. School obviously was not proving itself to be very relevant. This also is evidence that multicultural education, taking all students' experiences into account, is as important to a journalism class as any other. It does not signal the death of education as critics have argued, but its renewal. Young people are not blank slates. While most students were American citizens and this thesis does not show they were knowledgeable about the American government (precisely the opposite), these "disadvantaged" youth could be quite aware and concerned about political issues over the border. They said they were as powerless as the Mexican people to change things, but their knowledge of Mexico helped them value their own position in California. Perhaps they had more reason to be cynical about their schooling and society than upper-middle class youth because conditions were not as comfortable. In fact, they sometimes appeared less cynical. These moments actually could prove to be opportunities for the teacher to get students more interested in U.S. news and politics.

> SEA: What can you guys do about what's going on down there?
> Tony: Nothing. I don't know that we are in a way better position than they are, but by knowing that, I think our government is way better than theirs. So that even if we don't like the President or something, I think we're better off.

Not all were as naïve as the conversation that began this section suggests. The youth in this particular focus group could name President Bush and his rival Al Gore (a man they supported). They said they were liberals and they had faith in government officials.

This faith, of course, did not appear to extend to the direct school officials around them. But their liberal leanings and unique belief in politicians might have significant implications for U.S. politics were they to buck the trend of declining involvement and vote later as adults. The views of Latino students reflected trends noticed by political analysts and revealed in polling. Student views reflected the views of their families. On Hispanic adults, Mark Baldassare wrote in the California Journal (August 23, 2002):

> There are good reasons to expect Latinos to subscribe to a different point of view about government than most California voters. Latinos do not fit the profile of suburban, affluent college educated, issue-focused and more loosely partisan voters with 'post-materialist values' and thus are unlikely joiners of the 'New Political Culture.' Their demographics are more like ethnic voters of the American past – many are immigrants, have children, live in lower-income households, and reside in big cities – qualities that provide a focus on meeting basic needs and a desire for government to offer more public services to help achieve the American Dream.

Latinos, Baldassare wrote, "exceed all groups in California when it comes to faith in government." This assessment was confirmed to some degree when I asked Tony how much confidence he had in politicians, Tony said: "A lot. Because they are doing it all for us who are alive." Lupita added, "They are doing it for everybody. Everything that happens, everything that we have to do, it's because of them, the law and stuff happening."

This gave me pause, having heard so much doubt from more well-off teenagers:

CHAPTER 4: HOMESTEAD HIGH SCHOOL 181

    SEA: They have a lot of effect on your lives?
Tony: They have all the effect on our lives. Most of it. What we can't handle, the things we can't reach, that's all their fault if something happens.
    SEA: Like what? Are you talking about local politicians?
Tony: No, I am talking about all of them. The only effect they have on your life is the things you can't do yourselves. Like taxes. I guess they are doing all right because you are alive and eating and everything. Maybe they could be doing better, but I guess they are doing all right.

His lack of cynicism ended when Tony discussed his stance against the War in Iraq. Both he and Carlos criticized President Bush, especially his position of safety as the president. Once America goes to Iraq, "Bush will go hide in a tunnel," Carlos said.

Tony: That's true, huh? He's sending all the soldiers to get shot and he's just sitting at his desk.
    SEA: But isn't that the way it always is?
    Tony: Yeah, but it's wrong.
SEA: So he should be like George Washington out there on a horse. The true Commander in Chief?
    Carlos: That's how it should be.
Tony: I think he's not thinking about what he's doing. It's easy to sign a paper, but he is not really thinking about people's lives. He is thinking about himself and about the country but not about people in general.
SEA: Does the principal of the school think about every effect of his policies?
    Tony: No, he doesn't think about individual people.
    Carlos: They don't even know our names.
    Tony: They don't care.
Maria: Unless you get into trouble every day, then they know who you are. Otherwise, they probably don't even know you exist.
    (Field notes, February 25, 2003)

Tony explained that the reason many teenagers seem uninvolved is because adults do not consider their input or views to be significant, the same theory discussed earlier that Buckingham articulates (2000). "Students are not really concerned because adults don't involve them in anything! They are not involved because usually when you think of politics, you think of adults. Older people. Old rich people. So you don't really think about it. But if you were more involved then you would be thinking about it." Tony said politicians do not care about teenagers and compared this phenomenon to sports. "When there's sports, the players don't really care about the viewer. It's not going to change the way they are playing. It's the same with us. Politicians don't care. It's like we're nothing." The teens had grown used to a spectator role, in school or out. This may be unfortunate because the students' time is at hand. The white population in California fell below 50 percent for the first time in the state's 150-year history, according to the 2000 Census. Other research by the Public Policy Institute "suggests that Latino voting power may very well double in size during the next 40 years, promising a far more significant role in policy decisions and leadership positions for Latinos," wrote Jack Citrin and Benjamin Highton, the political science professors who conducted the study of voting patterns for the Public Policy Institute of California. Many Hispanic voters are fiscal liberals and social conservatives, the opposite of the rest of the electorate, and their growing population could cause significant shifts in state politics during what has been described as "the Latino Century." This remarkable opportunity to effect change is not something that should escape the notice of the young, as they are the very people the politicians will need to target in adulthood. The subject needed to be explicitly addressed.

The Latinos' trust in government may help offset the cynicism of most white Americans, but their low participation rates now frustrate this idea. At the same time, the study indicates that Latino voters will still be outnumbered by white voters even when they represent a much larger share of the population." One of the reasons that Latinos have lower turnout rates is because they often do not register to vote, or may be ineligible because they are not citizens or fear the Immigration and Naturalization Service. The two professors suggest citizenship drives, but voter turnout rates also can be increased in the schools, by creating more active citizens who question their environment. These new voters could be born not only in American History classes, but also in journalism class.

Student newspapers as 'kiddie stuff'

Student newspapers do not have the same freedom of expression as newspapers in the community because "we're just kids, " said Susana. "[Outside newspapers] believe they have that right because they are adults. We are minors." We had this conversation:

> Susana: The high school newspaper is just kiddie stuff.
> SEA: You are not taken seriously?
> Susana: Yeah, they don't take us seriously.
> Tony: Adults are probably thinking we just write to fill up space. That's why we write it.

SEA: Is that why sometimes students in the class don't take yourselves seriously? I mean, do you think you take yourselves seriously as a newspaper?
Susana: In some kind of way, we do take ourselves seriously as students, But some students who are not serious about their grades or anything, It probably hasn't hit them or they just don't care.
(Field notes, November 12, 2002)

The students' practice of a spectator role worked against Mrs. Webb. Shortly after the terrorism edition was finished, she tried an experiment. She told Lali, the quiet, Samoan editor in chief and a senior:

Mrs. Webb: OK, [Lali] whenever you're ready.
Lali: I'm ready, [Mrs. Webb].
Mrs. Webb: You are taking over, remember?
Lali: What am I supposed to say?
Mrs. Webb (to the rest of the class): "We are planning for the next edition so give her some ideas. What are some things we want to cover that will be interesting? Our winter edition, before the break, before the Christmas holiday, before New Year's. We have New Year's coming up and then we're gone.
Lali: OK, c'mon, give me some topics.
Female student: Are we going to include Culture Night?
Mrs. Webb: It depends.
Female student: Culture night is Nov. 22.
Mrs. Webb: yeah, we could do that.
Silence.
Mrs. Webb: So nobody has any ideas? Ms. Amster, do you have any ideas?
I said nothing but wanted to hear their ideas.
Maria: We can do an editorial on what the holidays mean to us.
Lots of silence.
Tony (a bit irritated): We could do stuff! I don't know.
Lali: You guys can't think of one topic, anything, anything going on? Do you have calendars in front of you?
(Field notes, November 12, 2002)

The only idea students came up with was taken directly from the school calendar, but silence was their main approach to the brainstorming session. The scene was repeated as late as March when they planned their senior edition in June because Mrs. Webb was soon to go on maternity leave. She had prepared a pink sheet giving them directions on what to do. The particular stories and pages where they were to go were spelled out. Lali and Mrs. Webb wrote down the ideas on the white board, such as profiles on the salutatorian and valedictorian. They started to fill in names next to stories and asked for volunteers, facing a silent class. Mrs. Webb told her to fill in names of those not listed more than once "Can you put in names?" Lali asked Mrs. Webb. "I don't want to."

A disgusted Carlos retorted, "Just do it! You're in charge."

Lali struggled with being a leader. The exchange was either proof of poor self-confidence and lack of assertiveness or an unwillingness to be Mrs. Webb's lackey. The ability to put herself forward was an ingredient essential to reporting and writing, also to editing others, but there is no way to ignore its connection to college, career and all the other issues she would soon face after graduation. Many students could not envision themselves in someone else's shoes, being someone else and doing something else in any other place, which also limited their horizons. Mrs. Webb knew this and tried to praise them when she could. At one point, they needed to revise their stories on substance abuse, rewriting information taken from the Internet, talking to actual teenagers and making their prose sound less like research papers. She said she had gotten no response to their previous edition. "I haven't heard anything so we're fine. . . I thought you guys did a good job." She lauded Ana, who wrote about diet pills, a way of getting to the subject of body image another way. Then she turned to Carlos and told him he was a good writer and could do the assignment on steroid use, a problem no one told him they were seeing at the school. "It's important that you guys use your own words because you guys are writers and you can handle it." A big problem was that the students did not appear to believe her that they were writers, but seemed to take the comments as one more empty adult speech (Field notes, February 18, 2003). It also went against how they thought she actually felt.

Manny, a 17-year-old senior who hoped to become a lawyer, mentioned the idea of his having a voice near the end of senior year. This had been a long time coming for a young man who had struggled with English vocabulary, Spanish having been his first language. The journalism class had served as an entry point for his thoughts of freedom (of course, he also was about to leave high school), but the conversation was about resistance. He and Tony were not considering the news itself, but who should have editorial control of the school newspaper. The subject came up because a student had asked Mr. Perez whether the paper could print a small classified ad from a senior who said his favorite memory of school was "senior ditch day." This was in a section with many other such "senior wills." Mr. Perez had responded that he would have to ask the assistant principal. The two boys were seated at a table in one corner of the newsroom:

CHAPTER 4: HOMESTEAD HIGH SCHOOL 185

Tony: We have a voice here. This is a student newspaper. Why do we have to ask permission? We should be able to write what we want.
Manny: Una voz.
Tony: They don't have to ask (referring to the students in another part of the classroom). I would stand up, but if I do, there goes my grade.
Manny: So we better be quiet.
Tony: We better do what we have to do.
Manny: Uh huh.

D. Conclusion: Una voz?

Teenagers in Homestead's journalism class often felt they had little control over the newspaper. This was yet another sign that they were unimportant. They did not really seek such control because it would have meant more responsibility, which they feared they could not handle. Family troubles sometimes made them feel numb. TV news reports made them feel numb. The idea of terrorism frightened them even more. Adults and students daily waged a struggle for control of students' own bodies, their manner, the way they dressed. Some pierced themselves out of a desire for influence or the sensation of pain. Friendship groups were made along common interests and beliefs. Yet when a freshman was killed by a drunk driver at the end of the year in 2003, Mr. Perez again was aghast at student indifference, at what he called "their stoicism." Some members of the journalism class had known the student, but they did not weep or hug, though freshman Ana had visited the girl's home the night before she died.

If students seemed indifferent to unexpected death, they also were unconcerned about other events that affected their lives or at least they did not feel as though they could alter them. Students often ignored signs of news when they heard about it around campus, such as the day the principal announced the school was getting its six-year accreditation visit. Mrs. Webb simply told her students to be on their best behavior. The way to stimulate political thinking would have been to discuss what this visit meant for students and how the state viewed the school. How should the visit be covered?

This type of trigger journalism is essential to getting working-class students to become more aware and self-actualized despite their circumstances. The job of journalists is to make others aware of the news and this was obviously not a priority in the journalism classroom. There were a number of issues the teacher did not want to address with students. This mattered because the students needed to see themselves as important actors in the world. For Hispanic students in California it was doubly important because changing demographics mean they are poised to assume more power at the ballot box and need to learn to use it. At the same time, the very concept of politics needed to be enlarged to make space for subjects and people most compelling to young people.

Working-class Latino students share some of the same problems of alienation from the news and politics as upper-middle class youth. They are all viewed as inconsequential simply by virtue of their being young. Yet students' sense of disempowerment in the very class where they should feel more powerful because of the connection to a school newspaper was more totalizing. They had grown accustomed to exclusion from decisions related to school operations. Their involvement in the school newspaper, which is supposed to provide an outlet for student expression, was ritualistic. If students truly believed that the class was about journalism, perhaps the damage would be longer-lasting and harder to reverse. In his study of schooling for early adolescents, Everhart argues that adolescence itself is an ideology perpetuated by the schools.

It may be impossible for schools to help adolescents become critical thinkers as long as they are in institutions that treat them as naturally dependent and inferior, he contends, asking what if our society could integrate youth into the political system and test their competencies by asking them to solve community problems? "Our schools, by maintaining adolescents in a dependent state for so long, are hardly an adequate preparation for the independent, assertive life that our culture romanticizes" (265). A high school newspaper class can do just this, identifying school problems and editorializing about solutions, but the journalism teacher never asked the question of what students would like to see changed in their school? To be fair, fears of a regressive principal may have inhibited the teacher from encouraging students' political involvement in school.

This study examines teenagers' views of the news and the way these ideas are affected by journalism programs in both upper-middle class and working-class communities. Most students at Homestead were confronting enough turmoil in their lives to justify disinterest in the news media, which seemed intent on hammering them with reports of turmoil in other locales. Teenagers turned away from daily reports of world turbulence because these stories seemed to intensify their own problems and feelings of insecurity. This orientation proved challenging for the teacher, but ultimately the structure of the class also turned the students off to the news. They were not encouraged to explore the stories of student life that they knew, the lived experiences of immigration, for example, or what it was like to attend Mexican schools and the differences between the American schools and the schools in Tijuana. Was Homestead succeeding or failing and how could students tell what their education was worth? What was the nature of its problems with illegal attendance from Mexico? Such stories were important and a critical discussion of their impact might make the newspaper and its journalism more authentic.

Students needed practice in conducting interviews and taking detailed notes because most seemed to lack experience in this area. The art of writing would improve as their collection of details improved. They also could improve their confidence by approaching and interviewing others. More than that, they needed to talk about how to recognize a newspaper story. The most newsworthy events in the journalism classroom were often the events closest to students' lives. Stories needed to spring from there, but these turned out to be the stories most disregarded. Student work was not measured against established rules or a firm standard. Mrs. Webb's fear that her students were most content doing nothing led her to push stories from the school calendar in which they had no interest. She needed to develop her own definition of news to expect students to have one. For most students, trouble coming up with ideas had to do with learned helplessness that transcended one journalism class or a teacher. They were never taught how to find ideas, dig for information or approach an interview subject. They sat quietly and waited.

A mix of societal factors were to blame for this. Although the factors did not foreclose a student from succeeding, they made it less likely. In *Managing to Make It* (1999), a study of poor families in Philadelphia, Frank Furstenberg Jr. et. al write that poor families were just as "caring, concerned, or invested" as any others. What they lacked was "adequate knowledge of the middle-class world to guide their children in how to succeed and they rarely had the resources to subcontract with those who had the knowledge." The authors write that family practices had a negative impact on youth and did not seem to be changed by teachers in schools, all of whom were preparing students for a past rather than future world (226). "Most of the youth did not sufficiently understand that they were being vastly underprepared to perform in the middle-class world – a realization that often only dawns upon them when they reach adulthood."

Such work puts Homestead's slogan, "Make It a Great Day or Not – The Choice is Yours" in a new light. It builds the case of Furstenburg and his colleagues that "family differences in social and cultural capital are in turn a byproduct of economic advantage and education. Unless children have fair access to the educational system, choice is a political pretense for maintaining privilege." Such disparity was apparent between the schools in this study and Homestead. Journalism classes and the newspapers they produced could not afford to foster the pretense of choice. False journalism may be worse than no journalism at all.

Notes

[1] Mehan et.al suggest that poor parent involvement in the schools happens because of "a mismatch" of expectations: Solutions require parent programs "sensitive to the social conditions and cultural arrangements of low-income and minority parents." The more educators grasp the strategies of poor families, the less they will rely on stereotypes (178-183).

Constructing Professional Journalists

The journalism program at Creekwood Canyon High won scholastic press honors regularly, including a Gold Crown award from the prestigious Columbia School Press Association, a feat the institution touted on its website under "2003 All-Star Accolades." This was a laundry list of student achievements, from high-test scores and sporting championships to honors in science and jazz. Students joined *The Comet* not for the love of news, but out of the belief that participation was "an elite thing to do" – an activity that satisfied the community and parental prescription to get ahead. Student rivalry, built into the fabric of the school, spilled over into the newspaper program by osmosis. Many had heard of journalism's stellar reputation from friends or older siblings and resolved to join even before setting foot on campus. They often received encouragement from competitive parents. This put the teacher in the unique position of having too many students who wished to write for the newspaper and too few openings.

The class had the trappings of prestige, including official press passes, trips to conventions, a bank of 35 computers (all with the PageMaker layout program and Internet access), and a lounge in the back of the classroom dubbed "the pub" for publications room. Here, students conducted meetings, raided a donated refrigerator, and relaxed on couches. Most appeared relaxed and in their element, a mini-Fourth Estate. The reality, though, was hardly stress-free or even comfortable. Only students who earned As and received the teacher's recommendation in the entry-level class could become staff writers for *The Comet*. The staff had beats and a firm hierarchy. They accepted assignments on deadline from section editors and stayed until midnight monthly to produce issues. They felt part of a special, powerful campus group.

The newspaper achieved autonomy from school officials not only based on its standing, but on students' and the advisor's awareness that adolescent writers had free speech rights under California law that adults could not dismiss lightly. This was a major lesson of the semester-long Beginning Journalism class that preceded newspaper membership. The result was that most students considered themselves journalists. They gained ideas for stories from such publications as the local daily, *The New York Times*, *The Village Voice* and *The New Yorker*. The attempt to follow professional standards boded well for the educational and occupational potential of the class, but hid an emotional toll because of the strain of being journalists and full-time students at once. This study focuses on the students who succeeded in making the newspaper and why, but it does not probe the weeding-out process that kept others from joining.

The apparent success of the class raised the question: Should teenagers become media professionals? Upper-middle class parents and their ambitions exacerbated purely journalistic pressures on students. Within *The Comet* staff, stress persisted in part because of the editorial board's hierarchal structure that is a genuine aspect of professional life. Too great a focus on recognition – another problem of journalists – sometimes caused students to forget the higher, public-service or democratic purposes of the class. Yet its similarity to a professional newspaper was among the reasons *The Comet* was judged superior. A top newspaper fueled school officials' obsession with image, but certain stories also irritated them. Ultimately, their awards and professionalism insulated students from undue interference. There were obviously positive features to the school's focus on achievement, college goals and competition. Staff at the low-performing Homestead High neglected such issues at students' peril.

The stress of academics probably had been familiar to the students since elementary school, where a local principal said the area's children aim to please their well-educated parents who know that "high achievement increases options" (Personal communication, October 22, 2003). Although many educational theorists see the effects of parent involvement in schools as positive, sociologist Lareau identified negative outcomes in children as young as first grade, from stress-related stomach aches to an unwillingness to try new things for fear of failure. Tension was evident in Lareau's study whenever upper-middle class children were performing below grade level. Lareau called this "the dark side of family-school relations" (11). In interviews, Creekwood Canyon students worried about measuring up to expectations, especially during the yearly selection of editors. This was a highly competitive and emotional month-long period of application, portfolio submission and interviews into which many students poured their entire sense of self-worth. Although the advisor Alexa Phillips said she did not support such thinking, she also compared the application process for editors to competition at *The New York Times*. Such hyperbole necessarily colored how students saw themselves and journalism. Students also were busy with their other courses plus after-

CHAPTER 5: CREEKWOOD CANYON HIGH SCHOOL 191

school jobs, sports like golf and track, dance, theater arts and SAT prep sessions.

Alvin Rosenfeld, M.D., author of *The Over-Scheduled Child* (2000) contends upper-middle class parents do harm by pressuring children and packing their schedules:

> Although her son was accepted for early admission by Boston College, we heard one mother, resident of a Cheeveresque New York City suburb known for having one of the most competitive public high schools in the country, describe her son as 'average, not all that bright.' It's unrealistic to expect every one of our children, (or frankly, even many of them) to earn straight As, captain three varsity teams, and staff the animal shelter on alternate weekends. We aren't all capable of superstardom – but that doesn't mean our lives should be viewed as disappointing (10).

Dr. Rosenberg blames the media for a constant barrage of parenting advice, along with stories of danger, giving parents the idea that they can achieve perfection. As a result, parents live with a constant sense of urgency and may micromanage their children.

Such qualities were noticeable at Coastal High School, but in the richer, more conservative and less diverse Creekwood community, they were rampant. Notes William J. Doherty, professor of family social science at the University of Minnesota (2000, 153):

> When our children become teenagers, competitive parenting makes us not want to deny them anything that their peers trumpet. What is wrong, we ask ourselves, with a television in their bedroom, with a private telephone line, with a closet full of expensive clothes?

Similarly, in *Ties That Stress* (1994), psychologist Elkind argues that many psychiatrists now see postmodern adolescence as a time of "sophistication" rather than "immaturity," causing adults to shirk their obligation to help young people grow. The false assumption, Elkind suggests, is that youth can do it all on their own -- without adult assistance. "The image of adolescent sophistication is a convenient way out," he writes (154).

In some respects, these books lend support for the contentions of conservative theorist Neil Postman (1983), who claimed that childhood was disappearing in the age of television, but they also make important points about the socioeconomics of childrearing. Buckingham criticizes Postman's desire to recapture childhood innocence and instead focuses on the preparation adults owe youth. A misguided Postman praises parents who strictly limit young people's exposure to TV, and he is especially adamant about the need for youth to defer to adults. He "urges parents to impress on their children the value of 'self-restraint in manners, language and style' and the need for 'deference and responsibility to elders,'" writes Buckingham in *After the Death of Childhood* (2000, 27). These views may reflect fears about youth gaining expressive power once intended only for adults. Teens' sophistication should not cause adults to inflict excessive restrictions or abandon their obligations. Creekwood students were expected to be instant adults.

At one point, when elections were not far away and too many students had missed deadline (Field notes, March 26, 2003), Carrie (16), the editor in chief, wrote their names on the front white board and asked:

> What happened you guys? . . . . If we haven't seen anything, any evidence of your story being on its way or something that's going to be substantial enough, your story kind of becomes worthless to us.

She encouraged students to get their stories in, later softening:

> Somebody got really stressed out yesterday, and there were problems. But it's not worth it. Don't let yourself get too stressed out. I know we just came down on everyone. Please talk to us about any of these things you are thinking about. We all make mistakes – even if we did come down on you today. I promise I won't keep this list.

At the same time, she informed students they would be watched more closely during the competition for editorships and that how much money they spent on their portfolios – on binding at Kinko's, for instance – would not clinch any job.

Her mother had encouraged Amanda (15), a shy Chinese-American girl, to join the newspaper and rise as high as she could after they had known another Asian girl in the neighborhood who became editor in chief. A sophomore, Amanda was a straight-A student who ran cross-country and played piano, but she experienced even greater angst from her mother when her science and math grades dropped. "She kind of holds it over me and says, 'OK, you don't need to pay so much attention to the paper if you can't handle other things.'" Amanda reflected that she did not enjoy journalism, except after the work was done. "It stresses me out, and I still do it," she said. "I don't know why."

During the year, student writers said many editors would discount their views. Only some people felt free to speak in class. When I asked a respected sophomore why he rarely spoke out after three semesters in the program, he replied:

> I don't have power in the class. A lot of comments come from the two editor tables. . . . in the future, I'd like to be a person that speaks out. Maybe if I become the editor or have power over the younger people, I will.

In this way, problems at *The Comet* reflected those at professsional, top-down newsrooms. At daily newspapers, news meetings usually occur in glass offices from which reporters are excluded, and decisions are not made democratically. Mrs. Phillips dismissed such issues, saying newspapers had been organized in hierarchies "since the beginning of time."

Mrs. Phillips needed only to point to *The Comet's* record of accomplishment to show that the highly structured arrangement -- in which everyone performed certain tasks – functioned effectively. A loosely organized system, accepting stories from students around the school, might be more democratic, but such a publication might not share The Comet's quality, seriousness, or staff training that made it one of the top newspapers in the nation (National School Press Association, 2003). The previous journalism and English teacher, Franny Eastwood, had divided the program in two courses, Beginning and Advanced Journalism, which meant as many as 70 students, 35 per class, could learn about journalism at any one time, although not all could achieve coveted spots as staff writers for *The Comet* and fewer became editors. "They practice shaking each other's hand," said Mrs. Phillips of Beginning Journalism. "Then they go out and do it." Students accepted to Advanced Journalism (as early as the second half of freshman year) could stay until they graduated. They received story suggestions and other guidance from the teacher but decided which 60-to-70 stories to cover each issue.

By 2003, the paper ran the same way each month with two weeks to write, a short period for story corrections (stories were turned in with six different copies for six editors), and three days of layout. Section editors controlled the content of their pages but gave instructions to other students to lay them out. In addition, every student was required to write two stories and sell two advertisements per issue to get an "A." What felt natural and self-directed to students actually came in a highly regimented package, one that could provide an easy but not necessarily certain transition to the corporate world. Usually 24 or 28 pages long, *The Comet* was funded entirely by advertising. Students showed journalistic spirit by writing longer, investigatory pieces and by supporting gay students, who were seen as a dispossessed group.

Mrs. Phillips let students explore any topic, as long as they acted responsibly. The principal Marla Hooper did not use prior restraint, but sometimes tried to convince students not to cover controversial topics. This usually did not work. Teachers attempted to create student journalists who were uncompromising and idealistic, less led by corporate interests and more by an ideal vision of journalism. The extent to which this succeeded was varied due to competing imperatives, such as academic, college and career goals that often conflicted with journalistic ones. Creekwood Canyon's program was almost universally admired by other journalism educators and students. This does not mean it was perfect. Sometimes students took shortcuts with stories because of harried schedules. A closer examination of its strengths and weaknesses may be useful to others.

Stories for *The Comet* were based on inventive ideas from students, the advisor and readers, provided a genuine picture of student life, and allowed students to include their personal reflections in columns in the features, opinions and sports sections. Students said they could afford to take risks because of the advisor's support and the status the newspaper had attained. The stories generally took significant reporting and writing effort. Students benefited from the newspaper by learning how to be assertive, communicate without wordiness, and function on deadline. They became more aware of the news. They formed bonds with other students and took part in motivational activities that fostered these relationships.

This chapter will explore (1) three case studies on issues of professionalism (analyzing the teacher's openness, investigatory stories, and the example of Isaac, a rule-violator); (2) the unusual coverage of a drag queen restaurant; and (3) student responses to the Iraq war. Within *The Comet's* structure, there was limited room to make mistakes and get in trouble, all of which happened. Students often discussed journalistic errors so that they might learn from them. As in a newsroom, they focused on individual projects. The class was different from real-world journalism: Professional reporters do not sell advertisements and editors rarely write stories. Yet the layout nights included a quality-control system of "checks" by editors and the advisor before the paper was "put to bed." Other high school newspapers review their copy for errors, but this program's vigilance – delineated in a step-by-step, meticulous list, was rare. The newspaper also attempted to help students balance newspaper routines with creativity and literary style.

Classroom use of *The New York Times* as a model suggested an effort to cater to more discerning readers. Many editors claimed to watch only limited TV, reflecting class-based biases toward "good" and "bad" media. "My family doesn't watch TV," declared Carrie, the editor in chief. "There's no time for TV. I listen to NPR." Other busy students made similar claims. The assistant editor Penny said she preferred the Internet to watching TV. "I actually try not to," she said of viewing TV. "I just don't have the time. I actually watch the news, and I read *The New York Times*. I try to read it every day." For story ideas, she would consult NYT.com and CNN.com, she said (Interview with Penny, March 29, 2003). Terry said he and his family mostly got their news online:

> Usually, it'll just be headlines that grab me. Yahoo has headlines and Google has a great news service that I am actually checking out a lot. I prefer getting my news online and from TV. What confuses me about newspapers is I'll open them and they will always get all over the place. I know some people just love the idea of getting up in the morning, having coffee, and opening up this huge paper. I have to spread my arms all out and bring it toward me and then some of the pages will fall out because it's not all stapled together . . . And then it'll say, 'Turn to Page E6,' and I'm like, 'What?' It's harder for me. We have this huge stack. I'm looking at it right now.

The Comet is smaller, more portable and more appealing to a youthful audience, he said.

A. Risks and Rewards of Professionalism for Youth: Critical Approaches to Reporting, Hierarchy, Fear of Failure, Dishonesty

Journalism is a political act. Reporters are supposed to represent average citizens who might not enter the places journalists go. Their stories should give readers enough information to make informed decisions about government (or school) policies and behavior. These traditional notions, both deified and derided by media theorists, were attractive to many high school students at *The Comet* and doubted by others. Reporters usually possess no formal knowledge that qualifies them for their jobs beyond college degrees. No state agency licenses them to act as professionals. They need pass no examinations to guarantee that all share a common body of knowledge. A journalism degree is optional and often not sought by newspapers at the upper echelons of the field. Yet like physicians or lawyers, journalists prefer to be judged only by each other. Theirs is a shared culture with expectations of what excellence in reporting and writing means. However, sometimes this separate status is seen as arrogance, standoffishness, or elitism.

The increasing corporate ownership of newspapers has eroded public trust in all forms of journalism, suggesting student newspapers – potentially separate from marketplace corruption -- could be critical sites for formative and hands-on lessons in press integrity. The inculcation of professional values, such as objectivity, fairness and balance, may begin in high school. When employed by schoolteachers and students, it is more difficult to argue, as has John Soloski (1997) that the objectivity standard masks corporate power. Soloski writes, "The tenets of news professionalism result in news coverage that does not threaten either the economic position of the individual news organization or the overall politico-economic system in which the news organization operates" (152-153). He is correct that the existing order is not upset by most news reports, but he fails to examine actual practices and treats all stories as equally defective. If youth learn professional norms without corporate pressure, perhaps the norms are less to blame for media failures than the corporate pressure.

The book *Manufacturing Consent* (Chomsky and Herman 1988) is one of many that attack the American press system, contending that even supposedly adversarial periods of journalism such as Watergate – still inspirational for young reporters -- only happened because elite interests were threatened by other elite interests. If this were the case, the tireless acts of individual journalists to expose abuse of power by the nation's chief executive would be irrelevant. Of course, they were not. The authors write (300):

CHAPTER 5: CREEKWOOD CANYON HIGH SCHOOL 197

> Powerful groups are capable of defending themselves, not surprisingly; and by media standards, it is a scandal when their position and rights are threatened. By contrast, as long as illegalities and violations of democratic substance are confined to marginal groups or distant victims of U.S. military attack, or result in a diffused cost imposed on the general population, media opposition is muted or absent altogether.

The authors contend that there was no scandal when it was revealed that the FBI had conducted illegal break-ins at the Socialists' Workers Party for more than a decade because the group represented no powerful base.

However, the authors' analysis does not consider news judgment, in which editors weigh a story's importance based on their assessment of reader interest. There has been no viable Socialist candidate for president since the 1920s. If the Socialists' Workers Party was not afforded the attention of the Watergate break-in, it was because Watergate not only was of greater public interest, but it had a more destabilizing effect on American government. In my view, it was a bigger story. The FBI's acts against fringe groups merited coverage because they, too, demonstrated the abuse of power. What they were not, as Herman and Chomsky put it, were "a violation of democratic principle far more extensive and serious than anything charged during the Watergate hearings" (299). High school students, including those at Creekwood, heard another version of the Watergate story, the more historically accurate account of persistent inquiry that helped derail a presidency, marking a change in the way the media and public regarded politicians. Had *The Washington Post* failed to chase the Watergate story or discounted it, it might have died in June 1972, changing the course of history. The two authors are correct that American coverage of international news is often pitiful, but only a sliver of the press can cover such news for lack of resources.

More cognizant of the complexities and vagaries of journalistic practice is Herbert J. Gans in *Deciding What's News* (1980). In evaluating news stories, the first judgment is that of Importance, Gans confirms. He finds that journalists tend to favor official sources for stories and inadvertently may slant their coverage in favor of the upper-middle class. Yet he argues that repairing these issues requires specific attention to sources not otherwise covered. He also discusses the systemic forces that work against reform, writing, "Although journalism does not lack its share of heroes, news organizations and firms are not often heroic" (289-290). Many youth might ultimately discover that news organizations are sufficiently hierarchical to enable executives and journalists at the top to make changes. However, journalists rise to the top by being cautious, and proposals for drastic change must be cleared with management, which is not paid to take unnecessary risks.

Although Gans studied the national press, his work is relevant to this study in that he found journalists translate information about "what individuals and groups do to and for each other in a wide range of institutions, agencies and communities. But as they translate that information into news, they frame it in a national context and thereby bring the nation into being" (298). Similarly, teenage reporters "bring their high schools into being" and need to seek myriad sources and rely on many solutions for improving coverage.

Some critics, including James Fallows (1996), fault the media for being out of touch with the rest of society, a problem as they evaluate stories. Reporters too often cover politics as a game and ignore substantive issues, he contends, pointing to a group of high school students who asked deeper questions of President Clinton after a State of the Union speech than did the press corps. "There was no overlap between the questions the students asked and those raised by the anchors," he writes. "None of the questions from these news professionals concerned the impact of legislation or politics on people's lives. Nearly all concerned the struggle for individual advancement among candidates." Thus, Fallows sees a gap between the way the public and reporters envision news. News and entertainment have been conflated, he argues. "The discussion shows that are supposed to enhance public understanding may actually reduce it, by hammering home the message that issues don't matter except as items for politicians to fight over."

If *The Comet* faltered, it was because it did not try to find out what the audience wanted from its newspaper and how students defined the school's educational mission. This might have gotten classmates more involved in considering the proper operation of their school, but the newspaper relied on the usual reader input, letters to the editor. This is true of other newspapers in high school and beyond. *The Comet* might have benefited by holding panel discussions of students, a technique used in "public journalism" to increase reader interest and reignite the civic purpose of the press in an age where many people consider newspapers extraneous. The idea of public journalism, practiced in different ways since the early 1990s, is credited to Jay Rosen, a Columbia University journalism professor who now directs the Project on Public Life and the Press. Arthur Charity writes (1995), "Surely one of the reasons public journalism arose when it did was that by the late 1980s, something new was in the air. In journalists' communities, forums, study circles, salons, town halls, and 'listening projects' were multiplying at the grass roots. At the same time, writers from several walks of life began to converge on the central question of what makes democracy work or fail" (3).

A positive trait of the journalism program at Creekwood was that young reporters learned the tools of investigation, and they could use these skills to cover the news, employing sources both from the margins and mainstream. The hope was that the more students relied on professional standards, the less interference they might expect from school officials. This was not always the case. However, the assumption of the value of a free press was built into the course in such a way that most students said they regarded the job of the media more positively – as a public good -- after the two-part instruction. This was not a characteristic of the two other schools in this study. Cynical instruction about the media at Coastal and Homestead did not allow students to engage seriously with the dilemmas journalists face.

Critical Approach?

Many reporters at *The Comet* assumed an adversarial or critical stance when dealing with school officials. Mrs. Phillips said she told students to think deeply about sources' responses during interviews – "not to be naïve and just accept everything they hear or read or to expect a source to just pour forth information – they should be inquisitive and dig beyond the surface of questions and answers." The teacher said she did not interpret her approach as encouraging an adversarial relationship with school authorities, but some students felt differently. While some also had a different Beginning Journalism teacher, long-time advisor Mrs. Eastwood, Mrs. Phillips' said there was little difference between them. Explained Penny:

> In journalism, we were taught from the very beginning that people will lie to you, all of the top people, I guess the authorities at school, the school administrators. We were taught in Beginning Journalism that they were going to lie to you, or they weren't going to tell you everything because obviously, they don't want you to know.

Many working journalists hold a similar skeptical attitude. Although it may appear healthy from an educational standpoint for students to question what they are told, the culture of schools may not be amenable to such self-interrogation.

Mrs. Phillips revealed her critical pedagogy during class discussions by speaking with candor, as an ally of students. During a discussion of the school's potential cancellation of student trips to journalism conventions because of state budget cuts, the teacher told students the most she could, though school officials may have preferred less:

> Mrs. Phillips (standing before the class): I'm going to tell you this, and I don't know if it's supposed to be a secret or not. The Portland trip and all the other conventions are in serious jeopardy because of budget cuts. There are a lot of political negotiations going on. We may not be able to go on conferences. Next year, there will be no out-of-state trips. (With a nervous smile) the principal may walk in here any second (classroom laughter). The administration doesn't understand that you guys learn so much during your convention -- it was not being considered educational. They thought of it more as a team event.
> Penny (sarcastically): Yeah, let's cancel all the football team's trips. We win more awards than they do!
> Mrs. Phillips: Now they understand the value. The funding part is their concern. The only expense comes out of the ASB budget. There's lots of philosophical discussions. I just wanted you guys to be aware of it. . . Teachers are upset about it and they say we should keep it quiet, *but I'm not into keeping secrets around here. You know that.*
> Carrie: It's not the administration's fault.
> Mrs. Phillips: Lots of schools are losing teachers. Some places are not buying paper towels for the bathrooms, just toilet paper. Female student; Can't we take a journalism trip not related to the school?
> Mrs. Phillips: It is actually a school-related experience. I have been thinking about it, though. What would happen if I called in sick for two days, but the liability is just too great.
> Female student: Can we ask for foundation money?
> Mrs. Phillips: That comes from parent money.
> Male: Can't we just sell candy bars?
> Business manager: Sell ads!

CHAPTER 5: CREEKWOOD CANYON HIGH SCHOOL 201

Mrs. Phillips: Part of the problem is the idea of equity. It's not a matter of how you pay, but the school district must pay my sub and the philosophy is people see us spending money on a luxury when a lot of places in the same school can't afford it.
Female (to classmates): The Superintendent and the School Board say it's not fair that you can afford it.
(The room explodes in discussion, as students consider this).
Mrs. Phillips: *I can't bring this up* so listen! [The Superintendent's] philosophy is students at [Creekwood Canyon] don't take journalism because they can't afford to go on the trips so they feel left out and don't take the class. I said we have scholarships. I never went on trips as a kid. We couldn't afford it, but the philosophy is you shouldn't have to go for a scholarship because you shouldn't have to be told you are poor. It's demoralizing. I say the only place you are challenged is national conventions because here . . . you are always the best.

The discussion (Field notes, January 29, 2003) reflected a heightened self-consciousness of the students' own prosperity – in which parents could afford to pay for out-of-state trips, but it also showed the class they could depend on the advisor to be forthcoming when she had information that was relevant to them. The principal was supposed to stop by the classroom that day but didn't, and the students and advisor were edgy during the complicit talk in which the advisor felt she might be taking chances professionally should an administrator walk in. A belief in public school journalism meant, to Mrs. Phillips, exposing information to students for discussion and debate. It also meant providing her support to them when they took on more controversial subjects, even when the school principal explicitly had asked them not to. Still, it showed restraint that the principal did not insist on certain press behavior as the Coastal principal had done. Mrs. Hooper allowed students to be investigative journalists, although it was not easy for her. At times, it was clear she had significant reservations about a free press running around her high school.

The ability to admit mistakes and learn from them is part of professionalism and so is aggressive effort, which led to in-depth feature stories and longer investigations. The newspaper in the 2002-2003 academic year included at least two investigations, along with a variety of opinion pieces, feature stories and humor. The two investigative stories did not portray the school positively and in fact, shed light on embarrassing mistakes by named school officials. For instance, the front-page investigative story in December 2002 carried the headline, "Intoxication at Homecoming." An earlier front-page story the month before by photo editor Nadine (17) actually had glossed over incidents of drunkenness at the school event and presented a much less controversial account, entitled "Dance Goes on Despite Delays." It focused mainly on the selection of the Homecoming King and Queen, which had left the King temporarily Queenless. The lead discussed the fact that rain had postponed the traditional royalty presentation. The suspension of some students for intoxication was mentioned in the second to last paragraph, without additional information. However, the newspaper did not leave the issue at that, a decision that might have suited other school publications.

Carrie, the editor in chief, conducted an investigation of drunkenness that included details of why all but one student, even those who could not walk and were vomiting, ultimately went unpunished by school officials and police. A police breathalyzer was not working. The front-page layout included a graphic of a police car with the steps involved in taking a breath sample. The piece was not sensational, but the subject itself was controversial, and the story placement assured more readers.

The involved girls had gotten drunk at a party before the event. The lead stated:

> One arrest and several suspensions were made at the Homecoming dance after an investigation traced alcohol use to one limousine of approximately 20 senior girls.

The second paragraph discussed the school's phone call to 911, which came after many of the girls had already left. The condition of one girl required paramedics. Carrie's method of reporting the story required persistence because the incidents at the dance were "so hush-hush." Just tracking down the police officer involved was a challenge that required calls to different stations, Carrie said. Among campus sources,

> nobody wanted to talk about it. I had to talk to zillions of people. I had a lead of two girls' names and that's what pretty much started me off, and then I talked to multiple administrators and various students, the students who organized the Homecoming dance, and

the final confirmation I received from the police officer who responded to the call. It was a lot of guessing when interviewing these people, not being quite sure the role they played . . .

An editorial column in the same issue criticized the administration for making no effort to detain students and blasted both students and parents for a careless attitude toward alcohol. "The bottom line is that administrators allowed students to get away with their illegal actions." The column also blamed parents for treating their teenagers as children in need of protection and allowing them to lie and manipulate school administrators. "Most disturbing is that those students, when caught, refused to take responsibility for their actions and ran away from the problem, sheltered by their parents as if they were children. . . It is troubling that such irresponsible and immature people represent [CCHS] and that they will soon hold more responsibility as adults."

Newspaper advisors at other schools have told Mrs. Phillips that they would be fired for what she allows students to print, but Mrs. Phillips said she often receives no criticism on highly controversial stories handled in a comprehensive and balanced way. Mrs. Phillips' editing was not taken as arbitrary censorship. Students needed to justify their work based on journalistic principles. Regarding the Homecoming story, she said, she waited for criticism once the issue was distributed, but the criticism never came. "Everyone knew there was nothing to say because what are you going to say?" she said. "The story is true. I'm mad at you for writing it?'"

An earlier newspaper investigation after a graffiti incident ("Officials fail to communicate," October 24, 2002) pointed to "breakdowns and holes" in the system that "undermine current vandalism prevention efforts." A student inquiry found that an assistant principal did not notify the school policeman of the vandalism. The Comet reported this in a way that directly held the school official accountable, again by name. "That was a failure that came from my office," the assistant principal said, and his words were lifted for a larger outquote on Page 3. The story also discussed a plan to install surveillance cameras costing $25,000 "in places where we have a history of a lot of vandalism." The students did not appear shy about direct confrontation.

An adversarial culture in the journalism class was not surprising because such a culture is supposed to be part of the field, having begun in the early 1920s with the start of public relations and early news management techniques by the government. The approach grew stronger during the Vietnam era when the government lied to manipulate American public opinion, such as about civilian casualties (Schudson 1978). The deaths of Martin Luther King Jr. and John and Robert F. Kennedy as well as the impeachment of President Richard Nixon led American society to expect a more critical press, he contended. Arthur Sylvester, the Pentagon spokesman under Kennedy and Lyndon Johnson, was infamous for his defense of government lies as necessary in a cold war age that contained the nuclear threat. New journalism "challenged straight news accounts of what sources said by turning to" muckraking and literary journalism, but it was mainly the province of magazine journalism, Schudson finds (187).

Causing controversy?

Some students resisted adversarial journalism and said they would prefer a newspaper – Nadine said "a newsletter" -- that was not always trying to cause controversy, trip up school authorities, or incite them (See Nadine's comments in the later section on the Iraq War). These students were a minority, but they held important positions. For example, the news editor Maggie (17) felt she had established a good relationship with the principal. This may have been because of her unusual practice of showing Mrs. Hooper controversial stories in advance – something that professional newspaper reporters would never do and the advisor told me did not occur. The curriculum appeared to form tougher student journalists than those at the two other schools in this study, but appearances could be misleading. The news editor had a reputation for being soft on the administration, which may have lost her the election later that year for editor in chief. Most other students could flout sources when necessary.

The sheer number of stories required to fill the newspaper forced students to be creative if they wanted to engage their student audience. Student journalists at *The Comet* knew that they were expected to do the extraordinary – the source of some stress. They wanted to exceed the performance of previous years and remain competitive among other schools with top newspapers. The teacher gave them the message that they needed to stay vigilant "to bring the paper further ahead of the pack that is clearly gaining on us" (Letter to newspaper staff after the selection of new editors, May 15, 2003). The class was made up of serious students, mostly in honors classes. Their writing was strong before entering the class. As a sample in June 2003, the front-page contained the requisite story about the new prom queen but also news on legal action delaying the school's stadium project and the dismissal of more than 40 bus drivers because of California's fiscal crisis. Opinion pieces called for greater racial integration in school and defended the quality of a public education. There were features on the practice of tongue-splitting (with a photo of a piercing shop worker's bisected tongue), students who have plans that do not include college (such as professional dance or entrepreneurialism), and love relationships that include an age gap (such as 20 and 15)."I've been in a relationship where I've technically been statutorily raped," said a girl, speaking under cover of a pseudonym. "He was 20. He was a little worried about it, but I wasn't. Maybe that's because it was my parents who might have pressed charges, but I wasn't going to let them find out."

A story about methamphetamine addiction had a photographic of a boy with a needle in his arm. Two formerly addicted students were quoted, but the writer used pseudonyms to protect them, a common practice in the hard-edged newspaper. "The very first time you do it, you are the luckiest person in the world," one student says. "Everything in your life is perfect." Past stories the paper has covered included such delicate topics as the approval of RU 486, written by Penny in her sophomore year. "In our school, kids get abortions, you know?" said the advisor of the reasoning for the story:

> You don't see kids walking around pregnant . . .but you also always hear kids talking about sex and talking about abortion. So I said, 'We should cover that story.' I knew it would be controversial and we would be stepping into territory that more conservative parents would go crazy with. But we're careful about how we cover these kinds of things
> (Interview with Mrs. Phillips, December 23, 2002).

RU 486 was only the first of the touchy stories Penny would author. "My lead was 'It's the pill that's licensed to kill.' It was the top story, and that got a lot of people upset." The lead grabbed attention, but it should not be taken as evidence of a pro-life stance, Penny said. The rest of the story was written in an informational style. "It wasn't really an opinion story. It was all news, but people were like, 'that's your opinion,' and they got really upset. We actually took that issue to competition, so it was kind of a big deal."

Through the stories they wrote, students showed daily that they were competitive with each other and goal-oriented. Their actions often revealed that they were vying for the teacher's approval. At a layout session in May 2003, Terry took on as much extra work as he could and stayed until the end of the night in attempt to show the teacher the extent of his commitment. It was time for the selection of new editors. He produced a slick, spiral-bound portfolio, gaining the job of new centerfold editor in spring 2003. When he first was introduced to the newspaper staff, he recalled, "I said, 'Wow, this is really one of the top things you could be doing here [at the high school]. . . It's stimulating to be around so many people that are really hard workers and that really write well, and it makes you want to work hard and write well, too" (Interview with Terry, March 22, 2003).

During the January class when students and teacher discussed the convention trips, they also considered a front-page story ("Teenagers' hit and run incident leaves local man in critical condition," *The Comet*, January 16, 2003) that was an account of three boys who had thrown eggs at a car, injuring the driver. After the boys threw the eggs, the victim pursued them, trapping their vehicle on a dead-end road. Angry, the man got out of his car and pounded on the boys' vehicle, then jumped on it. As the boys drove away, the man fell off, suffering severe head trauma. In an interview (March 30, 2003), the story's author, Cole, said the principal tried to get him not to write the story. His turning her down showed the value of the adversarial system:

> She effectively told us, 'I would really rather if you did not run anything on it.' She was afraid we would somehow damage the boys, or simply make the situation worse, but what I told her and what I did stand by – and what we did -- was that we were going to handle this in a mature manner. We were not going to go out with the intent of ruining these boys' lives simply to get a story. We were going to represent what happened in the same manner that any newspaper would. . . . Her concern was that we were going to be irresponsible and not take into account the possible impact the story would have on these boys.

Despite Mrs. Hooper's contentions, Cole made it clear the newspaper was determined to proceed. The story was accurate but ended up naming a paralegal, quoted extensively, as the boys' lawyer, in error. It was surprising that the news editor said she showed the principal the story a couple of days before publication. The advisor apparently did not know about this. The news editor also had showed Mrs. Hooper a sensitive story about a pro-Iraq War protest in which the principal was criticized.

Once the egging story ran, the paralegal complained, saying that only the lawyer was authorized to comment. His main concern was his own statement that "the boys will have to live the rest of their lives knowing their actions had the end result of severely injuring and possibly ending a life." Cole's attribution error was based on the advisor's representation to him that the man was a lawyer when she handed over the phone for the interview. This showed the extent of Mrs. Phillips' hands-on involvement with reporting. Cole said the paralegal "was pretty forthcoming with me," and Mrs. Phillips remembered him asking for the spelling of the source's name. However, as she did with other errors, she used this as an opportunity to inculcate professional values:

> I'm totally supporting you guys on this, but given the money or the mood, the lawyer may make an issue of this. . . . You must always make sure your sources are real, and interview situations are obvious. The entire newspaper rides on that, so I am just reminding everyone.

Mrs. Phillips guarded the newspaper's reputation, but there also were challenges to teaching bright, unseasoned young people. Sometimes she overestimated them.

Pecking order?

There were downsides to what students said could be a highly competitive and rigidly hierarchical environment. Had he not taken a year off to work in Congress, Leo (18) said he might never have realized what it was to be "on the bottom end of the food chain," the one whose opinions are not valued because he is not on the editorial board. In Beginning Journalism he was editor in chief of "the baby paper," a product that the class produces at the end of each semester as practice for the real thing. He enjoyed everything about the class – even the adrenalin rush of deadlines -- but he realized the program's flaws once he returned from Washington, D.C. as a senior:

> I not only couldn't stand the editors and their whole power-hungriness, it was more like I was sick of the constant pressure. It wasn't even the fun stress

anymore. It became one of those things where 'ugh, I have to write my story now,' and I wasn't enjoying it anymore. It's the type of people where you feel, 'If I wasn't here, would they really notice?'

After working for Congress during September 11, 2001, Leo felt high school was "small beans," but he did not quit the class because he had formed close ties with the teacher and did not want to let her down. At the same time, he found himself taking orders from "some snotty girl" (Interview with Leo, March 24, 2003).

The sense of autonomy in the class was so strong among students, they felt they could talk over the teacher or defy her at times. At one point, they left class in a big group for lunch without her permission, defying school rules. Often, Leo said, the teacher seemed to act the role of a peer. Some students had the attitude of "Oh, it doesn't matter. We'll control it [the paper," said Leo. "They really don't respect her. At the beginning of class, when she is talking, [a girl] will say, 'I really don't want to do this right now because we have to get to work.' Then [Alexa] just sits down." This may have been Leo's response to the teacher's effort to cede power to students, who sometimes misused it. "I just wish she would take her place," he said of Mrs. Phillips.

The issue of authority and how it was used irked some students, including both Henry (16) and Nadine (17). But the issue of authority for students may have been central what appeared professional about the program. Nadine felt the newspaper contained the stresses of real journalism. She was afraid such a career choice would make her "jittery" because of the need always to be on the alert. This was not necessarily a false worry. Some students put so much emphasis on the newspaper that they believed not becoming an editor meant they would not be successful in life either:

> Just the environment we're in, our parents. Just the need to succeed, like, I bet kids think that if they don't succeed in this little hierarchy that they're not going to survive in the hierarchy of life, so I mean you just see that this is it for these kids. They think that if they do not become editor in chief today then they are not going to amount to anything. (Interview with Nadine, April 28, 2003)

Henry wrote in his application for an editorship (he did not get one) that students were often too focused on their own positions of power to remember what it was like to be a staff writer who has ideas or needs advice. "In the beginning, everybody was talking about journalism," said Henry. "We're a family, we're on staff together, we're close, we're tight knit, but nobody -- it's one thing to say we're together and we're friends and we're family, but it's another thing to prove that" (Interview with Henry, May 6, 2003).

The paper takes a risk giving "a small clutch of people a great deal of power," he said. "Sometimes, when you rely too much on the hierarchy, especially in a high school environment where sociology is so important, it does get discouraging." Henry was a gifted and offbeat character whose portfolio application for centerfold editor included a barely clothed woman. "As much as this is a newspaper, it's still inside a high school," he said as if to remind me. "That's basically the definition."

The spring of 2003 was especially tense because Mrs. Phillips and seven senior editors were forced to choose 14 editors from among 20 talented juniors and eight sophomores. It left some disappointed youth, such as a highly talented girl who wanted to be a photojournalist one day, but did not get the photo editor spot or the two other applicants for editor in chief. The day editors were announced was an emotional one, with tears, threats of quitting, and editors who lost their jobs. Sirena (17), one of the few staff writers intent on becoming a journalist, had applied for an editorship but said it would not be the end of her life if she did not get the role:

> I know that for some people, it would be a big shock if they didn't get it. Editorship is very important to some people and I'm not, I mean I'm not going to kill myself over it and a lot of people feel that way. A lot of people feel that there is so much riding on this. If they don't do this right, then it's over.

She questioned how two losing editor in chief candidates would work under their rival.

The Case of Isaac

As feature editor, Henry felt responsible for what the advisor saw as the most egregious ethical lapse she had to police as advisor of The Comet thus far. The incident would prove to be a crucial test of the staff's dedication to professionalism. Isaac, a staff writer, penned a story for the September 26, 2002 issue's feature page (8). It carried the headline, "College acceptance withdrawals become dreaded reality." It read:

> The college withdrawal is sometimes dismissed as an urban legend, a frightening bedtime story created to scare Senioritis infected 12th graders into maintaining decent grades. However, stories of students being denied admission to a college after already being accepted are not all tall tales.

The story went on to discuss a 2002 graduate, an athlete and student leader, who was already accepted to a top college but let his grades drop to include a D in Calculus during second semester senior year. The only problem was Isaac apparently had never interviewed the student for <u>The Comet</u> and never specifically identified himself as a reporter. "He had heard from his friends about what happened to the student, and he had talked to the student in passing at some point but not for the newspaper," said Mrs. Phillips (Interview with Mrs. Phillips, December 23, 2002). When she and an editor asked him if the story's sources had been interviewed, he told them they had. The incident illustrated conflicting issues confronting journalism practiced within a public school. How far do the rights of student journalists extend? Isaac apparently had collected the information through deceit.

After the story ran, the senior complained to the principal that he had not wanted his name and grade printed. Mrs. Phillips judged Isaac's conduct to violate the newspaper's ethical standards, taught in Beginning Journalism. His lies to her also were disturbing. It is illegal for institutions that receive federal funds to disclose student grades under the Family Educational Rights and Privacy Act. Isaac's journalism put the newspaper -- and probably the school -- in legal jeopardy. The information was factual, and professional journalists might choose to print statements made by a public official that the official intended to be private, before a speech. But a minor is not a public official. When deciding whether to print such material, many media "weigh the importance of the information and whether it can be obtained without the deceit," wrote David H. Weaver and G. Cleveland Wilhoit (1996, 158). <u>The New York Times'</u> policy is not to use false identification during reporting under any circumstances, wrote Weaver and Wilhoit. Isaac's acts were serious when high standards are applied. The newspaper also used unnamed sources, and it asked readers to trust its reporting.

In her quest for professionalism, Mrs. Phillips faced resistance from school officials who could not support the application of such standards to adolescents. She ended up having all students sign a document that was a combination of the Society for Professional Journalists' ethical code (1996) and the school rules for extracurricular activities. The incident – particularly Mrs. Phillips' effort to remove Isaac from class -- touched off a major debate that would pit classmates against one another. Carrie, the editor in chief, described it this way: "Our entire staff disintegrated at that time. People took sides, and everything was really polarized... To really work as a paper, unity is critical, and when you lose that, you are pretty much screwed" (Interview with Carrie, March 31, 2003). However, some students including Ken (18), the digital media editor who had his own confrontations with the advisor, said even a professional journalist would have been given a second chance. His father was news editor for a local TV station. Amanda said the pressures in the class were extreme at times with students being held to adult demands of professionalism. She knew she would never become a journalist but the class might teach her to be assertive. Amanda felt Isaac was punished primarily because he had been caught. Other students have attempted to meet deadlines by cutting corners, she contended, and occasionally students claim to be quoted in stories when they have never spoken to anyone from The Comet. "I'm disappointed that Isaac did that, and I definitely think he was wrong. I'm sure he could have just called up [the student] and gotten his consent and put it in, but it's not like he was unique, like he was the only one who's ever done it."

Ken, a senior with Isaac, accused Mrs. Phillips of bias -- of hoping Isaac would quit when he did not get an editorship at the end of his junior year. He compared her harsh treatment of Isaac to her hesitancy later that fall to oust a girl who used the newspaper's account for personal film developing (Interview with Ken, April 21, 2003):

> She just has never been very fair. Isaac made big mistake with this whole misquoting thing and lying about that, but that's, I mean, a journalistic mistake. And we're student journalists and student journalists do make mistakes and he gets completely kicked off staff and then a girl goes and steals like $500 worth of film-developing and then we can't kick her off staff? We have to force her to resign through guilt?

Isaac's actions may have merited "extra oversight," but not dismissal, Ken said. At first, the principal did not permit Mrs. Phillips to remove Isaac from the class that he had worked hard to enter. She felt removal was too harsh. He was suspended, told to write a paper on the First Amendment, and restricted from having contact with the staff for a period of time. He ended up showing up during a layout night, saying he was "just dropping off information for someone else," Mrs. Phillips said. "I said, 'You have to go home right now.' Then later I find out he took a photograph for another issue of the newspaper . . . Somebody else put their name down as the byline. That was another whole breach of all the things you are supposed to do." She found it difficult to explain to an assistant principal why the photograph was a serious issue journalistically. Isaac was told to write her a letter of apology, which became "an attack on me and an explanation of why he did nothing wrong. So at that point I was like, 'You're done here.'"

After this second transgression, the principal agreed to the boy's removal, but his parents appealed the decision to the Superintendent. Isaac was placed in an independent study class of Advanced Journalism, where he was allowed to continue writing for submission to the paper. The Superintendent's decision came after a series of fact-finding and information-gathering meetings. "This boy feels that I am a bad advisor and that I suppressed his First Amendment rights when really I was trying to protect the other students from somebody who continually makes bad decisions." The Superintendent's decision ultimately had little effect because Mrs. Phillips and the editor in chief were determined not to print anything he wrote, Mrs. Phillips said, "He did a very, very irresponsible thing, but he was also, as a student, creating a lot of problems. He had a lot of issues with being disrespectful." The two had had previous arguments about copy the advisor felt was racist. At one point, he wanted to write a story on circumcision, Mrs. Phillips said. "For a parenting magazine, I could see debating the benefits of circumcision but for a high school newspaper, it's just to get your advisor to say penis a whole lot of times." I suspected that gender was a factor in the advisor's irritation with Isaac. Just less than two-thirds of the class was female so that males were a minority.

Newsrooms operate on trust more than many journalists admit. The case of *New York Times* reporter Jayson Blair proved that self-monitoring of journalists according to professional standards does not protect any newspaper from problems. The public saw that even the gray lady, 'the most powerful newspaper in the world" according to *Newsweek* (May 26, 2003, 41-51), was capable of false and shoddy journalism. Blair's exploits ultimately led to the resignations of executive editor Howell Raines and managing editor Gerald Boyd, who both had encouraged the African-American reporter as a rising star. Jonathan Alter wrote the worst part of the Blair debacle was that the public was unfazed, seemingly believing all journalism is lies.

Similarly, top-rated student newspapers are not immune from problems. They may be more responsible than professional publications, many of which also are heavily staffed by young journalists. Blair, then 27, who got interested in journalism during high school, ultimately was fired for fabricating stories, including some of the biggest news stories of recent memory. He made up interviews with unnamed "informants" about the Washington, D.C., sniper case. The Times did not fire Blair despite repeated warnings about his stories from middle managers until he plagiarized a report by a *San Antonio Express-News* reporter. During his four years on *The Times*, Blair's stories required 50 corrections. The Times' inaction may have been due to a poor record of minority hiring. Blair credited a high school journalism class for his becoming a reporter – a cautionary note for journalism educators. Those who worked with him in his early years described him as charming but unreliable. Isaac's troubles were not the clear breach of journalistic standards Blair had committed (they did not involve fabrication or stealing), but they demonstrated the challenge of teaching students to be professionals.

B. The Story of "Licks" –
'This is not the big, bad wolf talking to you'

It was the second day of pre-layout, the next night was the long layout night, and a page of the entertainment section, which included a sensitive story, was stuck with masking tape to the front white board. Editors were working on the final version. I looked at the layout with the advisor, who shook her head. The story involved Licks, a drag queen restaurant that welcomed all ages. The wait-people were clothed suggestively, and the place was very risqué, the advisor said. "When they told me they wanted to write a story about it, I thought it was a joke. They meant it." I asked the advisor if she would ever talk about the story, a restaurant review, with the principal in advance. "Oh, God no," she answered. "She's going to hate it. I hate it. I don't think it should go there."

As I began to read the story, she said, "That's the version that needs to be edited. I am kind of anxious. There's a huge conservative community. The first thing they'll say is the First Amendment allows anything but obscenity, but that's not what this is." Mrs. Phillips refused to censor the story based on the inclusion of homosexuality, but was considering it on the issue of sexuality alone. "There are a lot of young, naïve students and protective parents here."

Penny, the assistant editor, had authored the Licks story, and there were versions marked up in her handwriting, with comments from Mrs. Phillips and Carrie, the editor in chief. The entertainment editor, Maureen, also had edited it, having issued the assignment. The students were supposed to take their pages off the board to incorporate the notes of the advisor. She had to take a few layouts from the board to hand to students because some had disregarded them. "Sometimes, I don't care, but most of these comments were pretty good, so . . ." (Field notes, January 13, 2003).

The advisor's comments on the Licks story included reservations about the words "Black Bitch," the apparent nickname of a drag queen maitre de. "This is probably more trouble than it's worth," she wrote and in a discussion with the students, she said, "The words 'black bitch' are not going to play very well at all. I think it's OK that we are writing this story, but just based on the topic alone, we are going to get a lot of flak. I want to have the story, but not risk losing our rights because people get hyper." Responding to a line that said there were men drinking with men and women drinking with women at the bar, Mrs. Phillips wrote, "Clarify that heterosexuals are there, too."

Another questionable section of the story came when the drag queens handcuffed a customer to his chair, removed his shirt, and:

> put whipped cream all over him. Once they finish that, they try to get his girlfriend from the audience to lick it off him. She doesn't do it, but the rest of the audience is entertained nonetheless, and it is made apparent that [Licks] is not an appropriate dining establishment for every type of audience.

Ultimately, students included not bitch, but b****, the typical way of printing expletives.

Mrs. Phillips suggested that Penny add more descriptive detail to give readers a sense of the shock that the restaurant and its theme might give them. This was possible because not all youth are equally familiar with adult sexual issues. For the Beginning Journalism class, I was asked to speak about some of the stories I have written as a daily newspaper reporter and I delivered a lecture that included a feature story I wrote on prostitution after which one boy raised his hand and asked,

""What's a john?" This showed there is no such thing as assumed knowledge with teenagers (Visit, February 19, 2003). Mrs. Phillips' request for more detail about Licks from Penny was a sample of the way she taught journalism -- as literature. "There's pictures on the walls," Penny recalled, trying to figure out how to expand on description. "I can call them [the restaurant]."

Indeed, G. Stuart Adam focuses on the literary teaching of journalism in his essay, "Notes on a Definition of Journalism" (2002). "Journalism is made," he writes (36). "It doesn't just happen. . . The study of journalism practices should be invigorated by the spirit of art and the humanities. The humanities, properly understood, celebrate creation more than power." In Literary Journalism (1995), Norman Sims writes that the genre "has become widely discussed among writers and general readers, and has been taught in ever-increasing numbers of college and high school classes. Its appeal has grown from the solid foundations of the form – immersion reporting, narrative techniques that free the voice of the writer, and high standards of accuracy" (3).

Similarly, Roy Peter Clark of the Poynter Institute for Media Studies, demonstrates how narration can be an effective way to write news because people enjoy stories. This may be better than an over-reliance on the inverted pyramid style, the typical way of ordering news, not chronologically but based on importance. Some reporters at The Comet grasped this as they experimented with different forms more expertly and with less trepidation than those at Coastal High School. Clark writes (2002, 46):

> The newspaper has always played a role in America as the book of the masses. My grandfather, as far as I could tell, didn't read novels, nor books for that matter, but he read as many tabloid newspapers as New York City could offer, and he read them not just for the racing form or the straight news reports but for stories, narratives of life in his city, written at times with the technique of fiction.

Mrs. Phillips' effort was part of journalism's role to evoke emotion – to present real stories so that they put pictures in readers' minds – a creative aspect of the field.

Yet some Creekwood Canyon students were as young as 13. They brought the newspaper home to parents and younger siblings. Not everyone reading this would be a jaded senior with one foot out the door toward college. Not every parent was as liberal as Mrs. Phillips. She braced for the community reaction. She had decided to let the students run their story not only because they could but also because students go to this restaurant, she said, and she did not think censoring the story was justified. She believed that the story might prove comforting to gays and lesbians on campus because they would feel less marginalized. That may or may not have been the case (critics might reply that the story actually reinforced stereotypes by presenting an extreme and atypical picture of gays). At the same time, the story made the newspaper engaging to its adolescent audience. Young readers probably saw the place as an oddity, something offbeat for them to experience, perhaps as a lark after a formal. Penny wrote:

> From the street, [Licks] is innocent. Its presence is simply indicated by a small pair of red lips . . . Cashmere, the hostess, sits at the entrance to the restaurant, trying to fool visitors with a girlish voice and revealing slit that reaches all the way up her leg. After seeing this, the shock kicks in and it does not take long to figure out that she is wearing a wig. That she is a he (18).

The story ran in the January 16, 2003, edition in the middle of a five-page entertainment section, next to Nintendo game reviews and above a story evaluating a teen dance club.

Was this a genuine test of the student newspaper's freedom, or simply a validation of adolescent immaturity, with the real aim to make adults uncomfortable? The story would run, photos and all, despite its controversial nature, and it would be interesting to observe just how damaging it was, as some would claim, or how harmless. Would such a story be deemed "professional" enough? Although not all gay people like to dress in drag, the inclusion of the story on Licks in a student newspaper demonstrated greater toleration toward information about sexual practices. A newspaper editor might question whether the story was in good taste. The problem with this is that such appeals can mask deeper prejudices.

A story in the September 26, 2002 edition of *The Comet* (9) discusses the difficulty of being gay, lesbian and bisexual at Creekwood Canyon, where such students have a fear of getting beaten up or teased mercilessly. Often, their homosexuality is heavily closeted by necessity. The story includes a photograph of homophobic graffiti ("God hates all fags") on a stall in the boys' bathroom. The author quotes a student who rails against being gay and calls it immoral. A bisexual student comments, "I told a good friend of mine [that I was bisexual], and next thing I know he is going around telling people to be careful because I will rape them." A leader of the school's Gay-Straight Alliance comments that unless people stand up against discrimination and stop using such phrases as "that's so gay" to mean stupid, "homophobia isn't going to end."

Students saw their principal as conservative. Marla Hooper never had visited the classroom with anything but passing compliments for the newspaper before, although some students said she had applied pressure privately. With every one of those confrontations, Mrs. Hooper was getting easier to face and defy, which may be what is asked of a student editor, Carrie said. "Personally, I think she supports us on a surface level. But if it comes down to any conflict whatsoever, that support seems to decline rather rapidly." This was despite the fact that a press association had given her an award for being a top journalism administrator. "It's always clear when you know your rights and you know that you stand in the right. It's no longer really difficult for me. If I know what I am doing is right, even though it doesn't receive the administration's approval, I will still do it." Penny said this about Mrs. Hooper (Field notes, March 29, 2003):

> Penny: All she cares about is PR for the school.
> SEA: And is this why she got so upset about the Licks story?
> Penny: Yeah. She just wants the school to look good.
> SEA: But doesn't every principal want their school to look good?
> Penny: I guess, but it seems like that's ALL she cares about.

This time, after the Licks story appeared, a complaining phone call from the parent of a 14-year-old girl raised the principal's unease and prompted her to visit the class. First (Field notes, February 6, 2003), she tried to demonstrate her good intentions by distributing chocolates. "Just don't throw it at me when I'm done talking." She told students she had no plans to act as a censor, but just wanted to express her opinion. She had phoned Mark Goodman at the Student Press Law Center, who advised her "the students had done nothing illegal but that they were certainly 'pushing the envelope.'" Just the fact that she was willing to phone Goodman showed she believed students had legal rights that exceeded those of school officials. This is not something the principals of Coastal and Homestead high schools would do as they considered

Goodman's interpretation of student press law too liberal. Mrs. Hooper said she is:

> not allowed to operate that way as a principal [as a censor]. I've never really done this before, talked about an article. You have to be prepared for the reactions of people and you need to explain why you did what you did. I treasure the relationship of trust we have and I don't want you to be afraid of me. I'm kid-oriented.

But Carrie later would say the principal "overstepped her bounds" and the visit was intended as a threat. "When you step back and look at her reasoning for coming in, it is pretty clear that she did not want us to print anything in the future that did not receive her approval. Although it's not strictly prior review and she doesn't have that power, I think she was telling us that she would like to have that power to some degree."

My field notes include this account:

> Mrs. Hooper: I wanted to let you know what it feels like to be me and then I want to hear what you think. I think it [the Licks story] was done for sensationalism, and we went from having a newspaper that was on par with the Los Angeles Times to put it on par with The National Enquirer. I've talked to you before about the fact that at this school, we have conservative 13-year-olds and mature 18-year-olds...
> Penny (identifying herself as the author of the story): A lot of students go there so it doesn't seem so far-fetched. It's not that bad of a place.
> Mrs. Hooper: Why the inclusion of the b-word and the stuff with the whipped cream?
> Penny: I felt it was important because if we didn't, kids might have thought the place was perfectly innocent, and we'd get in more trouble. It would have been poor reporting.
> Mrs. Hooper: Why not emphasize the place is open to all ages?
> The entertainment editor, Maureen: That was the purpose of 'the teaser box,' (which contained the restaurant's address, hours, meal price, and the words, 'Reservations Required, All Ages.)'
> Mrs. Hooper: I totally missed the teaser box. I was caught up with the b-word.

When Mrs. Phillips asked the principal how the story harmed the student body, the question encapsulated the age-old debate over media effects, explored in Marjorie Heins' book, *Not in Front of the Children* (2001) in which she argues eloquently that proof of harm to young people from printed information about sex is so inconclusive that censorship is the more detrimental act. Teens often get treated the same way as elementary-age children despite that older children are capable of significantly more understanding. Heins' book demonstrates that the principal's concern is a historical one in existence since the time of Plato. It is largely symbolic, focusing on what young people should read, see and know about sexuality. Usually, this has been a matter of safeguarding information about sexual intercourse and birth control, but now school officials were confronting issues of transvestitism, cross-dressing and entertainment in drag. In their attempts to censor, adults reflect their own fears about the loss of an imagined rather than real childhood innocence, Heins writes. Such concerns are "not really fear of any demonstrable psychological harm" but have more to do with "notions of morality and proper socialization."

Mrs. Hooper was advocating censorship – albeit self-censorship. Removal of the Licks story, as Mrs. Hooper preferred, actually might rob young people, in Heins' words (256-257):

> of the ability to confront and work through the messiness of life – the things that are gross, shocking, embarrassing or scary. From children's fascination with 'dirty noses and dirty bottoms' to their pleasure in cartoon violence, adults' efforts to censor may actually get in the way of socialization. . . Censorship is an avoidance technique that addresses adult anxieties and satisfies symbolic concerns, but ultimately does nothing to resolve social problems or affirmatively help adolescents and children cope with their environments and impulses or navigate the dense and insistent media barrage that surrounds them.

In that sense, critical thinking and debate are the answers to combating social ills. Instead of endearing the journalism students to her, the principal's visit had the opposite effect.

Heins contends that restricting such youth from contact with bad ideas can "only make forbidden fruit more attractive." In addition, there is no sense in lumping teens into the same category as small children or as Heins writes, "into one vast pool of vulnerable youth." The teens at

Creekwood Canyon were experimenting with life issues using critical inquiry and written expression. The Licks story had not been placed on the front page after all, but buried on Page 18. Heins also finds concern about protecting children from sexuality to be rooted in European history. "Certainly, the 17th and 18th Centuries brought the West closer to contemporary ideas about childhood and sexual expression." He may have sentimentalized children in the 18th Century, but Jean Jacques Rousseau encouraged "an authoritarian" approach when he suggested sexuality instruction be postponed until the age of 20, Heins writes. She quotes Michel Foucault, who contends that only in recent centuries have adults targeted childhood sexuality as "sinful" and tried to control it. "One has only to 'glance over 'the architectural layout,' the 'rules of discipline,' and the 'whole internal organization' of secondary schools in 18th-century Europe to see that 'the question of sex was a constant preoccupation,'" Heins writes, quoting Foucault (20):

> The space for classes, the shape of the tables, the planning of the Recreation lessons, the distribution of the dormitories (with or without partitions, with or without curtains), the rules for monitoring bedtime and sleep periods – all this referred, in the most prolix manner, to the sexuality of children.

Ultimately, according to Foucault, "a whole literature of precepts, opinions, observations, medical advice, clinical cases, outlines for reform and plans for ideal institutions" emerged to guide and manage youthful sexuality – an effort that today's schools have not entirely shed.

The Licks story continued a present-tense descriptive style, providing a close approximation of what the drag queen restaurant looked and felt like, reprinting sexual references such as "Viagra Falls" that appeared on the menu. Two photos showed sleekly dressed "waitresses" in drag. The story criticized the food and high prices and discussed the wait-staff's rudeness (the waitresses threw menus at guests):

> Once dinner is served, Kiki announces to her tables that there will be two fashion shows plus a dessert show. Half the crowd is excited. The other half is nervous. The music gets louder, and the tall thin hostess makes her way up onto the stage. She lip-synchs for a while, followed by other drag queens who work at the restaurant, mouthing popular songs such as

CHAPTER 5: CREEKWOOD CANYON HIGH SCHOOL 221

the theme song from 'Chicago.' When Kiki comes on, the crowd breaks into laughter when she starts dancing with, and on top of, the innocent people eating at the table next to her. With this, it is made clear that their intent is to shock people, which they definitely succeed in doing.

It was clear that the story was not the typical fare of high school newspapers, but was it damaging? Ultimately, high school teachers and officials at all three schools in this study employed so-called "journalistic standards" to regulate certain types of sexual expression, whether or not there was any proof such standards were followed by professionals.

Coastal High School teachers and parents were upset by the sex survey students wished to conduct and Mr. McCormick called for the removal of swear words contained in a non-fictional school play. Mrs. Webb at Homestead, backed by Mr. Frank, was very careful to purge sexual language that she felt was inappropriate, once excising the word "orgasm" from a column by the editor in chief that was not referencing sexuality. Mrs. Hooper said did not see the Licks story's "journalistic value." Mrs. Phillips told the principal that she and students took the story seriously and discussed what it should include and why. This took some courage because advisors at the other schools simply would have squelched the story, possibly before it was ever reported or written.

In her appeals for restraint, Mrs. Hooper did not face a sympathetic audience: "I just wanted to let you know what I was thinking and I wanted you to cogitate on it. Its purpose was not really to educate. It was sensational was all I could think of it." Maureen, the entertainment editor, had her arms folded across her chest throughout the class. "These are not things that don't happen," she said petulantly. The principal's visit proceeded this way:

> Mrs. Phillips: Do you object to the whole concept of the story or just those two lines [including the word bitch and whipped cream]? That's what they need to know.
> Mrs. Hooper: It's both. I appreciate that you say kids are going there, but kids go a lot of places you wouldn't write about in the school newspaper. The content is controversial. I don't know how to say it any better than I've said it.
> Carrie: It's not good to go through life with your head in the sand. Really, this article allows you to get educated, to know that this is out there and to make your own

choice about it. I don't think there's any place that kids go that we shouldn't write about in this newspaper.
Mrs. Hooper: I'm not sure it doesn't inflame instead of educate.
Nadine (a conservative in student government): I think as a school, we have so many different story ideas that this was a strange pick. It was something impertinent, kind of obscure. I'm not trying to bash the staff but -- "
Cole (who would be editor in chief next year): To question the story's journalistic value is not fair. It draws reader interest. From a journalistic standpoint, it's a good story. It's written in an objective, lucid, documentary-style. You don't want to be a censor.
Mrs. Phillips: The subject is going to make some people uncomfortable. At least they'll know it exists and it's part of [the city]. The topic and subject matter may be offensive to some, but I thought if it was done in a proper manner. It did have merit.
Mrs. Hooper: I know you had a conversation, but it was a half-page story on drag queens! Think about it and think about if that's what you want to be broadcasting.
Penny: It's a restaurant review. That's what we were going for.
Mrs. Hooper: I remember the whipped cream on the guy's chest. I don't remember the food. It's the culminating effect of drag queens and whipped cream on the guy's chest. I wanted you to know I didn't like it . . . This is friendly, not the big-bad wolf taking to you.
Mrs. Phillips: We have received feedback from people in the lesbian, gay and bisexual community who said they felt validated that a lifestyle not typically represented was in a mainstream school publication. It's a straightforward review of a restaurant that just happens to involve drag queens. They felt that was nice, that it was a relief to have a story just reviewing a restaurant. We have received that feedback, too.
Mrs. Hooper: I think the issue of drag queens was a parody of gay and lesbian people that I didn't like. It's important for you to hear that feedback. Don't be mad at me. You are not mad at me are you? You are sitting there with your arms crossed (addressing Maureen). My intention was just to come here and give you chocolate.

After she made this disingenuous statement, she left. Mrs. Hooper's effort to handle high school students as "kids" did not go over well.

Besides Carrie, Penny and Maureen, among others, Ken said he had no respect for the principal when it came to her claims "that we are not journalistically sound because she has definitely backtracked on quotes that she's made on the record, and I don't really appreciate that." The principal has never been comfortable with the newspaper's presence on campus, he contended. Mrs. Phillips was effusive in her praise of the students' conduct after the meeting with the principal. "May I tell you guys that I love you and I think you did a really good job? And what I said about the gay and lesbian community, I did not make that up. It's true."

The gay and lesbian community actually appeared not upset but ambivalent toward the Licks story, according to Jennifer, the 2003 president of the Gay-Straight Alliance, a 16-year-old lesbian student who described herself as "half in and half out" of the closet. If anything, students felt the story was funny; the newspaper's other coverage, however, was more representative of high-quality reporting portraying gays and lesbians realistically (Interview, November 17, 2003). "Overall, other stories [*The Comet*]] has done promote tolerance and a better view of gay high school students, but the [Licks] story showed the student newspaper does have a lot of freedom. At the same time, the administration is more conservative."

Although the majority of those who spoke out in the principal's presence were editors -- all but one backing the Licks story -- there actually was a diversity of opinion in the classroom. Leo, a Democrat, the boy who had spent his junior year working for Congress, felt the story was about student editors displaying their power, rather than serving readers. The advisor should not have allowed the story but "she wants to make it seem like she's our peer, but at the same time she wants to make it seem like she's a lot older than us and she has all this power. Yet she doesn't exercise it." He said nothing about his opposition during class because Maureen was going to do "whatever she wanted." "I am for the most part fairly liberal and I was really opposed to that story," he said. "We just crossed the line way too much, and was it really necessary to do that? Was it really necessary to test the authorities, or do we already have what we want?"

Amanda portrayed the visit by Mrs. Hooper not as disquieting but "fun" because it demonstrated that students had pushed the limits. For her, the visit was an example of the adversarial nature of the students' journalism. It gave the class enough collective strength to defend their opinions but also may have reduced their respect for school officials.

"You don't care very much about what the principal was saying?" I asked her:

> Amanda: I don't know how much bearing it had on us. I see why people would object to some of the stories, like last year, we had an addiction centerspread that got a lot of flak because parents were calling in and saying, 'My kids don't have any problems. Why should I be reading about it?' And sometimes with those kinds of things you have to know when you're wrong and when you're right. When you're wrong, you know, you have to admit it, but when there's nothing really wrong, I don't know if we need to be too worried.

Penny agreed that the principal's visit "didn't affect us in any way. If anything, it made us feel cool because we stood up for ourselves and I guess kind of like won the fight. Not that it was a fight but I think everyone had really good things to say."

As soon as the principal had left, students quickly returned to the business of the newspaper. Carrie handed back student copy for the coming edition, telling new entrants, "Don't all feel bad. A lot of you have a lot of red marks on your papers." She told them how to put "he said" at the end of each quotation and that "opinions in any article except an opinions article are really bad. Be really, really careful of describer words. Make sure you don't have any opinions. You never speak directly to the reader. You are not talking directly to them, but you kind of are." There was no dwelling on the principal's visit. There wasn't time. Objectivity was a goal, but in this conservative community, the students had acted in a political way merely by supporting gays and lesbians in the newspaper. Printing the Licks story broached the borderline of acceptability. It was a subjective act. They had taken sides.

After Mrs. Hooper criticized the Licks story, Ken commented, "She could say, 'I didn't like the story,' but basically, what she came off as sounding like was that 'I don't like gay people and I don't think they should be in your newspaper. . . I just think she sounded like a homophobe." It might not have been fair to judge Mrs. Hooper homophobic when she did not object to the newspaper's other coverage of gay issues. Yet in his book <u>Homophobia</u> (2000) Byrne Fone, a New York scholar of gay and lesbian studies, argues that even seemingly tolerant heterosexuals have significant trouble accepting gays and that discomfort with gays and lesbians is "the last acceptable prejudice." He writes (419):

> The increased visibility of lesbians and gay men is said to have made inroads against homophobia. But visibility can also erode tolerance. An encounter on the street – two women kissing, two men holding hands – is still disturbing as revealed by a poll that asked people how they reacted to such sights. Half of those polled said that they were 'very bothered.'

In fact, two high school girls in Clarksville, Md. got suspended when they jumped on a cafeteria table, shouted "end homophobia now" and kissed for 12 seconds (ABC News.com, November 13, 2003). The public kiss of a same-sex couple, however, might be less bothersome than drag queens, who push the boundaries of propriety much more. It was ironic that students so closely followed The New York Times because the paper had its own struggle to accept a more tolerant approach to the gay community. For decades, it was known for its failure to recognize the legitimate social place of gays and lesbians – a trend charted by media scholar Larry Gross in Up From Invisibility (2001).

Gross traces the start of *The Times'* shift to Max Frankel taking over as executive editor in 1986 (118). He soon allowed for greater coverage of the AIDS epidemic. Before that, Abe Rosenthal had refused to even use the word "gay" in stories. The elevation of Arthur Sulzberger Jr. to publisher in 1992 institutionalized the paper's commitment to diversity so that gay reporter Jeffrey Schmaltz was assigned to cover gay affairs in 1990. The assignment provoked a reassessment of journalism's ideal of objectivity and the admission that gays can write about gays with the same objectivity as anyone else. Gross writes (125):

> In a profession dominated by straight, white males, it is well known that editors worry about whether the nonwhite, nonmale and/or nonstraight journalist can be 'objective' in writing about people who share their distinctive attributes. Presumably, conventional wisdom implies straight white men are capable of objectivity in all circumstances.

The Comet did not seek gay writers to explore homosexuality but like The Times, the student newspaper made regular efforts to include gay issues and students in its newspaper. Jennifer, the GSA president, said she had never known a story about gays to be written by a gay student (although there had been gays on the newspaper). She described The Comet as "as good as a newspaper can get and in some ways better than the local paper for reflecting student culture in the most tolerant way." For example, besides the September story on discrimination, a month after the Licks issue, the newspaper also ran a centerfold on dating, with stories on blind dates, date rape prevention, and gay dating. The story on gay dating was printed below the headline, "The Gay Dating Scene, Inside and Outside the Closet." The story began:

> Ashley is afraid to go on dates. She cannot talk on the phone with the person she is dating for fear that her parents will find out her secret. She sometimes lies in order to dodge questions about her significant other. Ashley is a lesbian. 'I'm not allowed to talk to [my girlfriend] or see her. We had to go to winter formal secretly, but it was worth it.'

In a sense, student journalists were employing an important principle of muckraking or at least investigative journalism – the coverage of the dispossessed. Although some drag performers are not gay, they also are not accepted as part of mainstream culture. According to Fone, gays often have used outlandish attire and cross-dressing to represent themselves and express a new version of reality, yet the choice of "outrageous style" has only served to further enrage "an unsympathetic public" (378).

In a magazine exploring school journalism (Summer 2003), Mrs. Hooper wrote that she wanted a school newspaper that is both respected and respectful. "I will go into the journalism class and talk about the impact of the article to our school. I believe we will agree to graciously disagree with one another, but I further believe it is important for both sides to be heard [those for and against the Lick's story] have an opportunity to talk about the situation." In the same edition of the magazine for teachers in which Mrs. Hooper wrote, the advisor authored a column, saying that "the principal wishes that I had told the students not to run the story and that they had trusted me enough not to do it. I never told them they could not write it. That is not my job." Mrs. Phillips' advice leaned in both directions, but she did not block controversial material easily.

During a layout May 6, 2003, Sirena, a staff writer and junior, struggled with the question of whether the newspaper should print the cover of the Placebo CD, "Sleeping with Ghosts," because of its sexual explicitness. The album, released in April 2003, depicted a man in jeans holding a naked woman, whose genitals could not be seen. "I am a coward and I would push for something like this but I just don't have the time." The fact that she was running for a position as centerfold editor also made her reticent because she was afraid people would accuse her of poor judgment. Several students in the class had experience with the attitudes of other countries on sexuality, which were very different than in America where youth are more ignorant and isolated than in Europe, Sirena said. Mrs. Phillips told the students to print the CD cover with two others (all could be seen in any record store), but the top editors disagreed, pulling the CD cover.

Mrs. Baker, the Beginning Journalism instructor, said that the nature of a newspaper advisor's job is tricky. "There are ways to steer them [the students], There are the constraints of bad taste. It's the job of the newspaper to push the envelope, but they need to understand that a certain degree of caution is necessary. That's why Alexa is in the hot seat all the time."

C. Iraqi Freedom? 'Keep in Mind, We Are Going to War:' How – and Why -- the Class Covered the Conflict

Students in the journalism class were extremely interested in the news. It was not clear if this interest had existed before the journalism class or developed because of it. The students also knew that many others – their teenage readers – did not share their interest in the world or even national events. This was an important reason the journalism class required that most stories have a "tie-in" to school. The tie-in to school also was necessary because student journalists lacked access to major figures in national or world news, and lived with a slower publication schedule that made covering timely events more challenging. Sometimes, the tie-in could simply be a reaction story to what was happening: Students and teachers gave their responses to particular events. Other times, it was a matter of being creative, of using design and images to attract young people's attention, indeed, to trick them into reading the news. Events like the Iraq War and the Columbia space shuttle disaster were deemed important for students to know about, and this gave *The Comet* an educational mission that extended beyond the aims of improving English literacy or allowing student journalists to practice their First Amendment rights and responsibilities.

At times, they moved beyond covering the news to changing readers based on judgments about what they needed to know. This was not a marketing goal, as it might be in a profit-driven newspaper, but a philosophical one.

The "tie-in" is an attempt "to relate everything to students' immediate world," said Carrie, the editor in chief. "And I think that students are more apt to read about themselves so we try to include multiple quotes and we try to get a wide array of people and that increases our readership and more high school students probably read our newspaper than they would a regular newspaper." A professional newspaper has the advantage that "it's more accepted that people do read the news and people read it no matter if it relates directly to them or not, where we have to take that into special consideration." While Carrie was accurate to a certain degree, professional newspapers also recognize a dire need to increase readership because of declining circulations and a disinterested public with more harried lives. Still, she had made the important point that serving a teen audience usually brings greater obstacles.

The centerfold in December 2002 – not long after the Homestead journalism teacher had pressed her students to produce a terrorism section – was dedicated to a possible war on Iraq. Beyond the attractive full-color design, there were significant differences in the coverage between Creekwood Canyon and Homestead, mainly because of the Homestead teacher's inability to convince students to do sufficient first-hand interviewing. The similarities also were striking to the degree that the coverage showed mainstream sensibilities, with both schools reprinting the American flag. The Homestead work was inauthentic because it had been largely teacher-directed – the students were used to doing what teachers told them -- making other classroom structures hard to achieve. In contrast, the Creekwood Canyon students had developed the centerfold on their own, without duress, based on what they had learned about journalism. As a result, they took more pride in their work. They were motivated to do it after having been socialized in particular ways. In this way, Mrs. Phillips had an easier job than Mrs. Webb. At the same time, for an anti-war group of students, interest in the conflict may have been rooted in sentiments against the large number of conservative, Republican parents in the community and anti-parent aims held consciously and subconsciously.

Most coverage strove for balance, though particular stories may have leaned one way or the other in emphasis. One story discussed the possibility of a student's military father being called for duty. "If he were to go, we would get really short notice," said his teenage daughter. " It would be a call saying 'pack your sea bag' and then, just like that, he'd be gone." A graphic "An Expert Talks" was based on an interview with a retired Marine Corps general. "We will win Iraq, quickly and swiftly and the [Iraqi] people will rejoice. Saddam Hussein is a ruthless dictator killer and neighboring countries will be happy that he's gone." There also was a story on student efforts to find peaceful alternatives to war.

The class response to the teacher was different than at Homestead. Students were more open to her cue March 18, 2003: "Keep in mind, we are going to war tomorrow."

"It's really important," responded the opinions editor immediately. "Can we cover it and not have a high school tie?"

Class discussion on war coverage began with the teacher – she provided certain provocative bits of information -- but student voices, mainly editors, quickly took over:

> Mrs. Phillips: A story could be on the teachers. Maybe part of the tie-in is that we are not allowed to send any e-mails that have political content. And we are not supposed to discuss anything political that shares our views with our students, but I know there are teachers out there whose views are pretty obvious when you walk into their classroom or when they talk.
> Boy: So anti-war talk is illegal?
> Mrs. Phillips: I don't know about illegal. Well, maybe. I don't know. But there are teachers in other states and in other districts that are being chastised for wearing – somebody wore 'President Bush is Not My President' on their jacket, and they got in trouble for it and it made CNN.
> Opinions editor: The other thing I have is about gas prices and it's a way you can make a tie to [Creekwood Canyon High School] with carpools. I know someone who has a Suburban who just spent $100 for a tank of gas.
> Carrie, the editor in chief: I want to talk to you guys about war and what your opinion is on how we should cover it. Next issue, we may be at war. So what do you guys think is too much coverage and what is not enough?
> Boy1: I think we shouldn't put too much importance on gas prices. Some coverage needs to be done on it because it's part of the economy, but an obsession with

it would just be in poor taste because people would be dying.

News editor: I think that when we go to war, we are a newspaper, but at the same time, we are not <u>The New York Times</u> or [the local city paper], and we need to balance it. Students need to find out about it, but we need to make sure it's not overpowering or overwhelming.

Mrs. Phillips: Our newspaper is not going to be where they are getting their news about the war because we finish on a Tuesday and come out on a Thursday. But that's not to say we can't write news about the war because the war affects you guys as teenagers in a different way than it does on the front page of <u>The New York Times</u>. . . . I think for our stories, there are definitely students and parents in the Middle East right now. There are husbands and wives and family members who are going off to war. It affects our school because there are teachers who say, 'OK, I've got to get all my stuff done before the war starts because who is going to pay attention?' You have to find a way to cover it that ties it to [Creekwood Canyon], that ties your lives as teenagers to the war.

Features editor: I think we should cover it, but I don't think we should let the idea of war dominate the paper.

The teacher and students were cooperating in an effort to generate ideas for the newspaper. The teacher gave the students suggestions, but she was not dictating them. When she indicated that the local area was a possible terrorist target, the students reacted to this information casually, as news professionals whose job was to inform the student body. It was clear to students that the teacher's contributions were merely suggestions and their point of view was paramount. The teacher often said that she did not like keeping secrets and she showed that she was quite willing to share whatever information she knew about the official treatment of faculty at the school. There was none of the kind of out-and-out resistance that the very idea of war coverage had faced at both Coastal and Homestead High schools. Teacher and students showed equal commitment to the project of the newspaper. Students also had the advantage of having spent a full semester preparing for their roles. The class continued this way:

Cole, the future editor in chief: We should absolutely explore it to the extent that it affects the student body.

We should acknowledge it but we should also run all the other stories that are important to the [Creekwood Canyon] community.

Mrs. Phillips: And there are people who don't know. Even in one of my classes, I heard, 'What? Really? Tomorrow?' If you didn't watch the president's speech yesterday, then you don't know that that's happening. So you might run a mini-info box, a 'how we got here' kind of thing.

Leo: That's what I was going to say. Some people don't get a newspaper at home or bother to watch or bother to learn, but when [the paper] comes to their classroom, they leaf through it at least. That is the only way they are going to learn, but I don't think there should be an extensive, in-depth story. Maybe an info box. When it's relevant.

Mrs. Phillips: But I don't think that should always be there. Like if we need to write something that has a [Creekwood Canyon] connection.

Photographer: We just need to be conscious of the fact that it seems very far away, and it seems very like, 'oh, this is national news . . ." But we live in a city that has four Navy bases. I mean, it's such a big part of the economy, and it's not far away. It could be your next-door neighbor or the guy sitting next to you's father could be on a ship halfway across the world. So that's the part that will really affect us.

Mrs. Philips: And that might be part of your story, too, the fact that we've got the Marines and Navy and so much military here. This is a pretty obvious target in the United States for terrorists. That might be our angle as well.

Carrie: So what's been assigned so far?

Opinions editor: I think there should be a pro and a con, for and against the war. The argument goes both ways. That the classroom is the place to make kids aware and also that we shouldn't because this is a school where we are supposed to be learning.

Mrs. Phillips: [One teacher], she always thinks that if anything ever happens the best thing to do is continue on with her lessons.

Boy1 Maybe we can do a feature on how teachers feel about the war.

(Field notes, March 18, 2003)

The class discussion reflected the fact that there was not necessarily agreement about how much the war mattered to students. The discussion reflected a sincere wish to make the war in Iraq comprehensible to the student body and live up to the newspaper's reputation as a top high school publication. There also was enough openness that participants felt comfortable thinking aloud. Both teacher and students shared their own experiences in hopes that this would trigger more ideas and deeper debate. There was recognition that war was a serious matter but also an understanding that it should not be treated merely as an eye-catching subject because the tactic could frighten younger readers. If any criticism was possible, I thought more student voices could have joined those deemed most powerful.

When the U.S. was poised to begin a war on Iraq in March 2003, students actually were very divided in their political views, but notions of professionalism made some editors reluctant to discuss their positions openly. They took themselves very seriously as students and journalists. By the time of the discussion on the eve of war, Amanda had already covered a front-page story on a March 5 walkout by high school students nationally, known as the "Books not Bombs" protest against military intervention in Iraq:

> Protesters affixed 'War=Death' flyers to their T-shirts, applied black-and-white face paint and laid down on the ground as part of a 'die-in. Others . . .stood up to share their views on the war, the Bush administration and Iraq.

She also wrote about passers-by who disapproved of the protest and wished to support the soldiers at war. While Amanda said she was liberal, the news editor Maggie would not reveal any political affiliation, a decision similar to those made by many professional journalists, who register to vote as independents – or may not vote -- to maintain a neutral appearance. Student reluctance to discuss their own political views was reminiscent of the furor caused by Kent MacDougall, whose socialist status (and work as a writer for radical publications) was revealed after 25 years as a reporter for *The Los Angeles Times* and *The Wall Street Journal* (Reese 1997, 1990).

MacDougall was accused of violating boundaries and distorting the news. However, his editor at *The Los Angeles Times*, John Lawrence, said that "being a Marxist does not necessarily have to detract from his journalistic integrity. Every reporter comes to a story with some level of bias. The question is: Are they capable of rising above that bias to write a fair story?" This reminded me of the opinionated news editor at Coastal High who had made a very similar argument. Amanda probably showed her bias – at least in her choice of anti-war stories. The next issue April 3, she authored a feature entitled, "The memo read around the school," which interviewed teachers about their responses to a school district policy that directed them not to discuss their personal opinions about the war with students or allow them class time as a platform for protest. The story quoted a teacher who gave students time to discuss the protest a few days after it had occurred. "I tried to act more as a facilitator, although I'm sure I say some things, too. I think a lot of times it's indirectly, and they notice your facial expressions, and they read it as if you had spoken," an English teacher remarks in the story.

Amanda's feature on teachers' views of the war was written in an informational style, but the juxtaposition of the story with the points of the administration's memo made it seem untenable for teachers to leave their political views out of the classroom. The story was printed atop a blank memo form from the school district, and the writing interspersed with sections of the actual policy. Above the section on the English teacher, for instance, is the part that reads, "In the classroom, we must put our personal beliefs aside. Remember that we have staff and students whose loved ones are going to be serving our country if we are at war" (9). Amanda's story stretched the boundaries of the news paradigm and objectivity. No staff editorial took a stand on the Iraq war, and Carrie said if it had, most staff likely would have opposed U.S. involvement.

The majority of print journalists "are left of center politically," but surprisingly, the Creekwood Canyon class was led by conservative Republicans. Franny Eastwood, Mrs. Phillips' predecessor, said most of her students were liberals over more than a quarter of a century. "In the early 1990s, journalists were much more likely to consider themselves left of center politically, and much less likely to claim to be middle of the road," found Weaver and Wilhoit (1996). "There was also a slight increase in the percentage of U.S. journalists considering themselves pretty far to the right politically" (15-16). Of the 26 students in the class who filled out a questionnaire asking them their position on the Iraq War, exactly 13 or half were against U.S. military action, and 11 supported it. Two were undecided. There were roughly an equal number of liberal Democrats as conservative Republicans in the class, but there were more top editors who considered themselves sympathetic to Republican causes. Given their position of authority, they were more vocal about their views. At least 10 students claimed they identified with no political party or ideology, but this may or may not have been true.

In Ken's view, his classmates seemed heavily to favor liberal politics despite some outspoken conservatives. One needed only to examine the popularity of the student anti-war protest and walkout of March 5, 2003 to understand the extent of anti-war sentiment among the high school's students. The newspaper reported that 225 students walked out, but Ken contended many were ill informed. Ken was a member of the campus Young Republican Club and helped plan a counter-protest in support of the troops to voice opposition to the usual liberal voices around school, he said. "Every single person who walked out, save maybe one or two, had no idea why they were doing it and no good reasons to support their actions," he claimed, adding:

> We didn't want the peace protesters to be the only voice on campus, so we decided that instead of having a pro-war rally, which we thought would be distasteful and just offend people, we wanted to do something to just support the troops and then we decided that having people sign pledges would be a good way to go about doing that.

The plan was to get the pledges to the troops, probably through a local Congressman. However, as students distributed flyers promoting their cause, an assistant principal stopped them. He told them that the school district required clubs to have pamphlets reviewed by the administration before they could hand them out.

Ken said that students knew the administration's action violated their Constitutional right to freedom of expression and a 9th Circuit Court of Appeals decision *Burch v. Barker* (1988) that found schools could not review material prior to its distribution, only punish students afterward for disrupting the educational process. The ruling, based on the distribution of an underground newspaper in Washington state, affects any non-school sponsored literature (861 F. 2nd 1149; 1988 U.S. App. LEXIS 15585). Aside from the legal issues, Ken said the administration seemed to display a bias by treating the pro-war students who staged the walkout lightly. Teachers were told to take a second roll after the students left, but many teachers refused to do this. The teachers were then told to handle the discipline themselves, which meant there was little action taken. The Superintendent eventually promised that she would revisit the policy of reviewing student material before distribution, but only after Ken and his friends caused considerable embarrassment for the principal, who was apparently concerned about the school's and her own image. The Republican students spoke on a local radio talk show and gained the aid of a lawyer who volunteered to help them sue. They ultimately dropped any such plans. "[I called because] I wanted an opportunity to clarify this issue," Principal Marla Hooper told the radio station after the students spoke. "The boys have a right to hand things out on campus. The administration just needs to review the information."

Yet the boys disagreed that the administration needed to practice prior review.

The stresses of a real newspaper always questioning her, the protests over the Iraq war, the phone calls from parents, public criticism of her leniency toward anti-war protesters, all may have proved too much for principal Marla Hooper by June of 2003. She announced that she was stepping down from the job one day after the newspaper had printed its final issue. Ken said "she was probably fed up with dealing with the school bureaucracy and the pressures of confronting rich kids' parents. The parents practically run the school." Schools in less wealthy areas have more freedom from parental oversight, but this may be to the students' academic detriment.

The journalism students were polarized on the issue of Iraq, with strong opinions on each side. This probably reflected the deep divisions in American popular opinion, particularly as soldiers continued to die after the president declared an end to major combat May 1, 2003. The American public already had proven itself to be divided in the election of 2000, when approximately equal electoral votes went to the Republican candidate as the Democrat, with the Supreme Court deciding the outcome in Florida. Among student comments against the war (Response sheet, May 12, 2003):

- " I don't feel there were immediate reasons for us to go." – 17-year-old boy
- "I felt that it was necessary for the USA to receive support from the United Nations. It is highly probable that countless have died as part of the 'collateral damage' category." – 16-year-old boy
- "Why use violence to show people that using violence is detrimental to society?" – 15-year-old girl
- "There are other ways the problem of Saddam Hussein could have been dealt with." – 15-year-old girl
- "We have no right to police the world and tell everyone that we are the only ones who are right." 17-year-old girl

The views that students expressed were intelligent but also reflected the debate nationally, probably because the students obtained significant information from the nation's major mainstream media, along with family and friends. The community in which they lived was more conservative than others in California, but that did not mean their identification with this conservatism was automatic, as political identities are complex. While studies on younger American children have found stronger notions of political affiliation, Connell (1971) argued that political ties among youth in Australia are light. His interviews with younger adolescents indicated that they took parents' judgments as grounds for their own opinion, rather than "simply reproducing" those views. Parent-child correspondence in party preference is not "a mass phenomenon" but applies to a "small minority of cases."

While younger children are isolated from one another, adolescents develop their political views in communication with each other. "By the age of 15 or 16, a majority had formed political outlooks which, despite some incoherencies and contradictions, had an inner unity and could be characterized as wholes" (89), Connell writes. Ultimately, journalism classes in which students discuss their views on the news and politics may be essential training grounds for democracy because the formation of a personal ideologies is social, requiring both "a strong stimulus from others" and reflection on the political beliefs of "the groups the person moves in." Political beliefs in youth are not constant.

Those teens in favor of the war did not appear to have been brainwashed. They were convinced of the threat posed by Iraq's supposed weapons of mass destruction and the cruelty with which the Iraqi people were treated by their own government. "It was time to get Hitler II out of power, with or without the United Nations," wrote an 18-year-old boy on his way to Yale. "All of the worldwide organizations had been dissolved due to inaction, and I don't support appeasement," said a girl, also 18, who would go to a University of California campus. A 17-year-old girl wrote, "I wish we could have charged Saddam with war crimes, but since that seemed like an impossible scenario, war was the next option. Paul Wolfowitz, the main planner, is brilliant." The knowledge of Wolfowitz, the Deputy Secretary of Defense, was impressive, as the girl's command of information may have surpassed the average adult without time or inclination to learn basic facts.

CHAPTER 5: CREEKWOOD CANYON HIGH SCHOOL   237

Nadine, a fellow member of the Young Republicans Club, felt that the attitude of her friends was much like the adversarial stance student journalists often maintained when dealing with school officials:

> I kind of wish that we had more of a newsletter, just to inform the students of what's going on on campus. Not really to start things. I think that we're always trying to start things. . .I think it's really cool that we are able to use the First Amendment in our favor, but I don't think that it's really necessary. [Licks] was an example of that, she said. "There was no reason we had to put that article in the paper. It's not like we have a drought of story ideas. It just seemed like we wanted to show how powerful we are. . . People criticize the administration on campus. I think it's more of just the trendy thing to do.

During the meeting where students planned the pledges for U.S. troops, Nadine argued "it was no big deal to have the administration approve" the flyers. The protest planners were like, 'No, no, you don't want to do that, and I said, 'it'll take like five minutes.'"

The class had convinced her she will never be a journalist because "it just seems like we're always trying to find stories that make people look bad. . . Like I was telling my parents, I'd rather be making the news than writing about it. I could never have a career where I am always on call. . . Ever since I've joined these people, I've noticed that I'm a much more intense person." Despite Nadine's criticisms, it was telling that she also found the students in the newspaper class -- that they read a newspaper every day and their persistent involvement in all aspects of school -- "incredibly reassuring." We had this exchange:

> SEA: That's an interesting word to use, reassuring. What do you mean by reassuring?
> Nadine: Reassuring that our generation is going to actually persevere and that we have kids that are going to go out there and do stuff.

D. Conclusion: Professionalism and *The Comet*

The professional standards that made up the core of the journalism program at Creekwood Canyon High School can be traced as far back as the turn-of-the-century Progressive era when writers first saw themselves as paid specialists and public servants, no longer members of the literary elite. While trade groups called for increased standards during the period that encompassed the first muckrakers, sensational journalism undoubtedly was more valuable to emerging commercial bosses who pressed employees for "exclusives" (Wilson 1985 17-35). The more important point is the extent to which newspapers increasingly were large bureaucratic organizations where writers were expected to learn their craft "of ritualized routines, careful sounding of the market, and hard work," writes Christopher P. Wilson in *The Labor of Words*:

> Professionalism's appeal accompanied the growth of the modern university and responded to the process by which independent entrepreneurialism had given way to rationalized and highly structured careers within bureaucratic work environments.

The managerial trend in newspapering of the 1880s and 1890s, instead of encouraging professionalism, led some reporters to fake events in what came to be known as "yellow journalism, writes Wilson (37). However, the journalistic tradition of objectivity originally responded to these perceptions of abuses in journalism. The teacher at Creekwood Canyon faced some of the same challenges that journalism has had over almost a century of pursuing objectivity, which she called "the key of good journalism." Students were taught "that it is their job to report other people's stories, not inject themselves into everything they write."

According to Robert Miraldi in *Muckraking and Objectivity: Journalism's Colliding Traditions* (1990), muckraking is about storytelling and reforming society while objectivity is about observation and neutrality, the balancing of perspectives. Muckraking largely disappeared around 1912 as the nation tired of the relentlessly critical reporting and prepared for World War I (journalists also lived in fear of libel lawsuits). But a new form of investigation – mixing factual detail and interpretation -- began in the late 1950s with Edward R. Murrow's exploration of the plight of migrant farm workers and became a permanent feature of journalism. Bob Woodward and Carl Bernstein, who continue to be heroes of the field, also are considered muckrakers. It is appropriate then that most high school journalism programs spring from English departments, and that students experiment with literary methods as they investigate stories.

The Comet adhered to contemporary newspaper layout standards, such as a five-column front page, fixed typefaces for section fronts, distinct fonts distinguishing news from opinion, and modular designs built around dominant photographic art. The journalism program made an effort to retain the rich literary history of journalism and the high authority newspapers had held before the introduction of *USA Today* (1982) and before the more contemporary onset of corporate conglomeration in newspapers. Barnhurst and Nerome (1982) write that newspapers between the wars sought to act as maps rather than mirrors of the world for readers. "A streamlined and rationalized front page with hierarchical story placement told the reader what mattered most in the world of news," they write (21). Sections of Wilson's book discussing the rise of the reporter could be written about today's journalist who also may be "fighting a valiant but losing battle" to increasing rationalization of the news-gathering process. Reporters must still confront workplaces that may be more competitive than collegial and "the pseudostatemetns of public officials" (Wilson, 37). Reporting in the 21st Century is probably even more fraught with "the tensions of bureaucracy, the pressures of status and job security, the anxieties that come with being 'radically institutionalized'" as Wilson phrases it about Progressive Era journalists. *The Comet* staff got a taste of these tensions as they learned what it meant to be professional and writerly at once.

Participation in the student newspaper created both excitement and anxiety for young people. The paper may enhance the overall quality of journalists, although any students who developed a sense of journalistic integrity in this environment could face a rude awakening if they decided to enter a professional world less swayed by democratic values than the corporate bottom line. Perhaps they could change the world that they entered if high school journalism offered more integrity than the real thing. The students did learn about corporate concentration of newspapers in Betsy Baker's Beginning Journalism class. Mrs. Phillips emphasized the need to sell advertisements, but this tended to strengthen the newspaper's sense of independence. Very few students planned to be journalists in the class, but their improved respect for journalism would last a lifetime. Unlike students at both Coastal and Homestead, who saw high school as a waiting period to be endured, students at Creekwood Canyon felt it was an opportunity to get places, and this attitude fueled their reporting and personal drive.

The poor and working-class Homestead students in this study had lower expectations placed upon them and probably would have a difficult time competing with this upper-middle class group. In fact, Homestead students had a great deal of catching up to do. It was hard to grasp how far they had fallen behind students who often started out with similar potential, but received much greater training and ended up with a stronger command of literacy. The distinctions were immense between journalism programs comprised mainly of white, upper-middle class students and one made up of Latino teens from underprivileged backgrounds. Of course, the reasons for this are complex, but I often found myself wishing there could be some kind of newspaper exchange program. How much would a week or a month spent in this entirely different setting do to broaden the outlooks of students from other schools? The fact that the students at Creekwood Canyon grasped and produced outside and high school news would make them more functional as democratic citizens.

Several students at Creekwood had experiences that were unlike the majority of their classmates. One was Bella, an Armenian youth who had spent her childhood escaping discrimination in the Soviet Union before immigrating to California. She had started out in a different district at an elementary school populated mostly by the children of poor Mexican and Southeast Asian immigrants. Quiet and thoughtful, she had almost achieved my imagined exchange program. She said upper-middle class students believe:

> you do everything in a prescribed way, Most of the kids in the class would think that you can't stoop any lower than going to a community college. In reality, there's nothing at all wrong with it, but it's wrong for them because they have tons of money. . . . What I am taught is that basically you make your own future and if you go to community college, it all comes down to what you want to get out of it. Just because you go to Harvard does not automatically make you anything.

This was something most of the upper-crust needed to appreciate, but parental focus on SAT prep classes and other enrichment efforts to boost their children's competitiveness is a way that the social classes get divided early on.

Students who joined the newspaper to improve their college chances quickly learned they also needed to become thoughtful about conditions in the world. Poor parents do not have the time or resources to make their children's schools look like a Creekwood Canyon or even a Coastal High School, Bella said. "If you're thinking about what you are going to eat tomorrow, you don't care about a newspaper," she said. A high-quality publication provides students a route to power if they were not born with it. These journalism students were more likely to be among those who cared about the world's problems. The class had the most work of any other and a potentially negative effect on student

CHAPTER 5: CREEKWOOD CANYON HIGH SCHOOL

GPAs (it was not weighted like advanced classes), said another student who brought a different perspective to the class, having moved to California from a small town in Illinois. She had given up explaining to other students how they should be happy their parents bought them a car, rather than dissatisfied with the color. "Kids get BMWs and Mercedes," she said. "It's just normal." Many have the attitude of "make your money, help yourself. I think we should help others." She wanted to be a photojournalist.

The journalism program's positive and negative points mirrored the best practices and contradictions of professional journalism. Despite its flaws, the journalism program was doing what teacher rhetoric claims is most desirable. It prepared students to think critically, work with others toward a common goal, question the ideas of those in power, and articulate their own positions and those of others. Because of the active nature of the class, students put conceptual frameworks, such as their Constitutional rights, into immediate practice. It was hard to imagine a more worthwhile media exercise – most worthwhile because it was more than a simple exercise but carried intrinsic meaning. There were times students would actually forget that they were in a class and lose themselves in the project of newspapering. Yet *The Comet* might be an anomaly. Such programs may never exist at the majority of high schools.

CHAPTER 6: AFTERWORD

Prescription for a Better Future?

High school journalism is important. What is admirable as well as what is loathed about today's media begins here. The high school newspaper class shapes lifelong attitudes toward what the media are and what they may become. It is true that few people decide to be journalists in high school, yet media education either can build respect or disdain for the job of the Fourth Estate. Early experiences stick in the memory. Despite the subject's potential, American youth are offered arbitrary and conflicting messages about journalism and their own rights. While teenagers crave purpose, schools rarely offer them any.

What is the reason for information exchange in an open society? If educators truly want to teach youth critical-thinking skills, the answer should be readily apparent in high school journalism classrooms. While the results of this study are not all-inclusive – they could be criticized for applying only to a particular region and time – the collection of observations point to more universal failures of the educational system and other adult efforts to socialize young people. Instead of turning youth cynical, as is too often the case, high school journalism instruction can inspire optimism about the media.

Professional organizations do much to improve the status of high school journalism nationally.[11] Yet they reach only a sliver of the population of journalism advisors and students. There is a need for more deliberate instruction in journalism as in many other subjects. Journalism deserves to be taught at the highest and most comprehensive level possible. As far back as 1976, Judith Nault said quality journalism in high school means students must be given "latitude of experimentation" but not without the parameters of journalistic responsibility. She would have applied her prescription for high school papers nationally, but could have easily been discussing California today with its strongly worded high school press law. "To implement this delicate harmony, journalism programs will have to be defined in a context of professionalism," she wrote. "This context demands the observance of press law under the qualified supervision of publications advisors who are qualified journalists, by educational training or practical experience." Even when the law nationally seemed to support a free press in high school, Nault argued, "due to the censorship approach to supervision rather than the more realistic professional and legal approach, the student is burdened with nothing more than a 'pretend' journalism which not only limits his creative and ethical awareness but more importantly, destroys his educational development in journalism" (Nault 1976, 68).

Many southern California students never learn the parameters of their right to free expression, especially when teachers feel threatened by the idea of teenagers gaining power. On top of this, many students do not know certain forms of journalism allow for a high degree of creativity – when combined with organization and accuracy – because they have not been exposed to much other non-fiction. If students found the inverted pyramid form rigid, other variations may be less so. The journalism teacher's usual privileging of objectivity ignored the technique of storytelling, which is more interpretive and could have been introduced through contemporary works including Roy Peter Clark's "Three Little Words," a serial for *The St. Petersburg Times*. The story discusses the pain caused by a married man's revelation to his family that he had led a secret gay life. His three little words were, "I have AIDS." There are many other examples of exemplary serials running in daily newspapers that attempt to tell stories filled with human emotion. Clark's vision is that these stories about real lives will draw people to print journalism again. The series is also available on the World Wide Web.

Clark's method of teaching journalism to middle school students in Pinellas County, Florida, called for building upon their own knowledge and ideas about the world to avoid over-reliance on the teacher for story ideas. He showed how students might be overly concerned about adult perceptions of what they write, rather than with the construction of an authentic journalism. The assumed inadequacy of teenagers is among the problems that student journalists continue to confront. It leads many to micromanage rather than teach. This book suggests an eight-part prescription to improve high school journalism, including ideas employed successfully in the professional world. Other possibilities for change should be evident in my work, such as including more stories in the student press that are written in all of students' native languages. The suggestions below go beyond the usual appeals to create a more professional student press because this must be the foundation upon which all other reforms will rest:

• *Practice public journalism.* None of the three school sites included in this study had a way of eliciting reader opinion about the newspaper or what issues it should cover. All accepted letters to the editor, but tried no measures beyond that. Newspapers can sponsor and cover panel discussions of teenagers about particular school dilemmas, offering students a voice. Use of this idea might make student newspaper reports more meaningful to readers. For example, community newspapers have required staff to interview typical readers to discover their concerns, allowed typical residents to question officials, set up booths or "newsrooms on wheels" where the public could comment on particular issues, and held focus group discussions on such issues as teen violence or troubled neighborhoods (offering free pizza as a lure). Jay Rosen encourages newspapers to ask readers the main five issues on their agendas, but "also the top five troubles or problems in their own lives" (Charity 1995, 30). Internet blogs and online journalism allow for reader feedback that is instant, but many high school English teachers – including those in this study – are not familiar enough with the latest technology to help students create online versions of their newspapers.

• *Name a reader editor or ombudsman.* This would be an extremely helpful step for a high school newspaper, and it might help work through the conflicts that invariably arise with readers, sources and school officials as a result of reporting. In an unprecedented move for the newspaper and following "plagiarism and management scandals," *The New York Times* named its first public editor Daniel Okrent who has been followed by others.[2] The decision came amid a period of increasing discontent from its audience over what appeared to be lapses in professional standards. Some genuine connection with readers should become standard operating procedure in any journalistic practice that claims to serve the public good. That *The Times* lacked such a link was testament to the arrogance that has been so rampant in news journalism.

• *Offer expanded training for principals.* Some principals seem to believe that there is a national standard placing them at the helm of the student newspaper, but this is not necessarily true as far as California law is concerned. An invaluable publication for principals is *The Principal's Guide to Scholastic Journalism* (2002) published by the Quill and Scroll Foundation at the University of Iowa. The book calls for principals to understand why school officials should support First Amendment rights for students, why they should not practice prior review or restraint, and how administrators can ensure freedom of expression for school media. The book contains model guidelines for student publications from the Student Press Law Center and an Adviser Code of Ethics adopted by the Journalism Education Association (January 1996). The book provides principals with a list of practices to avoid, such as the adoption of vaguely worded codes that supposedly outlaw unprotected speech such as the phrase "material inconsistent with the shared values of a civilized social order" or "material offensive

to good taste." Principals also are told to avoid setting goals for student-run media such as "creating a wholesome school spirit."
• *Create transitional routes for working journalists to become full- and part-time teachers.* Many journalists probably figure they should not support any professional options beyond the newsroom for editorial staff, but this is a mistake. News organizations would benefit from a more standardized route between them and the classroom. Many journalists do not remain in the profession for a lifetime and one will find those who switched to teaching after years in the business in almost every newsroom. Even if there is no formal program to retrain journalists for the classroom, there can be short or part-time instructional opportunities or guest lecture positions. The growing number of charter schools, in particular, may have more leeway to hire professionals from other fields to teach a single subject. While a journalism teacher need not have been a full-time journalist, such teachers are valuable for young people and offer a different perspective.
• *Form exchange programs between urban and suburban high schools.* The stark differences that exist between newspapers situated in more privileged high schools and those isolated in poorer communities call for way of swapping students for a day or a week to allow them to learn the differences. Although the risk is that this could make some students cynical or disconsolate, the benefits are that they will be exposed to a range of new ideas. One might argue students could simply get this contact with another level of student journalism by attending conferences and conventions. However, it is often not feasible for many youth to obtain the financing for participation in such programs.
• *Offer AP credit for advanced journalism classes.* The Dow Jones Newspaper Fund once promoted a program called Intensive Journalistic Writing and trained at least 100 teachers to offer the advanced writing class in high schools. However, since 1990, after Dow Jones decided to fund other projects, retired educator Carol Lange has kept the program afloat, receiving money from a variety of sources, such as the Freedom Forum's Newseum and Virginia Commonwealth University. Dow Jones continues to offer short training workshops for teachers during the summer in intensive journalistic writing. Lange is planning to co-author a book that will include information about the high schools still offering the course, which combines journalism and literary techniques to improve writing skills. At the end of each course, students take the College Board's English Language and Composition exam and try to score 3 or better, which earns them college credit. Proof of the program's success was the fact that students who took the class actually

did better on the AP test than after other English composition courses.[3] "At the core of a strong journalism program is a well-trained teacher and a community that believes in First Amendment principles because if you are open to ideas and discussion, you are not going to be afraid of what students write," Lange remarked (Interview with Lange, April 1, 2004). Because of its potential, this program should be expanded and receive a reliable funding stream.

• *Establish district-level publications and online media that give students other places to publish their work.* In California, this is a good idea if the publications allow contributors the same freedoms high school newspapers are supposed to enjoy. In one example, a district publication in Southern California accepts submissions from student journalists and pays them for their work, but its adult creator said the magazine would not print anything critical of the school system, even if a student's reporting had won journalism awards. The focus of the magazine was on lifestyle issues. Readers are going "to pick up what they relate to – skateboarding, punk rock music, hip hop music," said the 30-year-old founder. "Whatever they're watching on MTV is what you want to emulate, but when you open up the magazine you are going to see very thorough articles on binge drinking, on what alcohol and tobacco, smoking, caffeine do to teenage pregnancies. Real strong health care articles -- I don't want to use the word -- but maybe sugar-coated in an MTV, Rolling Stone type of magazine." The originator's focus on improving teenage health was laudable, but this should not rule out coverage of other educational and school issues. The organizer claimed teens were uninterested in such matters. Without a wider focus, however, the magazine is more like a public relations tool than an additional forum for student work. The magazine, which began with a $40,000 district grant (the organizer earns a teacher's salary), expects to be self-sustaining with private contributors.

• *Use the journalism textbook carefully.* One of the most popular textbooks for high schools is the 493-page Journalism Today! (1997). The book is quite comprehensive, including such topics as journalism history, evaluation of the media, legal and ethical responsibilities, newsgathering, interviewing, all aspects of newspaper writing, photography and advertising. There are even profiles of different journalism careers students could pursue. However, the text also includes a section on the U.S. Supreme Court's Hazelwood decision that gives the impression it is applicable everywhere, when schools in some states fall under different restrictions. California student journalists deserve to know of their added protections. In two of the three locations

I studied, they did not. The best high school newspaper programs often do not even use a textbook but offer other material, some of it examples from real-world journalism.

None of these ideas is impossible to implement, and each might yield dividends for students and advisors trying to improve the quality of their publications as well as their relevance to the audience of youthful readers they claim to serve. For the reasons set forth in this study, a teenage population is among the most difficult to serve. They are absorbed with the challenges of becoming adults and more wedded to popular culture and peers. Lacking the vote, they are less invested in conventional politics.

This study also highlights the differences between schools in rich and poor settings. Young people in disadvantaged schools can use the student newspaper in their pursuit of social equity and for self-actualization but only with the help of adults who understand the newspaper's value. The problems faced by minority and working-class youth in accessing the political system have been recognized for more than 40 years. Fred Greenstein, author of <u>Children and Politics</u> (1969, 106) cites Robert Lane (1959), in discussing "class differences in available leisure and financial resources, in ability to perceive the personal stakes in public policy, in the tendency to belong to organized groups and have social contacts and in possession of the sorts of verbal skills that facilitate political participation." A variety of studies describe working-class lifestyles and have included barriers to political involvement. Greenstein writes (1969, 106):

> Explanations of class differences in participation also may vary in the depth of the psychological factors which are said to affect participation. Emphasis may be placed on surface factors of a sort which could be (relatively) easily remedied by increasing an individual's education . . .or encouraging him to change consciously held attitudes – such as 'voting is a waste of time' or 'votes don't really have much of an effect on what politicians do.' On the other hand, one may suspect that more fundamental less readily changed psychological processes are at work – for example, strongly held beliefs in one's personal inadequacy, deferential tendencies, constricted imagination.

These ingrained social issues were what teachers like Homestead's Mrs. Webb confronted, yet the passage of time has not offered much in the way of wisdom. Homestead avoided the worst cuts during the state's budget crisis in 2003 because of past fiscal conservatism by the superintendent, but the obvious differences between rich and poor neighborhood schools remained stark as ever. The journalism programs are just one warning sign. Research is sharply critical of public cuts in support services to families and communities that have taken place over the last decade at all levels. Similarly, the plan in California to make school funding equitable, the result of legal victories for the poor, ended up reproducing the same class divisions. As soon as a court decision required the Legislature to fund all schools equally, a conservative revolt, the Proposition 13 property tax cap, left schools with little.

Jonathan Kozol (1991) quotes a California legislator as saying: "This is the revenge of wealth against the poor. 'If the schools must actually be equal,' they are saying, 'then we'll undercut them all.'" Although the poor won their court battles, Kozol calls the resulting California system "a victory of losers." He writes (221):

> In affluent school districts, tax-exempt foundations have been formed to channel extra money into local schools. Afternoon 'Super Schools' have been created also in these districts to provide the local children with tutorials and private lessons. ... . The consequence is easily discerned by visitors.

The problems presented in my work – unequal schools, disinterested youth, cynicism about the future and censorship -- are large and not be easily resolved. However, a better high school journalism, rooted in critical pedagogy, can help youth explore their immediate world. Student journalists can highlight problems in their schools and offer solutions. In turn, they will be more able to access the political system and become engaged citizens as adults.

Notes

1 Such groups include the Journalism Education Association, the Student Press Law Center and the Dow Jones Newspaper Fund.
2 See *Newsweek*, December 29, 2003, Periscope, 12.
3 In 1991, 64.7 percent of students in Intensive Journalistic Writing earned a 3 or better on the AP exam versus a passing rate of 61.6 percent for students in English.

Works Cited

Abbott, Allan. "High School Journalism." *The School Review* (December 1910).

Abrams, J. Marc, and S. Mark Goodman. "End of an Era?: the Decline of Student Press Rights in the Wake of Hazelwood School District v. Kuhlmeier," *Duke Law Journal* (Summer 1988): 706-732.

Adam, G. Stuart. "Notes on a Definition of Journalism." *The Values and Craft of American Journalism*, Roy Peter Clark and Cole Campbell, eds. University Press of Florida, 2002.

Agnew, James Kenner. *Today's Journalism for Today's Schools*. Syracuse, NY: L.W. Singer Co. Inc., 1951.

Alsop, Joseph and Stewart. *The Reporter's Trade*. New York: Reynal & Company, 1958.

Altschull, Herbert. *Agents of Power: The Media and Public Policy*. White Plains, NY: Longman Publishers, 2nd Edition, 1994.

Anyon, Jean. *Ghetto Schooling: A Political Economy of Urban Educational Reform*. New York: Teachers College Press, 1997.

Arnold, Mary, "Student Freedom of Expression and High School Journalism Advisers: A legal and educational dilemma," *Quill and Scroll*. (December-January 1996), also Diss. 9513551 University of Iowa, 1994.

Atwood, L. Erwin, and Malcolm S. MacLean Jr. "How Principals, Advisors, Parents and Pupils View Journalism," *Journalism Quarterly*, (Spring 1967).

Austin, Erica Weintraub and C. Leigh Nelson. "Influences of Ethnicity, Family Communication and Media on Adolescents' Socialization to U.S. Politics." *Journal of Broadcasting & Electronic Media* 37: 419-35.

Baldassare, Mark. "The Latino Century Begins." *California Journal*, StateNet. 23 August 2002, http://www.statenet.com.

Barbrook, Richard. *Media Freedom: The Contradictions of Communication in the Age of Modernity.* London: Pluto Press, 1995.

Barnard, Malcolm. *Fashion as Communication.* New York: Routledge, 2002.

Barnhurst, Kevin G. and John Nerome. *The Form of News: A History.* New York: Guilford Press, 2001.

Barnhurst, Kevin G. and Ellen Wartella. "Newspapers and Citizenship: Young Adults Subjective Experience of Newspapers." *Critical Studies in Mass Communication* 8 (1991): 195-209.

Bempechat, J., E. Mordkowitz, J.T. Wu, M.A. Morrison and H.P. Ginsburg. "Achievement Motivation in Cambodian Refugee Children: A Comparative Study." Society for Research in Child Development Conference. Kansas City, 1989.

Bethel School District No. 403 v. Fraser 478 U.S. 675 (1986).

Bleyer, Willard. "Journalistic Writing in High School and College." *The English Journal* Vol. 8 No. 10 (December 1919): 593-601.

Blinn, John Robert. *A Comparison of Selected Writing Skills of High School Journalism and Non-Journalism Students.* Diss. 8304361 Ohio University, 1982.

Bloom, Alan. *The Closing of the American Mind.* New York: Simon and Schuster, 1987.

Bogart, Leo. *The Press and the Public.* Hillsdale, NJ: Lawrence Erlbaum, 1989.

Booth, Alan and Anne C. Crouter. *Does It Take a Village? Community Effects on Children, Adolescents and Families.* Mahwah, NJ: Lawrence Erlbaum Associates, 2001

Bourdieu, Pierre and Jean-Claude Passeron. *Reproduction in Education, Society and Culture.* Beverly Hills, CA: Sage Publications Ltd., 1977.

Bourdieu, Pierre. *The State Nobility: Elite Schools in the Field of Power.* Stanford, CA: Stanford University Press, 1996.

— *Acts of Resistance.* New York: New Press, 1999.

Bowen, John. "Captive Voices: What Progress, Change Has Occurred in 10 Years?" *Quill & Scroll.* (February-March 1985): 14-15.

Bowles, Dorothy. "Hazelwood v. Kuhlmeier: National press Reaction to the Decision and Its Impact in Tennessee High Schools." Secondary Education Division of the Association for Education in Journalism and Mass Communication, St. Petersburg, Fla. Midwinter meeting 1989.

Boyd, John Allen. "High School Newspaper Advisers in Indiana and Their Instructional Programs in Journalism." Diss. Indiana U: June 1960.

Branson, Richard Jay, *First Amendment Rights and High School Journalism: The Evolving Definition of Substantial Disruption,* Diss. 1329305 University of Oregon, 1986.

Brooks, David. *Bobos in Paradise*, New York: Simon & Schuster, 2000.

Broussard, Joseph E. and C. Robert Blackmon. "Advisers, Editors and Principals Judge First Amendment Cases." *Journalism Quarterly* 55 (Winter 1978): 797-799.

Buckingham, David. *The Making of Citizens: Young People, News and Politics.* London: Routledge, 2000.

— *After the Death of Childhood: Growing Up in the Age of Electronic Media.* Cambridge: Polity Press, 2000.

Moving Images: Understanding Children's EmotionalResponses to Television Manchester: Manchester University Press, 1996.

Buckingham, David and Julian Sefton-Green. *Cultural Studies Goes to School: Reading and Teaching Popular Media*, London: Taylor & Francis, 1994.

California Department of Education. Policy and Evaluation Division. Academic Performance Index Growth Report, 2001-2002.

California Education Code § 48907, 1977.

Campbell, L.R. *The Teacher of Journalistic Activities in the American Public High School*, Diss. Northwestern U. 1939.

Carey, James. *Communication as Culture*. Boston: Unwin Hyman, 1988.

Charity, Arthur. *Doing Public Journalism*. New York: Guilford Press, 1995.

Citrin, Jack and Benjamin Highton. "Who is Voting?" California Journal, StateNet. 1 December 2002. <http://www.statenet.com>

Clark, Roy Peter, *Free to Write: A Journalist Teaches Young Writers*. Portsmouth, NH: Heinemann, 1995.

Clark, Roy Peter and Cole C. Campbell. *The Values and Craft of American Journalism*. Gainesville, FL: University Press of Florida, 2002.

Coleman, James S. *The Adolescent Society*. New York: Free Press, 1961.

"Comment: Open Season on the High School Press." *Columbia Journalism Review*, 26 (March/April 1988), 6.

Connell, R.W. *The Child's Construction of Politics*, Melbourne, Australia: Melbourne University Press, 1971.

Csikszentmihalyi, Mihaly and Reed Larson. *Being Adolescent: Conflict and Growth in the Teen Years*. Illinois: Basic Books, 1984.

Click, J. William, and Lillian Lodge Kopenhaver, "Principals Favor Discipline More than a Free Press, " *Journalism Educator* (Summer 1988).

—— "Few Changes Since Hazelwood," *School Press Review* (Winter 1990): 12-27.

Comer, James P. *School Power*. New York: Free Press, 1980.

Cowan, Philip A. *Piaget: With Feeling*. New York: Holt, Rinehart and Winston, 1978.

Cranford, Robert Joshua, *A Sample Survey of the Attitudes of Iowa High School Seniors Toward Journalism and Careers in Journalism*. Diss. 0006500 University of Iowa, 1962.

—— "When Are Career Choices Made? *Journalism Quarterly* 37 (Summer 1960): 422-424.

Crow, Lorrie R. "The Impact of Texas High School Students' and Principals' Perceptions of Student Press Freedom Following the Hazelwood v. Kuhlmeier Supreme Court Decision," Unpublished master's thesis, U. of Oklahoma, 1992.

Darling-Hammond, Linda. "Restructuring Schools for High Performance," 144-194, *Rewards and Reform: Creating Educational Incentives That Work*, eds. Susan Fuhrman and Jennifer O'Day. San Francisco: Josey-Bass,1996

Davila, Arlene. *Latinos Inc.: The Marketing and Making of a People*. Berkeley: University of California Press, 2001.

Day, Louis A. and John M. Butler. *Hazelwood School District v. Kuhlmeier: A Constitutional Review or Sound Public Policy?* Association for Education in Journalism and Mass Communication Conference, Portland, OR, July 1988.

Death by Cheeseburger: High School Journalism in the 1990s and Beyond, The Freedom Forum, Arlington, Va., 1994.

Delpit, Lisa. *Other People's Children: Cultural Conflict in the Classroom.* New York: The New Press, 1995.

Dickson, Thomas V. "Attitudes of High School Principals About Press Freedom After Hazelwood." *Journalism Quarterly*, (Spring 1989): 169-73.

___ "Self-Censorship and Freedom of the High School Press." *Journalism Educator* (Autumn 1994).

Dillon, Charles. *Journalism for High Schools.* New York: Norle and Noble, 1919.

Dolbee, Cora. "A Practical Experiment in Journalism." *The English Journal* Vol. 13, No. 8. (October 1913): 518-520.

Doherty, William. *Take Back Your Kids: Confident Parenting in Turbulent Times.* Notre Dame, Indiana: Sorin Books. 2000.

Doppelt, Jack and Ellen Shearer. *Nonvoters.* Thousand Oaks, CA.: Sage Publications Inc., 1999.

Dressel, Paul L. *Liberal Education and Journalism.* New York: Teachers College Bureau of Publications, Columbia University, 1963.

Dvorak, Jack. "Characteristics of Journalistic Media and Journalism Educators in Inner-City High Schools." Paper presented at the annual convention of the Association for Education in Journalism and Mass Communication, Kansas City, Mo., Summer 2003.

Dvorak, Jack, Lawrence Lain and Tom Dickson. *Journalism Kids Do Better: What Research Tells Us About High School Journalism in the 1990s*, ERIC, 1994.

Dyson, Anne Haas. *Writing Superheroes.* New York, NY: Teachers College Press, 1997.

Eckert, Penelope. *Jocks & Burnouts: Social Categories and Identity in the High School.* New York: Teachers College Press, 1989.

Elkind, David. *Ties That Stress: The New Family Imbalance.* Cambridge, MA: Harvard University Press, 1994.

Emerson, Robert M., *Contemporary Field Research: Perspectives and Formulations*, Prospect Heights, Illinois: Waveland Press, 2001.

Erikson, Erik. *The Life Cycle Completed.* New York: W.W. Norton and Company, 1982.

___ *Identity, Youth and Crisis.* New York: W.W. Norton and Company, 1968.

"Evaluation of the Blueprint for Student Success in a Standards-Based System." Palo Alto, Ca.: American Institutes for Research, January 2002.

Everhart, Robert. *Reading, Writing and Resistance.* Boston: Routledge & Kegan, 1983.

Fallows, James. "Why Americans Hate the Media." *Atlantic Monthly* (February 1996) Volume 277, No. 2, 45-64.

Fetto, J. "Down for the Count." *American Demographics* 21 (1999): 46-47.

Fine, Michelle. *Framing Dropouts: Notes on the Politics of an Urban High School.* Albany, NY: State University of New York Press, 1991.

Fineman, Howard and Karen Breslau. "California in Crisis." *Newsweek*, 28 July, 2003.

"The First Amendment and Schools." *Educational Leadership.* (May 2001).

Fone, Byrne. *Homophobia.* New York: Metropolitan Books, 2000.

Foster, Charles R. *Extra-Curricular Activities in the High School.* Richmond, VA: Johnson Publishing Co., 1925.

Fredriksen, N. "The Real Test Bias: Influences of Testing on Teaching and Learning." *American Psychologist* 39, 1984, 193-202.

Freire, Paulo, *Pedagogy of the Oppressed.* New York: Continuum Books, 1970, 30th anniversary edition, 2000.

__ *Pedagogy of Hope.* 1992. New York: Continuum, 1999.

Frith, Simon. *Sound Effects: Youth, Leisure and the Politics of Rock n' Roll.* New York: Pantheon Books, 1981.

Fujishima v. Board of Education, 460 F. 2d 1355 (7th Circuit 1972).

Furstenberg, Frank F. Jr., Thomas D. Cook Jacqueline Eccles, Glen H. Elder Jr. and Arnold Sameroff. *Managing to Make It: Urban Families and Adolescent Success.* Chicago: The University of Chicago Press, 1999.

Gans, Herbert J. *Deciding What's News: A Study of CBS Evening News, NBC Nightly News, Newsweek and Time.* New York: Vintage Books, 1980.

Geertz, Clifford, *The Interpretation of Cultures*, New York: Basic Books, 1973.

Giddens, Anthony. "The Class Structure of the Advanced Societies," *Social Stratification.* Boulder, Co.: Westview Press, 2001:152-162.

__ "Elites and Power," 1973. *Social Stratification*, Boulder, Co.: Westview Press, 2001: 212-222.

Gilbert, James. *A Cycle of Outrage: America's Reaction to the Juvenile Delinquent in the 1950s.* New York: Oxford University Press, 1986.

Gillespie, Marie. *Television, Ethnicity and Cultural Change.* London and New York: Routledge, 1995.

Giroux, Henry A. *Theory and Resistance in Education*. Westport, CT: Bergin & Garvey, revised ed. 2001.

Gordon, C. Wayne. *The Social System of the High School*. Chicago: The Free Press, 1957.

Graves, Donald. *A Fresh Look at Writing*. Portsmouth, NH: Heinemann, 1994.

Greenstein, Fred. *Children and Politics*. New Haven: Yale University Press, 1969.

Gross, Larry. *Up From Invisibility: Lesbians, Gay Men and the Media in America*. New York: Columbia University Press, 2001.

Grusky, David, ed. *Social Stratification: Class, Race and Gender*. Boulder, Co.: Westview Press, 2001.

Grusky, David and Jesper B. Sorensen. "Are There Big Social Classes?" *Social Stratification*. Boulder, Co.: Westview Press, 2001, 183-194.

Gumbel, Andrew. "California Schools to Lay Off 25,000 Staff." *The Independent*. London, England, April 6, 2003.

Gunter, Barrie. *Poor Reception*. Hillsdale, NJ: Lawrence Erlbaum Associates, 1987.

Hafen, Bruce C., "Hazelwood School District and the Role of First Amendment Institutions," *Duke Law Journal*, 1988.

Hall, Granville Stanley. *Adolescence: Its Psychology and Its Relations to Physiology, Anthropology, Sociology, Sex, Crime, Religion and Education*. New York: D. Appleton and Company, 1904.

Hammersly, Martyn. "Ethnography and Realism," *Contemporary Field Research: Perspectives and Formulations*, Ed. Robert Emerson, Prospect Heights, Illinois: Waveland Press, 2001, 102-111.

Harter, Susan. "Self and Identity Development." *At the Threshold: The Developing Adolescent*, Eds. S. Shirley Feldman and Glen Elliott. Cambridge: Harvard University Press, 1990.

"Has School Reform Been Good for California?" *Research Brief* 30. (February 2000). San Francisco, CA: Public Policy Institute of California.

Hazelwood v. Kuhlmeier 484 U.S. 260 (1988).

Heath, Shirley Brice. "What no bedtime story means: Narrative skills at home and school." *Language in Society* 11 (1982): 49-76.

Hebdige, Dick. *Subculture: the meaning of style*. London and New York: Routledge, 1979 reprinted 1994.

Heins, Marjorie. *Not in Front of the Children: 'Indecency,' Censorship and the Innocence of Youth*. New York: Hill and Wang, 2001.

Herman, Edward S. and Noam Chomsky. *Manufacturing Consent: The Political Economy of the Mass Media*. 1988. New York: Pantheon Books, 2002.

Hill, Jim. "Proposition 187 Supporters Vow to Battle On. Parts of Immigration Measure Struck Down by Judge." 1995, CNN.com.

Hine, Thomas. *The Rise and Fall of the American Teenager*. New York: Avon Books Inc., 1999.

Hirsch, E.D. *Cultural Literacy: What Every American Needs to Know*. Boston: Houghton Mifflin, 1987.

Hollander, Neil. "Adolescents and the War: the Sources of Socialization." *Journalism Quarterly* 48 (1971): 472-9.

Holweger, Kimberly Ann, *High School Journalism Advisors' Perceptions of Control Over Student Newspapers*. Diss. 1351847 California State University-Fresno. 1992.

Horine, Don. "How Principals, Advisors and Editors View the High School Newspaper." *Journalism Quarterly* 43 (1966): 339.

Humes, Edward. *School of Dreams: Making the Grade at a Top American High School*. San Diego: Harcourt Inc., 2003.

Hyde, Grant Milnor. *Journalistic Writing*. New York: D. Appleton and Company, 1922.

"Identity in Adolescence: Processes and Contents." *New Directions for Child Development* 30. Ed. Alan S. Waterman. San Francisco: Josey-Bass Inc. (December 1985).

Jenkins, Henry. "Prof. Jenkins Goes to Washington." 7 May 1999. Online posting. <www.swiss.ai.mit.edu/classes/6.805/assorted-short-pieces/ henry-jenkins-goes-to-washington.html>

___ Ed. *The Children's Culture Reader*. New York: New York University Press, 1998.

"Judge Rules Prop. 187 Unconstitutional, States May Not Make Own Immigration Laws." *ACLU News*. (January/February 1998) San Francisco, CA.

Katz, Jonathan. "The Media's War on Kids." *Rolling Stone*. Nov. 1993); 47-130.

Keating, Daniel. "Adolescent Thinking." *At the Threshold: The Developing Adolescent*, Eds. S. Shirley Feldman and Glen Elliott. Cambridge: Harvard University Press, 1990.

Kimball, Penn T. and Samuel Lubell. "High School Students' Attitudes Toward Journalism as a Career II." *Journalism Quarterly* 37 (Summer 1960): 413-422.

Kingston, Paul W. *The Classless Society*. Stanford, Ca.: Stanford University Press, 2000.

Kliebard, Herbert. *Schooled to Work: Vocationalism and the American Curriculum, 1876-1946*. New York: Teachers College Press, 1999.

___ *The Struggle for the American Curriculum, 1893-1958.* New York: Routledge, 1995.

Kozol, Jonathan. *Savage Inequalities.* New York: Crown Publishers, 1991.

Knight, Robert P. "High School Journalism in the Post-Hazelwood Era," *Journalism Educator,* (Summer 1988).

Knott, David L. *Treatment in Selected High School Journalism Textbooks of the First Amendment as It Relates to the Rights of Students to Express Themselves in Print.* Diss. 8121655. University of Toledo, 1981.

Kohlberg, L. "Moral Stages and Moralization: The Cognitive-Developmental Approach" *Moral Development and Behavior: Theory Research and Social Issues,* Ed. T. Lickona, New York: Holt, Reinhart and Winston, 1976.

Kohn, Alfie. *Punished by Rewards.* Boston and New York: Houghton Mifflin Company, 1993.

Koslowski, B., and L. Okagaki, "Non-Human Indices of Causation in Problem-Solving Situations: Causal Mechanism, Analogous Effects and the Status of Alternative Rival Accounts." *Child Development* 57, (1986):1100-8.

Kristoff, Nicholas, D. "Freedom of the High School Press." Lanham, MD: University Press of America, 1983.

Krop, Cathy S., Stephen J. Carroll and Randy L. Ross. *Tracking K-12 Education Spending in California.* Santa Monica, Ca.: Rand Institute on Education and Training, 1995.

Lareau, Annette. *Home Advantage.* Lanham, Md.: Rowman & Littlefield Publishers Inc., 2000.

Lau v. Nichols, 414 U.S. 563 (1974).

Lauffer, Kimberly Ann. *Examining the State of High School Journalism in Michigan Nine Years After Hazelwood v. Kuhlmeier*. Diss. 1386875 Michigan State University School of Journalism 1997.

Liebes, Tamar. "Television, Parents and the Political Socialization of Children." *Teachers College Record* 94, (1990): 73-86.

Lipsitz, George. *Dangerous Crossroads: Popular Music, Postmodernism and the Poetics of Place*. London: Verso, 1994.

__ *The Possessive Investment in Whiteness: How White People Profit from Identity Politics*. Philadelphia: Temple University Press, 1998.

__ *Time Passages: Collective Memory and American Popular Culture*. Minneapolis, MN: University of Minnesota Press, 1990.

Mariscal, Jorge. "Lethal and Compassionate: The Militarization of U.S. Culture." *Counterpunch*, (3 May 2003) Alexander Cockburn and Jeffrey St. Clair, Eds.

Martin, Jane Roland. *The Schoolhome: Rethinking Schools for Changing Families*. Cambridge, MA: Harvard University Press, 1992.

McCauley, Clark. 2003, 10-32. "Making Sense of Terrorism After 9/11." In *Shocking Violence II: Violent Disaster, War and Terrorism Affecting Our Youth*. Springfield, IL: Charles C Thomas Publisher Ltd.

McChesney, Robert W. "September 11 and the Structural Limitations of U.S. Journalism." *Journalism After September 11*, Barbie Zelizer and Stuart Allen, Eds. London: Routledge, 2002: 91-100.

McDevitt, Michael and Steven H. Chaffee. "The Family in a Sequence of Political Activation: Why Civic Interventions Can Succeed." Association for Education in Journalism and Mass Communication, 2002.

McKee, Kathy Brittain, *High School Principals and the Student Press: Functions, Procedures and Regulation*. Diss. 9235453 U. of Georgia 1992.

Mehan, Hugh, Irene Villanueva, Lea Hubbard and Angele Lintz. *Constructing School Success: The Consequences of Untracking Low-Achieving Students*. Cambridge, UK: Cambridge University Press, 1996.

Mindich, David. *Just the Facts: How Objectivity Came to Define American Journalism*. New York: New York University Press, 1998.

__ *Tuned Out: Why Young People Don't Follow the News*. Oxford University Press, June 2004.

Miraldi, Robert. *Muckrkaking and Objectivity: Journalism's Collliding Traditions*. New York: Greenwood Press, 1990.

Modell, John and Madeline Goodman. "Historical Perspectives." *At the Threshold: The Developing Adolescent*, Eds. S. Shirley Feldman and Glen Elliott, Cambridge: Harvard University Press, 1990.

Moore, Michael. *Stupid White Men*. New York: Harper Colins Publishers, 2001.

Moser, Rosemarie Scolaro and Corinne E. Frantz. *Shocking Violence II: Violent Disaster, War and Terrorism Affecting Our Youth*. Springfield, IL: Charles C Thomas Publisher Ltd., 2003.

NDC Yellow Pages, Southern California directories, 2001.

Nault, Judith Therese, *Quality High School Journalism: Program Principles and Publication Guidelines Governed by Press Law*, Diss. University of Nevada, Reno. 1976, 1309665.

Nelson, Jack, Ed. *Captive Voices: High School Journalism in America, The Report of the Commission of Inquiry into High School Journalism*, Robert F. Kennedy Memorial. New York: Schocken Books, 1974.

Nelson, Richard Albert, *A Study of the Motivations of High School Students to Careers in Journalism*, dis. University of Wisconsin-Madison, 1976, Diss. 7620680.

Noriega, Chon and Ana M. Lopez. *The Ethnic Eye*. Minneapolis, MN: University of Minnesota Press, 1996.

Oakes, Jeannie. 1990. Multiplying Inequalities: The Effects of Race, Social Class and Tracking on Opportunities to Learn Mathematics and Science. Santa Monica, Ca.: Rand Corporation.

Ogbu, J. U. "Academic Socialization of Black Children." Society for Research in Child Development, Kansas City, 1989.

"Open Season on the High School Press." Comment. *Columbia Journalism Review* 26 March/April 1988: 6.

Overduin, Hendrik. "Civic Journalism and Objectivity: A Philosophical Resuscitation." Paper presented at the Association for Education in Journalism and Mass Communication. Conference in Kansas City, MO, July 30-Aug. 2, 2003.

Peak, L. "Learning to Go to School in Japan." Diss. Harvard Graduate School of Education, Harvard U, 1987.

Perry, Frances M. "The Supervision of School Publications." *English Journal* Vol. 8, No. 5 (May 1919): 299-301.

Piaget, Jean. *Judgment and Reasoning in the Child*. 1932. New Jersey: Littlefield, Adams, 1962.

Plyler v. Doe, 457 U.S. 202 (1982).

Postman, Neil. *The Disappearance of Childhood*. London: W.H. Allen, 1983.

"Poverty in the United States: 2001." U.S. Census Bureau.

Pritchard, Peter S. *The Making of McPaper*, New York: St. Martin's Press, 1987.

Private School Statistics. Rand California. Santa Monica, CA., 1990-2001.

"Private School Universe Survey." National Center for Education Statistics. Washington, D.C.: U.S. Department of Education, 1999-2000.

Profile of Selected Social Characteristics, Profile of Selected Economic Statistics, Value, Mortgage Status and Selected Conditions, American Factfinder, U.S. Census Bureau, 2000, Summary File 3.

"Proposition 187. Text of Proposed Law." 1994 California Voter Information.

"Public's News Habits Little Changed by September 11: Americans Lack Background to Follow International News." Pew Research Center for the People and the Press. June 9, 2002.

"Questions That May Be Raised by Proposition 227." Washington, D.C.: Office for Civil Rights, U.S. Department of Education, June 10, 1998.

Reddick, DeWitt C. *The Mass Media and the School Newspaper* 2nd ed. Belmont, Ca.: Wadsworth, 1976.

___ *Journalism and the School Paper*. New York: D.C. Heath and Company, 1938.

Reese, Stephen D. "The News Paradigm and the Ideology of Objectivity." *Social Meanings of the News*, Dan Berkowitz, Ed. Thousand Oaks, CA: Sage Publications, 1997.

Rojas, Gonzalo. "Report on the Compact: A Year of Growth." College of Education, San Diego State University, 2003.

Rosenfeld, Alvin and Nicole Wise. *The Over-Scheduled Child: Avoiding the Hyper-Parenting Trap*. New York: St. Martin's Press, 2001.

Sampson, Robert J. "How do communities undergird or undermine human development? Relevant contexts and social mechanisms." Booth, Alan and Anne C. Crouter. Eds. *Does It Take a Village? Community Effects on Children, Adolescents and Families.* Mahwah, NJ: Lawrence Erlbaum Associates. 2001.

Schudson, Michael. *Discovering the News: A Social History of American Newspapers.* New York: Basic Books, 1978.

___ *The Good Citizen*, New York: The Free Press, 1998.

Schlesinger, Philip. *Putting 'Reality' Together: BBC News.* London and New York: Constable & Company Ltd., 1978.

Scott, Alan. *Secondary School Journalism: Current Practices and Trends.* Diss. U. of Texas, 1955.

Seplow, Stephen. "Closer to Home," *American Journalism Review.* (July/August 2002): 18-31.

Sonstelie, Jon, Eric Brunner and Kenneth Ardon. "For Better or for Worse? School Finance Reform in California." San Francisco, CA.: Public Policy Institute of California, 2000.

Sherry, Susanna, "Responsible Republicanism: Educating for Citizenship," The University of Chicago Law *Review* 62. (1995).

Siebert, Fred, Theodore Peterson and Wilbur Schramm. *Four Theories of the Press.* Urbana, Ill.: University of Illinois, 1963.

Sims, Norman. *Literary Journalism.* New York: Ballantine Books, 1995.

Sigal, Leon V. *Reporters and Officials: The Organization and Politics of Newsmaking.* Lexington, MA: D.C. Heath, 1973.

Soloski, John. "News Reporting and Professionalism: Some Constraints on the Reporting of the News." *Social Meanings of News*, Dan Berkowitz, Ed. Thousand Oaks, CA: Sage Publications, 1997

Spradley, James P. and Brenda J. Mann. *The Cocktail Waitress: Women's Work in a Man's World*, New York: John Wiley & Sons Inc., 1975.

Spindler, George and Lorie Hammond. "The Use of Anthropological Methods in Educational Research," *Harvard Educational Review*, (Spring 2000): 39-48.

Spindler, George, ed. *Doing the Ethnography of Schooling*, New York: Holt, Rinehart and Winston, 1982.

Stigler, James W. "Individuals, Institutions and Academic Achievement." *Social Theory for a Changing Society*, Eds. Pierre Bourdieu and James S. Coleman. Boulder: Westview Press, 1991.

Strong, Marilee. *A Bright Red Scream: Self-Mutilation and the Language of Pain*. New York: Penguin USA, 1999.

Students Gazette. First Issue. Philadelphia, Pa.: Public Latin School. Norris of Fairhill Papers, Vol. 44, Historical Society of Pennsylvania. (June 11, 1777):1-5.

"Terrorism Transforms News Interest: Worries Over New Attacks Decline." Pew Research Center for the People and the Press, December 18 2001 report.

Tilly, Charles. *Durable Inequality*. Berkeley and Los Angeles: University of California Press, 1998.

Tinker v. Des Moines, 393 U.S. 503 1969.

Trager, Robert and Donna Dickerson. "Prior Restraint in High School: Law, Attitudes and Practice," *Journalism Quarterly* (Spring 1980): 135-138.

Tuchman, Gaye. "Objectivity as Strategic Ritual: An Examination of Newsmen's Notions of Objectivity." *American Journal of Sociology* 77 (January 1972): 660-679.

Uagas, Charmaine and Thomas D. Snyder. "Status and Trends in the Education of Hispanics." National Center for Education Statistics, U.S. Department of Education, April 2003.

Useem, Michael. "The Inner Circle" 1984. *Social Stratification.* Boulder, Co.: Westview Press, 2001, 223-232.

Valenzuela, Angela. *Subtractive Schooling: U.S.-Mexican Youth and the Politics of Caring.* Albany, NY: State University of New York Press, 1999.

Vasquez, Olga. *La Clase Magica: Imagining Optimal Possibilities in a Bilinqual Community of Learners.* Mahwah, NJ: Lawrence Erlbaum Associates, 2003.

Vonnegut Jr., Kurt. "Introduction." *Our Time is Now: Notes from the High School Underground.* Ed., John Birmingham. New York; Praeger Publications, 1970.

Vygotsky, L. S. *Mind in Society.* Cambridge, MA: Harvard University Press, 1978.

Waller, Willard. *The Sociology of Teaching.* New York: John Wiley, 1965.

Walling, Donovan R. "Meeting the Needs of Transient Students." Bloomington, IN: Phi Beta Kappa Educational Foundation, Fastback Series 304.

Walkerdine, Valerie, Helen Lucey and June Melody. *Growing Up: Psychosocial Explorations of Gender and Class.* London; Palgrave, 2001.

Warner, W. Lloyd, Marchia Meeker and Kenneth Eells. "Gradational Status Groupings: Reputation, Deference and Prestige, Social Class in America." 1960. *Social Stratification*, Boulder, Co.: Westview Press, 2001.

Warth, Gary. "Unfair Housing -- North County Neighborhoods Once Quietly Shut Out Other Races, Religions." *North County Times*, May 5, 2002.

Weaver, David H. and G. Cleveland Wilhoit. *The American Journalist in the 1990s: U.S. News People at the End of an Era*. Mahwah, NJ: Lawrence Erlbaum Associates, 1996.

Weber, Max. "Class, Status, Party," 1946 and 1958. *Social Stratification*. Boulder, Co.: Westview Press, 2001, 132-142.

—— "Status Groups and Classes," 1947. *Social Stratification*. Boulder, Co.: Westview Press, 2001, 142-145.

—— "Open and Closed Relationships," 1968, *Social Stratification*. Boulder, Co.: Westview Press 2001, 146-149.

West Virginia Dept. of Education. "A Guide to Journalism for Secondary Schools." Charleston, West Virginia, 1951.

West Virginia State Board of Education v. Barnette 319 U.S. 624 (1943).

Willis, Paul. *Learning to Labor: How Working Class Kids Get Working Class Jobs*. New York: Columbia University Press, 1977.

Wilson, Christopher. *The Labor of Words: Literary Professionalism in the Progressive Era*. Athens, Georgia: The University of Georgia Press, 1985.

Yancy, Kitty Bean. "Enough. As the anniversary of the attacks approaches, some say they can't bear to see it again." *USA Today*, August 22, 2002, "Life" section D.

Zelizer, Barbie, "Journalists as Interpretive Communities" *Social Meanings of News* by Dan Berkowitz. Thousand Oaks, Ca.: Sage Publications (1997); 401-419.

Zelizer, Barbie and Stuart Allen, Eds. *Journalism After September 11*. New York: Routledge, 2002.